The Global and Local Appeal of Kneehigh Theatre Company

The Global and Local Appeal of Kneehigh Theatre Company:

Brand Kneehigh

By

Catherine Trenchfield

Cambridge
Scholars
Publishing

The Global and Local Appeal of Kneehigh Theatre Company:
Brand Kneehigh

By Catherine Trenchfield

This book first published 2022

Cambridge Scholars Publishing

Lady Stephenson Library, Newcastle upon Tyne, NE6 2PA, UK

British Library Cataloguing in Publication Data
A catalogue record for this book is available from the British Library

ISBN (10): 1-5275-8660-X
ISBN (13): 978-1-5275-8660-4

CONTENTS

ACKNOWLEDGEMENTS

I would like to thank my former PhD supervisor Dr Libby Worth and the Drama and Theatre department at Royal Holloway University. Thank you to Dr Emma Cox and Dr Kate Dorney, who recommended I publish my research. I would also like to thank Sarah C. Jane at Falmouth University for providing access to the Kneehigh Archive. Thanks, should also be given to Kneehigh Theatre Company, for suppling materials during the early days of my research, and to former company members who participated in interviews. Thank you to my colleagues at Kingston College (South Thames College Group) and West Thames College.

Finally, I would also like to offer a heartfelt thanks to my family (particularly my mom, dad, and brother) and friends who have supported me on this journey, some of which have attended numerous road trips to Cornwall.

This book is dedicated to Kneehigh Theatre and to those who have been part of their theatrical landscape.

FOREWORD

This book explores Kneehigh Theatre Company's notions of 'Brand Kneehigh' in relation to theories of globalisation. It will define Kneehigh's theatrical brand, showing Cornish cultural identity as a core component while also working with international influences through cultural exchange. By looking at the history of this company, analysis of key productions will discuss the qualities attributed to 'Brand Kneehigh' and consider the 'local' and 'global' nature of their work. This research will contribute towards developing a knowledge base about Kneehigh spanning decades, offering a detailed (and durational) study of a theatre company. The selection of productions for examination reveals the changes and reinventions Kneehigh has undergone to incorporate shifting interests and socio/economic engagements. The book will explore Kneehigh's ambitions to establish themselves as a company delivering material that is 'popular' in appeal and that meets the needs of a Cornish (local) community and international (global) audience. However, tensions working between local and global interests will be exposed, with an investigation into Kneehigh's own cited solution, their self-created performance space, Asylum.

My research and structure for this book engages with theories of globalisation, adaptation, archives and spectatorship. This is conducted in conjunction with the use of the entire Kneehigh archive and attending a range of Kneehigh performances. Building on the analysis of the above theoretical frameworks, key productions will be used as case studies to explore Kneehigh's brand evolution and artistic practices. The case studies included within the following chapters, chart the development of the Kneehigh brand considering: productions exploring interests within local heritage; a project facilitating cultural exchange between European countries; material engaging with national and international collaborations, and; performances within the Asylum. Finally, productions post Rice's departure and recruitment of Carl Grose as joint artistic director, acknowledge and examine the work of Rice's new company, Wise Children and material under Grose's direction.

The chronology of the Kneehigh brand corresponds with the chronology of the productions examined as case studies in this thesis. Earlier emergences of 'Brand Kneehigh' are analysed in terms of localisation, affirming the company's affiliations with Cornish identity in the productions, *Quicksilver* (2002), *Tristan and Yseult* (2005), and *Blast* (2010). Progression of the brand within the realms of cultural exchange is seen in the Three Islands Project Case Study (2003-5) and *The Very Old Man with Enormous Wings* (2011). An exploration into national and international collaborations, displaying the dominance of Kneehigh's theatrical style, is examined in the productions: *Cymbeline* (2006); *A Matter of Life and Death* (2007), *Brief Encounter* (2008) and *The Umbrellas of Cherbourg* (2011). Performances of *The Red Shoes* (2010) and *Global Cornwall* (2012) are case studies considered within the home venue, Asylum, centralising and potentially strengthening the brand. These productions, spanning 2014 to 2020, chart a critical juncture for Kneehigh and Rice, reflecting a change of direction for both parties, a reconfiguration of the Kneehigh brand, and inception of Rice's own independent theatrical identification.

LIST OF ILLUSTRATIONS

CHAPTER ONE

INTRODUCTION

This book explores Kneehigh Theatre Company's notions of 'Brand Kneehigh' in relation to theories of globalisation. It will define Kneehigh's theatrical brand, showing Cornish cultural identity as a core component while also working with international influences through cultural exchange. By looking at the history of this company, analysis of key productions will discuss the qualities attributed to 'Brand Kneehigh' and consider the 'local' and 'global' nature of their work. This research will contribute towards developing a knowledge base about Kneehigh spanning decades, offering a detailed (and durational) study of a theatre company. The selection of productions for examination reveals the changes and reinventions Kneehigh has undergone to incorporate shifting interests and socio/economic engagements. This text will explore Kneehigh's ambitions to establish themselves as a company delivering material that is 'popular' in appeal and that meets the needs of a Cornish (local) community and international (global) audience. However, tensions working between local and global interests will be exposed, with an investigation into Kneehigh's own cited solution, their self-created performance space, Asylum.

Kneehigh is an important contemporary British theatre company to examine, running for forty-two years, before closing in June 2022. They have grown in critical acclaim and were recognised by the British Council as one of Britain's most exciting and innovative theatre companies. Kneehigh has displayed longevity in their career, negotiated by broadening their scope and ambitions to produce work initially for Cornwall, and then with the encouragement of Arts Council England, South West, amongst other funding bodies, to venture beyond the confines of their locality. This has seen the company use business models to grow stronger financially, taking their work to as many audiences as possible, enjoying high profile collaborations nationally and internationally. Additionally, Kneehigh has been acknowledged by educational examining bodies and institutions as influential theatre practitioners, with inclusion in GCSE, BTEC and A-Level specifications in addition to university study.

This book will present my research within the Kneehigh archive (held at Falmouth University, from April 2010), and attendance at the Asylum (since the first summer season in 2010). By using both performance and archive, I illustrate how the company has developed a brand that is a hybrid of local and global artistic influences and ambitions. The text will also explore the complexities Kneehigh experienced in defining and communicating Cornish cultural identity. My consideration of the Kneehigh Theatre archive triggers discursive responses to performance and archival research, offering an 'experiential' archive structure. I examine the 'experiential' environments that global brands and theatrical companies use to establish their identity, strengthen their product and reinforce their brand. Ultimately my argument establishes Kneehigh working towards an equilibrium between localism and globalism through cultural exchange.

My research and structure for this book engages with theories of globalisation, adaptation, archives and spectatorship. This is conducted in conjunction with the use of the entire Kneehigh archive and attending a range of Kneehigh performances. Building on the analysis of the above theoretical frameworks, key productions will be used as case studies to explore Kneehigh's brand evolution and artistic practices. The case studies included within the following chapters, chart the development of the Kneehigh brand considering: productions exploring interests within local heritage; a project facilitating cultural exchange between European countries; material engaging with national and international collaborations, and; performances within the Asylum. Finally, productions post Rice's departure and recruitment of Carl Grose as joint artistic director, acknowledge and examine the work of Rice's new company, Wise Children and material under Grose's direction. Within this concluding chapter the closure of Kneehigh will also be considered.

The chronology of the Kneehigh brand, corresponds with the chronology of the productions examined as case studies in this book. Earlier emergences of 'Brand Kneehigh' are analysed in terms of localisation, affirming the company's affiliations with Cornish identity in the productions, *Quicksilver* (2002), *Tristan and Yseult* (2005), and *Blast* (2010). Progression of the brand within the realms of cultural exchange is seen in the Three Islands Project Case Study (2003-5) and *The Very Old Man with Enormous Wings* (2011). An exploration into national and international collaborations, displaying the dominance of Kneehigh's theatrical style, is examined in the productions: *Cymbeline* (2006); *A Matter of Life and Death* (2007), *Brief Encounter* (2008) and *The Umbrellas of Cherbourg* (2011). Performances of *The Red Shoes* (2010) and *Global Cornwall* (2012) are case studies considered within the home venue,

Asylum, centralising and potentially strengthening the brand. These productions, spanning 2014 to 2020, chart a critical juncture for Kneehigh and Rice, reflecting a change of direction for both parties, a reconfiguration of the Kneehigh brand, and inception of Rice's own independent theatrical identification. It should be stated that Mike Shepherd, as founder and artistic director, has been in the role since 1980, maintaining a stable sense of leadership and artistic identity.

The research from the above-listed cases studies and theoretical analysis illustrates a company caught in international tensions; an experience still felt by many within the UK because of the EU referendum. In the Brexit referendum, Cornwall voted 'Leave' however the county stands to lose a huge amount of EU regeneration funding. The effects of Brexit and the emerging Covid 19 pandemic, have had a profound impact on Kneehigh, and will be discussed in further detail in the conclusion. The construction of their own branded space, Asylum, offered a sanctuary from global tensions and a place to fulfil their artistic vision. The Asylum also represented a physical manifestation of its growing brand. This study provides an opportunity to explore a company who contended with a range of divergent factors, while maintaining their interests and sense of cultural identity. These factors will be addressed in conjunction with the company's theatrical performance style, arguably the core component of the brand.

Kneehigh was a Cornish based Theatre Company, with a reputation for transforming classic fairy tales, popular films and literature into performance using song, dance, physical theatre, puppetry and multi-media. They have been creating theatre for forty years in the UK, maintaining a reputation as an inventive and enthralling theatre company. As described by the British Council:

> Kneehigh tells stories and creates theatre of humanity from an epic and tiny scale. It works with an ever-changing ensemble of performers, musicians, artists, technicians, and administrators, and is passionate about its multi-disciplined creative process[1].

Mike Shepherd, an actor, and former primary school teacher in Cornwall founded Kneehigh Theatre in 1980. He was inspired to create work for his local community and attain creative autonomy. Shepherd had become disillusioned with working as an actor in London, finding the work uninspiring. By returning to Cornwall, he could develop work on his own terms, discover new skills and form artistic connections with musicians, artists and anyone interested in making performances.

The company originally devised performances for schools, with children as their primary audience; hence the name Kneehigh, progressing into mainstream theatre by producing work aimed at a broader age range. Initially, Shepherd was sole artistic director, eventually sharing this role with Bill Mitchell who has since developed 'sister' company, WildWorks in 2005. WildWorks focuses predominantly on site-specific performance, named 'Landscape Theatre' on the Cornish coast. In 2003, Emma Rice became artistic director, holding this role for over a decade before moving on to The Globe in 2016, then forming her own company, Wise Children in 2018. Carl Grose (actor, director and playwright) was appointed the role of joint artistic director in late 2018. Despite the company's fluctuating fortunes and successes (which will be considered in more detail in Chapter 3), Kneehigh continued to maintain its creative identity until the very end of their career. In recent years, they have transcended their national reputation, gaining international interest and followers of their theatrical style.

My first encounter with Kneehigh occurred in 2004 at the Battersea Arts Centre London, with the production *The Wooden Frock*. A colleague and I were taking a group of college students to this performance with some trepidation; a long train journey to an unglamorous venue, and an even longer walk up Lavender Hill, to a dreary and uninspiring entrance. Neither of us had witnessed the company before and were daunted by the prospect of the show not living up to the critical gaze of our teenage tutor group. However, the production was both inspirational and entertaining: providing an introduction to the company. It also afforded the opportunity of engaging with a theatrical 'experience' and Kneehigh's 'branded' theatrical style; subsequently inspiring attendance to future company productions.

Brand Kneehigh

Years after attending my first Kneehigh production, a leaflet published in 2010 encouraged membership to their *Friends of Kneehigh Scheme,* to support the company's new performance venue, the Asylum. It provided an overview of a new environment that offered a complete night out featuring a range of shows, food, drink, and live music. The language used by Kneehigh in this promotional material for the Asylum shared descriptions with other lifestyle brands. In this aspect, it contrasted with literature used by other theatre companies to communicate their work and artistic vision. An invitation to eat, drink, dance and be part of a Kneehigh 'night out' asserted the concept of a 'total' leisure product. Within this document, the company introduced the phrase, 'Brand Kneehigh' to outline their ambitions for a recognisable theatre company with a range of performances and products. This phrase provoked connotations with globalisation;

encouraging my consideration of the company, noting their branded ambitions and observations of cultural exchange inherent in the work.

'Brand Kneehigh' is a term that encompasses a broad entertainment experience. I use it as an umbrella term which includes theatrical style; performance events, music gigs, entertainment at the Asylum, food and drink, merchandise, community projects, school tours and workshops. Although other reviewers and scholars refer to the Kneehigh theatrical brand, in most instances they are referring to the company's theatrical style. In some cases, there are descriptions of the Kneehigh entertainment experience which extends beyond the realms of onstage performance. For clarification, I will use the term 'Brand Kneehigh' to discuss the company's total entertainment experience (including theatrical performance). This will include entertainment events and experiences at the Asylum, food and drink, and merchandise. References to Kneehigh's 'theatre brand' or 'theatrical style', will focus more specifically on performance elements, seen on stage and within site-specific locations. I will also use their theatrical style as a term to reflect on their devising and adaptation processes. Although Kneehigh's theatrical style is part of the company brand; 'Brand Kneehigh' displays broader ambitions for entertainment and lifestyle.

The Kneehigh 'theatre brand', is a performance style which encompasses an eclectic mix of physical theatre, puppetry, Brechtian Epic theatre, music, and dance, that centralises on themes of love, loss, innocence and experience. The company tends to refer to fairy tales, myths and legends as stimuli for their work, but in recent years has drawn inspiration from classic films and literature, underpinned by references to their Cornish heritage. Although other contemporary companies use similar theatrical components within their performance, Kneehigh specifically uses references to Cornwall and Cornish cultural identity within their work. Performance is used by Kneehigh as a platform to discuss and define cultural identity, with a focus on Cornwall being central to their brand. This is matched with a commitment to storytelling within theatre.

Part of Kneehigh's theatrical style incorporates their devising and adaptation processes. Emma Govan, Helen Nicholson and Kate Normington in *Devising Histories and Contemporary Practices (2007)* provided a concise overview of Kneehigh as a devising theatre company, exploring cultural identity through storytelling and adaptation. Govan et al. clearly encapsulated Kneehigh's emerging reputation for storytelling, signposting their adaptations that incorporate a Cornish focal point.

Drama scholar Margherita Laera, proposes a model for considering adaptation which has been beneficial in the analysis of productions discussed in this book. Laera's notions on the importance of the 'cyclical nature' of repetition [2] within adaptation in *Theatre and Adaptation: return, rewrite, repeat (2014)* and the assertion of cultural identities within the storytelling tradition are comparable to Kneehigh's practice. Kneehigh will reprise many of their productions, shaping them to fit their company and shifting concepts of cultural and artistic identity, and sense of 'self'. I would also assert that the cyclical nature of adapting theatre can support the development of a theatrical brand and provide an opportunity to engage with a production missed in an earlier tour.

Theatre historian Kara Reilly, in *Contemporary Approaches to Adaptation in Theatre (2018)*, established the potential for theatrical adaptation to capture 'moments in history' [3]Kneehigh's more socially and politically themed productions have attempted this 'time-capsule' quality; notably *Kneehigh's Ubu! A Singalong Satire* (2019-20) referring to Brexit and the UK 2019 general election. The production, *946: The Amazing Adolphus Tips* (2016), portrayed the story of black American soldiers stationed in the Cornish town of Slapton during the second world war. Within the production programme and marketing campaign, Kneehigh highlighted the 'lost' historical narrative of this true-life story, documenting the 946 soldiers who were killed in a training exercise (unfortunately intercepted by enemy troops).

Heather Lilley, an academic in drama, describes Rice and Shepherd's stance on adaptation, and the company's process of adapting varied stimuli. Lilley signposts the importance of repetition through 're-telling', referring to Rice's preference for this phrase to describe Kneehigh's adaptive process[4]. Descriptions of the adaptation process of the company are outlined, fluctuating between devised group work and solo written adaptation. Interestingly, Lilley questions to what extent the company has 'co-authored' the work; but concludes that a singular modality of adaptation should not solely define the material generated.

> Placing works at either end of the spectrum reinforces simplistic notions of a singular, original source text and also the restrictive binary of devised theatre against text-based theatre, both of which are actually challenged and complicated by Kneehigh's work and Rice's desire to be a 'reteller' rather than an adapter. [5]

Lilley acknowledges Kneehigh's theatricality, seeking to explore different ways of devising and adaptation, beyond the text, embracing different sources and perspectives. 'Kneehigh' as a theatrical style is inclusive of all members of the company, but also associated with Shepherd and Rice's adaptation, devising and artistic direction. Duska Radosavljevic, discussed a 'shared' devising process in her interview with Shepherd, describing

Shepherd's ability to utilise the talents within the company. Irrespective of company members having agency over specific elements of the production, Radosavljevic states that it is still very clear who is in charge.[6]

Kneehigh uses the term 'magic realism' to summarise their artistic stance, highlighting the magical aspect of theatre and live performance. Colombian writer Gabriel García Márquez (and author of the story *A Very Old Man with Enormous Wings*) used magic realism as a way to tell stories, exploring people on the outskirts of society, providing critique for those with political power. Magic realism is a style of fiction which provides a view of the contemporary world, whilst adding magical, fantastical elements. This is implicit in the Kneehigh production of this story and can be seen in many of Kneehigh's shows. Notable examples can be seen in *Dead Dog in a Suitcase and Other Love Songs* (2019), with the appearance of a giant dead dog puppet in the finale highlighting the moral decay of society. Magic realism can be observed in *Tristan and Yseult,* capturing the intoxicating qualities of love by suspending actors in mid-air with wires; literally, rather than figuratively, 'high' on a love potion.

Despite the magic realist nature of these elements, Kneehigh is keen to engage the audience's emotions through moments of realism within the performance. The desire to tell a story, finding the emotional heart, human connections and shared commonalities within the narrative is core to their artistic vision and identity. Theatre Critic Patrick Marmion summarised Kneehigh's theatrical brand, identifiable by its creative qualities as well as the influence of Cornish heritage, as a hybrid of classic works combined with modern theatrical aesthetics. On describing the creativity and originality in devising a chorus of nerds who observed the love story in *Tristan and Yseult* (2005) from a distance, Marmion stated that the company had taken a classic story and embedded it with 'freshness and charm'[7]. Marmion's theatre review for the production communicated Kneehigh's ability to reinvent a story that both entertains and incorporates localism into a global product. Likewise, Marmion presented observations on Emma Rice's theatrical style that incorporated a blend of international performance techniques.

> Emma Rice's ebullient production is also an ingenious fusion of theatrical forms, from May Day mumming to circus, pantomime to German cabaret. Underpinning it is a hearty, honest-to-goodness Britishness – the sort that revels in meat pies and Morris dancing.[8]

Revealed within Marmion's commentary are further descriptors of Kneehigh's brand of theatre, fusing selected elements of Cornish and British identity, culturally blended with a range of international influences.

Like other successful brands, Kneehigh utilises the art of reinvention. The company achieves this by updating their ethos, promoting creativity, together with the capacity to reinvent and reinvigorate a product that has become outdated. Tom Gatti observed Kneehigh's ability to re-imagine classic stories and bring them back to life, suggesting that their recognisable brand is as 'theatre's foremost story resuscitators: they breathe new life into old tales'.[9] Through Kneehigh's flexibility and evolution of past and present brand associations, the company can be adaptable in producing work that may detract and change their core values. Such an example can be seen in Kneehigh's development from Theatre In Education (TIE)[a] into mainstream theatre and later in the company's transitions into other cultural stimuli. The selection of myths, legends and fairy tales as a basis for much of Kneehigh's work is a pragmatic choice for a company that started life as a TIE company. Developing these tales made the company marketable and appealing to their primary school age target audience, providing Kneehigh with the opportunity to explore what they perceive as 'universal' and timeless issues in their work. As the company has developed from school tours to adult theatre, Kneehigh has been able to explore these tales, emphasising the darker areas of the subject matter through their own theatrical style.

In many of the company's programmes, Emma Rice and Mike Shepherd stated their reasons behind tackling these stories, indicating that they are 'timeless' and global, thus relevant in the modern age. Shepherd has cited the research of psychologist Bruno Bettelheim as an influence on the company, referring to his work as an inspiration and artistic philosophy in production programmes and interviews. Bettelheim advocated the telling of fairy tales as important in child development, dealing with problems that are global and timeless in nature.

> By dealing with universal human problems, particularly those which preoccupy the child's mind, these stories speak to his budding ego and encourage its development, while at the same time relieving preconscious and unconscious pressures. [10]

This drive to consider 'universal human problems' is integral to Kneehigh's selection of stimuli, but also informs their theatrical adaptations. As I will explore within the case studies of productions, adaptation can include the physical aesthetics of the production, and specify the focus on worldwide

---

[a] (TIE) – This abbreviation stands for theatre in education and refers to work produced specifically for school tours. Productions can often be accompanied by a workshop to reinforce the themes covered in the main performance.

yet personal issues. In this cultural transaction, emphasis ranges from macro to micro, and vice versa: from personal issues to worldwide commonalities.

Reviews in *The Red Shoes Press Report, Edinburgh Festival (2001)*, documented Kneehigh's reputation as a company who focus on the universal and fundamental themes within classic folk and fairy tales (mirroring the concerns outlined by Bettelheim). Several reviews for this production argued that the company had returned to the 'original' and darker version of the story. They described the production as suiting all age ranges by not being too frightening for children, but 'thought provoking enough for sophisticated adults'.[11] Kneehigh's brand identity in developing productions based on fairy tales displays their ability to retain the darkness and edginess of the source material in their work, appealing to a range of audience members and age groups. Through this treatment of fairy tales and classic films, Kneehigh has emerged with a brand association for theatre that presents darker re-imaginings of myths and legends.

The desire to be a brand, in an age of globalisation and capitalism, prompts questions on Kneehigh's brand identity and their appeal to local and global audiences. This is a stance emerging out of their artistic philosophy, company reports and publicity materials for the Asylum. 'Branding' involved the development of a product that is recognisable and synonymous with their theatrical style, and its diversification into varied products and projects contained within the Kneehigh 'banner'. Theatre scholar, Kate Dorney, defined the company in branded terms: 'Kneehigh has a unique selling proposition (USP), a brand, that makes their work popular with audiences and funding bodies alike'[12]. Successful brands display the ability to appeal to potential consumers and investors who can offer financial backing. I have found Dorney's work useful in signposting the potential for the Asylum to strengthen Kneehigh's USP. I wish to explore the Asylum's impact on the Kneehigh brand within my research, exploring my own queries and areas of engagement.

Kneehigh's use of the phrase 'Brand Kneehigh' instigated my research into branding and globalisation. It provided a theoretical lens to clarify what 'brands' are, whilst underpinning definitions of business models and strategies. It is a significant area to look into since it relates to Kneehigh's own branded ambitions for local to global expansion, but also describes significant influences on contemporary society. Globalisation (associated with capitalism and neoliberalism) defines how we lived in the twentieth century and how we live now in this century. Emerging arguments for and against globalisation have developed; specifically, with argumentation against this social, political and economic process growing as a pervasive narrative in the later twentieth century. Both narratives for and against globalism display the impact on modern culture, but also represent the very same tensions Kneehigh contend with.

Kneehigh experienced a range of challenges in trying to create a global theatre product whilst staying true to their Cornish cultural identity. These tensions include; a pull away from creating work in Cornwall, pressure from funding bodies to create work that has national and international appeal, financial hardships forcing the near closure of the company, critique on the evolution of Kneehigh as a local and global company, and artistic backlash against Kneehigh's adaptation or 'retelling' of popular works. This book will consider the Asylum, as Kneehigh's solution to the difficulties encountered, and also as a venue to strengthen their product and reinforce their brand. Ultimately my argument establishes Kneehigh working towards an equilibrium between localism and globalism through cultural exchange. Just as I have focused on branding as a facet within globalism, cultural exchange is also part of a globalised process evident within Kneehigh's brand evolution. I use the term cultural exchange within Kneehigh's work to reflect on sharing of influences, narratives, communities, people and places, as a way to create work. The Three Islands Project (2003-2005) was established to form cultural exchange on an international level and will be considered as a case study in Chapter 4.

Research into globalisation was undertaken to establish definitions and investigate theories useful in considering the tensions navigated by Kneehigh, with the following texts and theorists being particularly instrumental in shaping the research. Phillipe Legrain in *Open World: The Truth about Globalisation* (2000) discussed the benefits of the brand. Within the realms of theatre and performance, many companies have also acknowledged and embraced the advantages of brand association. Joseph Pine and James H. Gilmore in *The Experience Economy (1998)* suggested an 'experience' within a self-contained environment can strengthen brand association, reinforce repeat custom, and transcend a product into a 'lifestyle' affirmation. Naomi Klein in *No Logo (2010)* offered an alternative view of companies who wish to expand their brand by constructing a 'world' as a powerful display of expansion, removing competition and critique.[13] Likewise, Klein outlined the backlash against high profile brands (Nike, Levi's, McDonalds, Starbucks, etc.). Starting in the 1990s, Klein illustrated a global awareness of the negative attributes of branded companies and brands; highlighting possible opposition by 'anti-globals' (those opposed to globalisation). Naomi Klein is, of course, a social activist. However, her work was of value in contributing to the global/branding debate explored within this text. Her argument provided a counter-argument addressing the negativity of brands, in contrast to Legrain's positive outlook.

Argumentation against branding and associations with market globalism are critical discourses facing many companies and genres of theatre, as well as Kneehigh. Immersive theatre company, Punchdrunk, has encountered critique for brand associations with Sony PlayStation and Courvoisier, in conjunction with high ticket costs. This critique was evident in reviews for their production *Sleep No More* (2012). A theatre blog in *The Guardian* by Miriam Gillinson titled, Punchdrunk's "Sleep No More: is this a sell-out which I see before me?" questioned the theatre company's artistic intentions in recreating *Macbeth*. The blog title itself underpins an 'anti-global' positionality, that reduces artistic appreciation, emphasising abandonment of theatrical 'principles' for economic gains. Gillinson found a number of aspects in the production as evidence of money-grabbing and self-promotion:

> In these cash strapped times – hell, in any time – why shouldn't a company engage with the business world if it helps them advertise their brand, or make great work elsewhere? But I do worry when these commercial concerns begin to undermine a company's own theatrical productions. [14]

Gillinson's shares concerns on the 'commercial' impact on Punchdrunk's productions: the very same concerns explored in relation to Kneehigh within this study. Punchdrunk, like Kneehigh, has experienced criticism for establishing and developing a recognisable brand, with negative associations formed between their artistry and neoliberalism. The 'McDonaldization' of theatre, specifically in relation to musicals produced by Cameron Mackintosh, as discussed in the research of Dan Rebellato and his phrase 'McTheatre' (Rebellato *Theatre and Globalization* 39), explores artistic hegemony and the dominance of the Cameron Mackintosh brand. This argument provided a further dimension to the context of 'Brand Kneehigh'; establishing the backlash against brands and capitalism, voicing a potential negativity towards Kneehigh's theatrical branding. I argue that 'Brand Kneehigh' mirrors both arguments, illustrating the dichotomy Kneehigh faces in its career and within the evolution of its brand.

Globalisation in Theatre

The areas of business, economics, and sociology have offered a range of extensive research and theories on globalisation. A selection of these theories are used as a frame or tool to consider Kneehigh and their work alongside research linking globalisation and theatre. Dan Rebellato in

Theatre & Globalisation recognised the immense range of work on this subject, indicating that: 'The literature on globalisation is enormous'[15] As introduced earlier, Rebellato discussed the homogenising effects of a global theatrical product described as 'McTheatre'[b]. McTheatre was identified as a globalised by-product of capitalism, citing musical theatre productions (or 'mega musicals' by Cameron Mackintosh) as prime examples of franchised theatre. These include *Phantom of the Opera, Cats, Miss Saigon, etc.* As described by Rebellato, original work was not displayed in opening shows around the world; offering instead new franchises of work already in existence. Referring to the uniformity of McDonald's products, with little local variation globally, the work inherent in these mega musicals follows similar terms. Likewise, McTheatre can include dramatic theatre productions beyond the realms of the musical.

Franchised theatre shows can include popular work such as *War Horse* (2007-2009), evolving its own brand identity beyond the National Theatre. *War Horse* was resident at the National Theatre between 2007-2009, transferring to the West End, and has been on a tour around the world since 2009, with reprised productions in 2018-19. In addition, *Ghost Stories* (2010-2020) has featured several reproductions since its premiere in the Liverpool Playhouse in 2010. Both productions received acclaim meeting popular audience demand. The term McTheatre suggests a process encountered by a show incarnated so many times (sticking to the original format) that it loses its uniqueness and innovative qualities. This is a dilemma faced by many theatre companies with several factors having a negative impact on their artistic and cultural sensibilities. Aspects related to globalisation and their impact on Kneehigh will be a central focus of this study. In an issue of *Contemporary Theatre Review* in 2006, dedicated to globalisation, Harvie and Rebellato suggest that theatre as globalisation is effective in its simplicity and is cheap to make. It has a global relevance in its construction:

> ...the primary stuff of theatrical work - creating images, transforming meanings, finding new ways of expressing ideas and experiences - has a far greater continuity with the every-day reality of most people's working lives than it has ever had before. [16]

Theatre, as a platform, has the potential to encourage communication and exchange, lending itself to sharing processes inherent in globalisation.

---

[b] 'McTheatre' is an unflattering term, underpinning the homogenised construct of global musical theatre. It has strong links with the business model of McDonalds, utilising the connection within the name. (Rebellato 2010).

Different arguments relating to globalisation outline the perceived benefits and limitations that this paradigm offers, and theatre can explore varied global opinions. Sophie Nield commented on performance or an 'event' and its ability to communicate an anti-globalist movement.

> 'Evidently, many oppositional protest events connected to global anti-capitalist activity have acutely considered - in order to exploit - the symbolic summary produced by the moment of the enactment or encounter.' [17]

Nield's description of the strategic occupation of public and local spaces to draw attention to globalisation, by the anti-globalist movement, illustrated the intricacies at work between global energies within local limits. However, this does not lessen the validity of an anti-global movement. It does illustrate the complexity of working within varying degrees of this paradigm; even when protesting against globalism, whilst using a platform which is arguably global. David Barnett described the difficulties artists face within a globalised world:

> ...artists have to ask themselves how they are to apprehend a topography of contemporary life in which long distance travel is not exceptional, corporations straddle continents, and the internet can connect two sides of the world in less than a second. [18]

These are challenges Kneehigh have faced within their work, artistic vision, and company ethos and are multi-faceted concepts to navigate. Examples are portrayed within the case studies of the Three Islands Project and *Cymbeline*. In these examples, contemporary life has been explored, spanning countries in the case of the Three Islands Project and engaging in performance across continents in reference to *Cymbeline*. This work has been undertaken to share artistic practices and encourage spectatorship internationally, provoking reactions that are rich in their range of variety and argumentation. As will be explored in more detail in the case studies for the above productions, the Three Islands Projects did establish cultural sharing and an examination of hegemony, whilst opening a debate on the true extent of exchange. *Cymbeline* initiated international recognition for Kneehigh's theatrical style, but also generated critique against its style's dominance over the source material.

Gabrielle Giannachi in 'Exposing globalisation' stated globalisation's ability to transform theatre into a 'new theatre that bursts the boundaries of the theatre of everyday life'.[19] The boundaries of theatre can be both physical (or real) and digital. Giannachi cites Critical Art Ensemble as such an example, describing them as a company who create work: 'both electronically and in 'real' locations.[20] The use of media in theatre mirrors the technological advancements of globalisation within other areas of modern life. Kneehigh, like other contemporary theatre companies, have incorporated digital elements within their productions and are willing to engage with them as both a stimuli and performance style. The company have broken boundaries between the digital and 'real' artistically in *Brief Encounter*, with live actors interacting with their digital counterparts. This was a production that developed material known globally, placing their own 'localised' branded style within their adaptation.

Definitions of 'local' and 'global' are indeterminate, as indicated by Paul Rae: '[In] the theatre, "somewhere" and "anywhere" are not so much mutually exclusive as mutually informing'.[21] Being a spectator in the theatre involves a transition from the theatre space to a fictional place on stage. This potential for fluidity in theatre can transform a space, by shaping and re-imagining local and global elements. It can do this by redefining them, developing imagined worlds on a physical and ephemeral level. Kneehigh's production *A Very Old Man with Enormous Wings* (2005) reconfigured their own local and global limits, producing a show (discussed later) in terms of international cultural exchange.

The work of Helen Gilbert has contributed to theatre and cosmopolitanism, post-colonialism and globalisation. Gilbert's research has focused on post-colonialism and indigeneity within theatre and performance. Although my research is not a study of post-colonialism, it does refer to Cornish cultural identity, which shares prevalent views in Cornwall about 'English' dominance. Shepherd has expressed similar views in press interviews and within production work. The Cornish struggles cited in *Blast* (2010) mirror colonialist oppression experienced in Ireland, as analysed by Gilbert and Tompkins: 'Ireland's centuries-old political and economic oppression at the hands of the British – and its resistance to such control – fits well within the post-colonial paradigm[22]. Similarly, to other 'colonised' people, Kneehigh produced plays which seek to communicate Cornish history.

> To refute the misguided belief that colonised people do/did not have a history of their own, many plays stage aspects of the pre-contact past in order to re-establish traditions, to lay claim to a heritage or territory, and to recuperate various forms of cultural expression. [23]

By communicating stories that have local importance, the 'local' has a new focus, a 'voice' or 'narrative' for consideration. Gilbert communicated the complex relationship between the 'local' and the 'global' and discussed concerns, shared by Kneehigh, in meeting the needs of local and indigenous communities.

Kneehigh's place within theatre and globalisation covers a number of areas, some of which are artistic, other areas include branding and entertainment. The company's theatrical style portrays a devising and adaptation process that engages with globalism. They actively seek international stimuli and collaborators, with the cyclical style of their work lending itself to reprisals, updates and further globalism. As a brand, their portfolio of experiences continues to grow. The same production can be reprised at different times, at different locations, offering different experiences and mementoes. In the case of *Quicksilver* (2002), the production could be seen within a tin mine, at a later point within a theatre environment with an accompanying 'gift'. *Tristan and Yseult* has been performed on the Cornish coast and in theatres around the world. Kneehigh, like other contemporary devising theatre companies, displays a notable theatrical style, offering experiences (within a range of locations) and merchandise as part of a performance. Kneehigh offers a specificity in aligning their brand with Cornwall and tourism within the county, whilst maintaining their artistic identity. Importantly, all of this is underpinned by the company's desire to tell a story, forming the 'heart' within the company brand.

'Brand Kneehigh' and Globalisation

An emerging by-product of globalisation, originating in the nineteenth century, is the brand. Legrain states that brands started in the nineteenth century as 'badges of quality and consistency'.[24] This allowed consumers to be more confident when buying products from strangers, rather than from their local community. 'Brands were the first piece of consumer protection'.[25] Legrain argues that this is still the case, with consumers willing to pay more for a brand name they trust, simplifying buying/ shopping decisions through brand loyalty. This focus on the brand with its associations with lifestyle and aspirations is pertinent to the current age of globalisation, with Legrain providing recent historical examples such as the virtual branding of Britain as 'Cool Britannia' in the 1990s: 'Companies provide their consumers with opportunities not merely to shop but to experience fully the meaning of their brand'.[26]

Gillespie and Hennessey in *Global Marketing* describe those in support of brands as 'Global Dreamers' who 'equate global brands with quality and are attracted by the lifestyle'.[27] There is an aspirational and idealistic tone to Gillespie and Hennessey's term for individuals and companies pursuing neoliberalist branding as 'dreamers'. Alternatively, the phrase 'dreamers' holds negative associations, emphasising the fantastical, non-tangible and unreliable quality of dreams. Despite these negative characteristics, Gillespie and Hennessey succinctly highlight the powerful aspirations maintained by 'brand' and brand associations. As described by Legrain, many companies (in pursuit of lifestyle branding) develop their products in a multi-purpose building that may contain many core 'leisure' activities such as shopping, cinema and food and drink. Other areas of leisure include branded travel, driven by the consumer identifying or even aspiring to a specific way of life.

> This is the meaning of lifestyle brand: living your life inside a brand. Brand-based companies are no longer satisfied with having a fling with their consumers, they want to move in together. [28]

This statement mirrors Kneehigh's own plans with the Asylum which it realised with its grand opening including; shows, live music, food and drink, art and photography exhibitions. Merchandise could be purchased, including books, CDs, even clothing. Like other lifestyle brands wishing to appeal to several areas in a consumer's life, Kneehigh has used their website to promote their live theatre work which is central to their brand while also advertising other merchandise which offers different forms of entertainment and experience. As part of the Kneehigh brand online, a 'consumer' can keep up to date with their next performances, buy their collection of plays, poetry or picture books which provide a historical overview with photography. Three CD's of Kneehigh's music are available on their website, including the soundtracks to their acclaimed RSC production, *Cymbeline* (2006), and *The Wild Bride* (2011), with the third CD featuring a collection of love songs from their shows. Likewise, areas of the website offered different levels of paid membership with Kneehigh, sharing many characteristics of other fan clubs, and allowing Kneehigh fans priority notification on performances and other events.

   If Legrain's argument that brands are a way of developing consumer confidence in the quality of a product is true, it is understandable why Kneehigh harnessed this view. They wished to develop a strong brand, one that displays excellent quality and creativity in theatre, encouraging loyalty in which customers will spend their money and come back for more. Economically this is a strong business strategy displaying tactics for self-preservation and a steady source of income. Developing a strong brand creates good publicity, attracting more custom. Kneehigh Theatre Company state in their literature (especially in their publicity about their home venue, Asylum), their ambitions to develop themselves into a recognisable brand, synonymous with their theatrical style and quality. Lyn Gardner for *The*

Guardian sums up the company's style of theatre which is central to their brand:

> What the company has created instead is an original brand of theatre, born out of Cornwall's lack of red velvet spaces and a need to engage directly with an audience, often outdoors without the trick of lights or effects. Its style is rough, irreverent and belligerent – and venues are queuing up to slot Kneehigh into their programmes. [29]

The Telegraph, in an interview with Shepherd and Rice in 2010, used similar language in defining Kneehigh as a 'brand' that is playful and irreverent, effective in storytelling and in demand by the RSC, West End commercial producers and 'abroad too'.[30]

Kneehigh has used the phrase 'to be truly universal you must be truly local', by Joan Miro, a Catalan artist[c], as a strapline on many of their marketing materials and production reports, claiming a global resonance and universality to their work. This quote underlines the ability to incorporate local needs with global/universal interests but places the heart of the process of globalisation within a local origin. However, this notion is problematic, reducing the differences between the local and global, just as globalisation has homogenising effects on local variations. Although Legrain himself is in favour of globalisation, he presents a balanced response to the opposing views of global sceptics, showing a move towards globalism as a choice, rather than an inevitability. Legrain highlights an area of globalisation which is limiting in its appeal, citing mass marketing and branding as having a limited shelf life and being unable to connect with contemporary consumers.

> Mass marketing has become a very hard thing to do because people don't like to be seen as 'normal' anymore – they all want to be seen as individuals…The bigger you become, the less appealing you become. It's a dilemma: somehow you have to find a way of exploiting the behind-the-scenes benefits of being big, yet at the point at which you touch the consumer, you have to be seen to be small. [31]

This duality between the global and the local, underlines the complexity of the individual and their macro and micro concerns and identifications. Kneehigh no longer used the above Miro quote on their publicity materials showing an aspiration to move away from the 'one-world' local is global

---

[c] Kneehigh have used this quote from this artist in the past. However, during my research using the Kneehigh Archive, I could find no rationale behind using this particular quote or any links between the company and Miro.

view of cultural identity. Arguably, this is a view that cannot communicate the multi-faceted nature of globalism.

Responding to a question I posed to Rice, about the difficulties the company may experience in aiming to work both locally and globally, Rice suggested that although people around the world have different experiences, 'we are all on the same emotional and spiritual level'[32] (Rice 2012). Rice commented on this former 'strapline', suggesting it is not an advertising campaign to underline their 'glocalisation', but a code that the company lives by:

> We often use a Miro quote which is 'To be truly universal you have to be local' and we live by that, but it doesn't feel like a tension to make work in a very precise, isolated place [Cornwall] and then take it to the world. [33]

This response presents the company's own aspiration to be connected to their own locality, which they see as important to their processes of working and intrinsic to them developing globally. Issues of dominant global businesses obliterating smaller local companies are concerns that Kneehigh know of and have taken on board in a variety of productions. The above issues are explored in *The Very Old Man with Enormous Wings* (2005) and in *Blast* (2010), with both productions providing a narrative platform. Acknowledgements of the differences between global and local culture are not recognised by globalisation, according to global sceptics. It should be noted that Kneehigh may not be responding directly to a local versus global dichotomy, but instead, acknowledging the differences between the local and the global in their own work.

According to Legrain, any product wishing to assert itself as a successful brand should aim to transcend being a product into a lifestyle choice and a form of self-expression:

> Expressing its aspirations, its soul, its sense of family, the brands humanised the corporation, lifted it from the land of goods and services up to an exalted moral plane. [34]

This stance is demonstrated as early as 2000, in an interview with Julie Seyer, the general manager of Kneehigh. Seyer stated Kneehigh's motive is to be more than just entertainment, but to empower people to 'make the most of their lives, planting a seed in people's minds that anything is possible'.[35] The tagline in the promotional materials for the *Summer Schools in Cornwall 2001* offered potential consumers the chance to 'Eat, sleep, breathe and dream theatre' (Summer School 2001). The statement affirms

Kneehigh's globalist 'ambitions' of becoming a lifestyle product, targeting the senses and allowing for greater participation.

In the report, *The Kneehigh Plan 1999-2001 Appendices* (written by the administration team at Kneehigh and based on company meetings), Kneehigh considered whether they should change their name to rebrand the company. They concluded with the realisation that the name is too valuable to lose in the search for further marketing opportunities:

> The reasons for change are outweighed by the benefits of retaining the profile and goodwill associated with the name Kneehigh. There is little point in changing Kneehigh to choose something which will be meaningless for a long time when the product is not being totally changed. [36]

Their name is clearly intrinsic to their identity, and pragmatically it would take a long time to build new connections with a different title. Arguably, Kneehigh has been successful in changing the branded connotations with their name from children's theatre, generating reinvented associations. Central to this book is the definition of 'Brand Kneehigh', and the company's 'rejuvenation' of their name from TIE to noted contemporary theatre, charting a formative yet seismic development of their artistic identification. Later, this section of the report discusses branding and marketing opportunities, outlining their future ambitions for the Kneehigh brand:

> Keep the name but consider it a brand. As a brand - like Virgin or Nike - Kneehigh can be a production company, one or more touring companies, a publishing company, a recording studios, a building, a performance style, a type of social or educational work - even a philosophy or ideology.
>
> There could be:
>
> Kneehigh 2 - a smaller company
> Village Kneehigh - organising own rural promotions
> Young Kneehigh - a youth theatre company etc.
>
> Recommendation: drop the words 'Theatre Company' and build up the brand. In ten year's time when Kneehigh is very well known for any or all of these things no one will ask what 'Kneehigh' connotes - everyone will know! It's the Kneehigh Experience! Names become transparent once the product they represent is well known. [37]

Disclosed and revealed within this section were Kneehigh's thought processes, exploring brand identification and embracing the facets they perceived are enjoyed by other brands, having agency over the diverse products developed and offered. Communicated within this text is their ambition to transcend the range of products Kneehigh can offer to become 'a philosophy or ideology'. This shares commonalities with Legrain's observations on brand, evolving beyond the product itself, taking on fundamental significance to an individual's way of life and ideals. There is also commentary on the possibility of 'dropping' theatre company from their title, to build up their brand and to communicate their vision, aiming to be more than 'just' a theatre company. Within the appendices, a new strapline is created: 'Kneehigh: The National Theatre of Cornwall'.[38] Although it is agreed that it would make an excellent strapline, it is eventually unused. Why this was the case was undisclosed (or not recorded as part of a company meeting), with no other references or reasons provided in the Kneehigh archive.

Changing a company name, to fit a developing identity (and product diversity), is an important development for many modern businesses. Using the above 'National Theatre of Cornwall' strapline marginalises them within local parameters, limiting their development as a cosmopolitan company. Interestingly, the company label themselves as the 'Kneehigh Experience!', provoking allusions to Pine and Gilmore's theories of 'experience'. In reference to Legrain's research, brands need rebranding, and marketing campaigns can become outdated or 'usurped, creating the quintessential lose-lose situation'.[39] Arguably, Kneehigh needed to create a company name and branded strapline which communicated their links with community and international work; their ambition to create a venue for theatre and non-theatre goers, whilst also generating a tourist attraction appealing to a range of visitors. It is my argument that Kneehigh has achieved these ambitions, considering their brand very carefully to ensure that they do not limit themselves locally.

Arguments against globalisation and branding illustrate a potential homogenising impact; effects considered positive and progressive by supporters of globalism. This, of course, assumes that globalisation is a natural evolution (of modernism and postmodernism) intruding on local communities. Global influences or cultural flows can invigorate local 'niches' rather than overwhelm them, and alternatively, local variations can play an important role in the larger global culture.[40] Homogeneity of culture may in fact enrich the artistic product by sharing cultural practices, developing it in the global marketplace. Kneehigh collaborates with a range of global artists. Rather than undermining their backgrounds and original local markets, they celebrate these localities by incorporating local influences and references within the performance.

However, Kneehigh has been accused of homogenising the source material of the productions; *Cymbeline, Brief Encounter* and *A Matter of Life and Death*. Theatre critics have observed the hegemony of their original qualities due to Kneehigh's brand assertions. In these instances, Kneehigh's theatrical style has been critiqued as being too dominant, overshadowing the primary stimuli. Alternative arguments suggest that this is, in fact, Kneehigh's adaptation process: creative partners and sponsorship seek out the company to develop the work within their artistic 'branded' scope. As will be covered in the case studies of the above productions later in this book; the Royal Shakespeare Company, British Council and the National Theatre (amongst other noted national and international theatre organisations and practitioners) have recruited Kneehigh, with the intention of the work being given Kneehigh's branded treatment.

Global sceptics (including Naomi Klein) highlight the arguments against globalisation, voicing fears of hegemony and the loss of cultural boundaries. Theatre reviews for *Cymbeline* and *Brief Encounter* shared an 'anti-global' critique in conjunction with Kneehigh's brand, raising objections over the branded treatment of the work, particularly in its dominance (or hegemony) over the source material. The analogy of globalisation as a 'melting pot' for different cultures, inducing a loss of regional traditions and local roots, is a fear expressed by the 'anti-globalisation' movement. Kneehigh, in their own artistic development, appear to be wrestling with these global dilemmas, trying to bridge the divide between local audiences and global appeal.

Global advocates or 'hyper-globalists' including Legrain, regard the processes of cultural exchange as being supportive of globalisation. In fact, cultural sharing is integral to the successful integration of globalisation, with cultural exchange an emerging by-product of globalisation.

Cultural Exchange

The material discovered within the Kneehigh archive at Falmouth University presented Kneehigh as a company facing difficulties when navigating local and global interests. It portrayed the company's ambitions to provide work for their local community, whilst developing their theatrical brand on national and international platforms. Evidence found within the archive displayed the company negotiating these tensions by engaging in cultural exchange. As a by-product of globalisation, cultural exchange allows for the sharing of different influences and experiences; although equality between influences is open for debate. This was most transparent in Arts Council Reports and company evaluations, displaying ongoing negotiations between the council and Kneehigh for funding, in conjunction with changing strategies for greater community and cultural engagement.

Revealed in *The Arts Council Consultation Paper* (2011-12), with relevant sections included within Kneehigh evaluative reports, was the incentive for theatre companies to consider different business strategies. There is an awareness by the Arts Council of developing strategies for collaboration and developing work with an appeal to a wider context and audience base.

> The traditional theatre business models are being rethought. Theatres and theatre producers are working more collaboratively, increasing their capacity to make inspiring work and to take it to more people. [41]

The Arts Council and similar organisations incorporated government aims and initiatives, some of which have a localised focus, situating theatre within national parameters. Encouraging theatre companies to develop 'inspiring work' for a wider audience to experience, facilitated the opportunities for globalisation and cultural exchange. Although financial benefits to this process are an additional bonus, the encouragement of increased audience diversity and collaborations between artists from varied cultural backgrounds is paramount.

In the Arts Council consultation paper in Goal 5, the following statement referred to developing a range of funding opportunities with the arts; 'We want to encourage new ways of working, new business models and new funding relationships'.[42] This consultation paper mirrored ambitions of neoliberalism, securing the best resources, working relationships and funding mechanisms to develop financially 'successful' artistic opportunities. Likewise, Kneehigh displayed similar ambitions to incorporate elements of globalisation, attracting high profile co-producers from the Berkeley Rep in California USA, The Lyric Hammersmith, and Arts Project Australia.

Kneehigh, as described in their Arts Council report in 1996-7, showed their unhappiness and concerns on being urged to take their productions outside the Cornish locality:

> Whilst it is gratifying to the company that it is possible to achieve money in this way there is concern that all of the money brings with it conditions specifying touring outside Cornwall. [43]

However, years later, the Arts Council influence is economically and artistically enriching for Kneehigh, with cultural identities merged to build a nationally appealing product.

Emma Govan, Helen Nicholson and Kate Normington described Kneehigh's ability to combine the local with the global, therefore ensuring a mixture of global artists respond to the complexities of community. In this capacity, the company is successful in creating a multi-layered theatrical community:

> Kneehigh Theatre in England, for instance, has responded to the local-global nexus both by re-examining its Cornish roots and by developing collaborations with performers whose work takes place in very different settings/situations from its own. For example, Kneehigh developed its adaptation of the Cornish folktale 'Tristan and Yseult' in 2004-5 into a theatrical experiment in responding to place through the Three Island collaboration between England, Malta and Cyprus. As the production travelled to these three countries, company members and local performers worked together on the play, developing and recycling it in new ways that drew upon indigenous forms of aesthetic expression, and engaged with the political concerns of the place of performance. [44]

Govan et al. observed Kneehigh's ability to engage with global (external) influences, whilst revealing sensitivity towards 'local' issues. Their inclusion of the Three Island Projects, in terms of cultural exchange, and *Tristan and Yseult* as an example of embedding Cornish identity within Kneehigh's theatrical style acknowledged the globalised/localised duality of Kneehigh's work. Both productions are important to include in this detailed study; as cultural exchange is embedded within the company structure, the devising process, and woven into the 'fabric' of the narrative of the source material through adaptation.

Kneehigh, in their appeal to perform in different countries, assert their role as cultural ambassadors, engaging in cultural exchange and sharing theatre practice. As discussed earlier by Harvie and Rebellato, the very construction of the theatrical art form is a successful form of globalisation and can contribute to the development and debate of this process. Theatre has the ability to impact actors and audience alike, through the experienced physical performance: '...creating images, transforming meanings, finding new ways of expressing ideas and experiences' (Harvie and Rebellato 4). Many of Kneehigh's reports to the Arts Council England and the British Council, including evaluations of productions *The Red Shoes* (1999) and *Cymbeline* (2007), presented the cultural benefits experienced through a mutual sharing process. This was established between Kneehigh and communities in China and South America (locations to which these productions toured). Although the Arts Council South West (is the administrative office for the devolved funding model) encouraged these exchanges to ensure further funding, they also contributed to the sharing of cultural practices between both parties. In the case of *The Red Shoes,* Chinese actors who were unfamiliar with Brechtian influenced contemporary western theatre, were encouraged to experience Kneehigh's performance style through post-show workshops. My interview with Andrea Pelaez-Lyons revealed opportunities for South American artists to work with Kneehigh on *Cymbeline* through the British Council, which facilitated future working relationships. These are practices Kneehigh wished to share and develop further, enriching their work. The cultural sharing processes experienced between the individual and the group can result in an intensification and acceleration of social exchanges. Kneehigh has utilised this acceleration to form new contacts and ideas; sharing and learning from artistic encounters.

The tensions experienced by Kneehigh and examined in this study, raise valid questions relating to the convergence and divergence of the local and global; and questions how cultures can co-exist or submerge one another. Such issues highlight the fundamental effects and impact generated by globalisation.

> Our lives are becoming increasingly intertwined with those of distant people and places around the world – economically, politically and culturally. [45]

As Legrain has observed, cultural exchange is a process of working which is 'intertwined' in our lives, forming core elements of a global business model, with an expectation to conduct theatrical cultural exchanges to recreate successful business strategies. This is a strategy utilised by theatre companies themselves, or by external funding bodies.

Kneehigh experienced tensions in their development as a company through globalisation and their placement in the cultural and regional landscape of Cornwall. These tensions are multifaceted with alternating opposition between a counterculture defending individuation and those in favour of globalism. However, cultural exchange provides an opportunity for globalisation and localism to coexist. Burke suggests that cultural adaptation occurs to assimilate cultural differences into a global framework.

> Cultural adaptation may be analysed, as a double movement of de-contextualisation and re-contextualisation, lifting an item out of its original setting and modifying it to fit its new environment. [46]

In this capacity, a complexity within culture and cultural influences can be exposed and acknowledged. Regarding Kneehigh's artistic and cultural identity, a range of influences are clearly displayed within their work incorporating the Cornish location and international cast and crew. These influences vary in each production, and despite the global range, Cornish identity remains at the forefront. Steger, in contrast with Burke, argued the redefinition of cultural/global identities, may induce a less stable sense of identity:

> Those commentators who summarily denounce the homogenising effects of Americanisation must not forget that hardly any society in the world today possesses an 'authentic' self-contained culture.[47]

Although Steger, and other theorists included in this research, put forward a strong case illustrating the power of globalisation, his statement on 'authenticity' exposes the polarisation between cultural influences. What is 'authentic' can prove problematic to define, and despite a varied range of influences, many cultures assert themselves as 'authentic'. What Kneehigh and other cultural groups have difficulty with, is communicating and having 'others' understand and perceive their identity. Notions of cultural identity aren't definitive or static. Steger, in his defence of globalisation, has 'reduced' cultural identity. Steger's commentary typifies the negative connotations of global perceptions - underestimating localised factors which construct a cultural identity and their ability to invent and reinvent themselves.

Dorney discusses the terms 'regional', 'local' and 'national', showing that these terms convey very different meanings, depending on their use and context:

> We have seen individuals, companies, buildings and organisations have tried variously to conform to, challenge and quantify this terminology to survive.[48]

Kneehigh embraced these terms to define their work to encourage further funding and to appeal to a wider audience. Dorney in, *The Glory of the Garden: English Regional Theatre and the Arts Council 1984 – 2009,* highlights the tensions of capitalist and global success for Kneehigh, underlining a issue pertinent for localism:

> For some, their move to a national and international platform is seen as a betrayal of their local roots, for others, particularly theatre journalists and commentators, it is proof of the power of regional theatre.[49]

The perceived abandonment of local roots in favour of global influences is an important issue, highlighting tensions experienced by Kneehigh from their local audience, due to making work that reaches out to an international platform. Tensions generated from local 'abandonment' were at odds with the potential to strengthen the company and increase its funds and popularity by 'going global'. Dorney suggests that touring companies like Kneehigh are successful in their ability to succeed within globalisation, as they are a global construct: 'Their product is a more successful commodity in an era of turbo-capitalism because it is essentially cosmopolitan in focus and approach' (Dorney 122). In fact, the desire to tour increases popularity, as companies like Kneehigh and Cheek by Jowl 'are tailor-made for the current funding emphases' (Dorney 119). The company reviews and Arts Council reports found in the Kneehigh archive, showed a company forming to create work in Cornwall for the local inhabitants, with a realisation they would need to perform work nationally and internationally to survive.

Examples of cultural exchange were discussed in my interview with former actor and company member Andrea Perez-Lyons. This mirrored Dorney's comments on the company, descriptions reiterated in journalistic interviews, and statements made by Kneehigh themselves.

> The cast work together as an ensemble for a long period before the show opens (and in many cases return to work with the company on a regular basis), and there is a company style which combines physical robustness with music and songs, and they still practice a kind of rough theatre. [50]

Perez-Lyons described the experience of working with Kneehigh in similar terms, with comparisons made with the 'festival-like' atmosphere generated whilst touring around South America with *Cymbeline* and the Asylum. Dorney hypothesised about the opportunities and continued financial support this new environment could provide:

> This will give the company's operation even greater flexibility, allowing them to continue serving rural communities as well as metropolitan areas, and thereby help them achieve a greater range of targets set by the national and local funding bodies. [51]

Dorney completed research on Kneehigh by 2010 (for the publication *The Glory of the Garden English Regional Theatre and The Arts Council 1984 – 2009)*, just before the start of the Asylum's first summer season. In contrast, the 'experiential' research described in this book began at the same time, including all seasons of so far. It considers Kneehigh's ambitions for the Asylum discussing the company's opportunity to control their rehearsal and performance environment. This environment serves the local community in the summer and provides the space for Kneehigh to offer a complete entertainment package. This entertainment product strengthens the brand, acting as a model for when the show is on tour. Kneehigh premiere new shows at the Asylum, in front of a local audience, before they go on tour nationally and internationally. Dorney states that touring regional theatre is a global product, allowing the touring company to publicise and reinforce their product:

> It offers a recognisable brand, a hand-crafted and high-quality product using ingredients delivered to a discerning audience, but available anywhere if you have the money to pay for it. [52]

Dorney notes that touring the product outside its creative locality provided an availability to the consumer like other global products. In the summer season held in the Asylum, some audience members (including myself) would make the journey to experience Kneehigh's home venue. As a consumer, I was first attracted to Kneehigh's theatrical brand through their touring work. Their theatre brand has since then encouraged me to see their work in a range of venues, culminating in travelling to the Asylum to 'consume' more of their work. Through consideration of Kneehigh's local and global tensions, I discuss the notion of what is 'local', revealing the difficulty in defining this term. However, perceiving cultural identity as an ever-evolving map, a journey, as opposed to a fixed point with non-negotiable characteristics, provides a resolution. I contrast notions of the 'local' and cultural identity to discussions on the 'global', in relation to 'Brand Kneehigh'. Despite Kneehigh's ambitions to take onboard global business models, my assertion is that this company resists global homogeny, maintaining their Cornish cultural identity and while also engaging in cultural exchange.

Brand Chronology and Case Studies

The chronology of the Kneehigh brand corresponds with the chronology of the productions examined as case studies and the structure of this book. Chapter 1 has sought to introduce Kneehigh and key theoretical frameworks and terms within the fields of globalisation. Chapter 2 discusses research methodology, engaging in my use of archive and Asylum. This chapter also examines research into spectatorship, archives and adaptation: areas which have been fundamental to my work. Chapter 3 considers Kneehigh's 'local' components within their work. It explores the earlier emergences of 'Brand Kneehigh' in terms of localisation and Cornish identity in productions *Quicksilver* (2002), *Tristan and Yseult* (2005), and *Blast* (2010). The production *Quicksilver* (2002) explored the history of the Cornish mining industry, providing a voice to express local history, staged within the environment of the Cornish Landscape. The show was developed as a comedic western, set in the nineteenth century, addressing Mike Shepherd's concerns to share the history of Cornwall and its people within the county.[53] *Tristan and Yseult* (2005) is perceived by many followers of Kneehigh's work as a 'classic' within their theatrical productions and was important to include in a discussion about their branded theatricality. The production demonstrated Kneehigh's translation of a mythical legend, underscoring Cornish origins with a contemporary and somewhat cinematic interpretation. The production has positive associations with landscape theatre, with a memorable and acclaimed performance of *Tristan and Yseult* in 2004 at the open-air Minack Theatre, situated on the cliffs of Porthcurno, Cornwall. The production *Blast* (in the first season of the Asylum in 2010) encouraged the examination of oppositions between the 'local' and the 'global'. It displayed this through a comical look at Cornish history and suppression, with Cornish characters willing to commit an act of terrorism. The performance featured the main characters planting bombs in the theatre, creating a public platform for their collective 'Cornish' voice.

Chapter 4 looks at the progression of the brand within the realms of international cultural exchange in the *Three Islands Project* Case Study (2003-5) and *The Very Old Man with Enormous Wings* (2011). Global branded ambitions, forming partnerships with national and international collaborations, demonstrates the development of the brand on a wider platform. The project utilised Kneehigh's Cornish heritage and identity as a basis for multi-cultural collaboration with productions in Cyprus and Malta, recruiting company members from all three islands. The Three Islands Project was extremely important for Kneehigh; displaying their abilities to create a production which could connect different European countries on a collaborative, social and culturally sharing process. In addition to building relationships between European countries, it fostered an appreciation of Kneehigh as a Cornish global export, redirecting attention back to the Cornish county.

Chapter 5 examines the national and international work/collaboration with RSC and NT, and Michel Legrand. It considers the critique concerning the dominance of Kneehigh's theatrical style in the productions: *Cymbeline* (2006); *A Matter of Life and Death* (2007), *Brief Encounter* (2008) and *The Umbrellas of Cherbourg* (2011). The production *Cymbeline* (2006) toured South America (financed by the British Council) as an example of creative contemporary theatre from the UK. The Royal Shakespeare Company worked in conjunction with Kneehigh as part of the *Complete Works Festival*[d], with productions being performed around the UK before

---

[d] Complete Works Festival - the first time that all 37 plays, the sonnets and the long poems have been performed in one place. The RSC have produced 23 productions,

Cymbeline embarked on the South America tour – commissioned by the British Council. *A Matter of Life and Death* (2007) was the first time the company adapted a film. It exposed the company to critique from the Powell and Pressburger estate, theatrical reviewers and audience members. It continued an ongoing high-profile relationship with the National Theatre, attracting well-known actors such as Douglas Hodge to the production. This project also displayed an artistic shift embracing devising work (found commonly within Kneehigh's work on fairy tales), and adaptation (developing classic films, literature and television for theatre). *Brief Encounter* (2008) was the company's second re-imagining of a classic film by Powell and Pressburger from the 1940s and displayed Kneehigh's ambitions to create an immersive brand experience extending further than the stage/performance area. The production appeared to 'celebrate' the original film by embracing multi-media within the performance, rather than generating a theatrical adaptation which tried to omit or completely transform the primary source. *The Umbrellas of Cherbourg* (2011) proved to be a problematic 'globalist' endeavour as the production closed after a few weeks in London's West End. The production provided evidence of the company's work of adaptation. However, as a researcher considering the work of Kneehigh, it raised questions of artistic 'value' and 'worth' when considering it in terms of globalisation and cultural exchange.

Chapter 6 considers the Asylum, exploring branded worlds to reinforce their product and repeat custom. The chapter will also discuss my experiential archive and spectatorship within this space. Performances of *The Red Shoes* (2010) and *Global Cornwall* (2012) are case studies considered within the home venue, Asylum, which I suggest centralises and strengthens the brand. *The Red Shoes* (2010), first performed in 2001-2 and reprised in the Asylum in the opening season, illustrated an important stage for Kneehigh's branding in conjunction with Emma Rice's directorial skills. The first performance of this production secured Rice a theatrical award for directing and arguably initiated a new 'age' for the company, achieving recognition for their theatrical style globally. Kneehigh held *Global Cornwall* in July 2012, instigating a political and cultural debate on Cornish identity and its place within the world. Despite the global connotations in the title, the company were keen to establish a localised approach to their business strategy for this event by supporting local cultural identities in selecting 'homegrown' companies. This is an important event to analyse,

---

with more than 30 visiting companies, 17 from overseas, including Yukio Ninagawa's Japanese *Titus Andronicus, Macbeth* in Polish and *Twelfth Night* in Russian. (https://www.rsc.org.uk/about-us/history)

portraying Kneehigh's willingness to engage with a political global debate, centralising Cornwall's and the company's place within this discussion.

Finally, Chapter 7 considers the latter stages and closure of Kneehigh Theatre and progression of Emma Rice (in leaving Kneehigh, joining the Globe and eventually creating her own theatre company, Wise Children), discussing changes within both companies and the socio/political landscape within which they operate. Spanning the period, 2016 to 2020, these case studies offer a detailed reflection on the 'splintering' and development of the brand, and the emergence of Rice's own theatrical trademark. Rice's directorship had been synonymous with Kneehigh's performance style for many years. This case study takes this into consideration and reflects on Rice's individuation – and eventual emancipation from Kneehigh. Arguably (before Kneehigh's closure), Rice with her company, Wise Children and Kneehigh stood to benefit from links and associations with one another (as did WildWorks). In light of Kneehigh's closure, former company members may now create new relationships with Rice and her company.

This book engages with a journey-like analogy of cartography, a mapping of an important contemporary British theatre company, facing cultural and economic tensions shared by many other theatre companies at the time of writing this text. As a researcher, I have found the evolution and fulfilment of 'Brand Kneehigh' revealed and supported by the Kneehigh Archive fascinating. The archival narrative reinforced the company's endeavours to create a recognisable USP, while simultaneously exposing the dilemmas they and other theatre companies contend with when working with local and global interests.

References

[1] British Council, *Kneehigh Theatre*, Theatre and Dance, <https://theatreanddance.britishcouncil.org/artists-and-companies/k/kneehigh-theatre/>

[2] Laera, M. *Theatre and Adaptation: return, rewrite, repeat*, Bloomsbury, 2014. Pg-2.

[3] Reilly, K. *Contemporary Approaches to Adaptation in Theatre*, Palgrave Macmillan, 2018. Pg- xxiii.

[4] Lilley, H. "Kneehigh's Retellings", Reilly, K (ed). *Contemporary Approaches to Adaptation in Theatre*, Palgrave Macmillan, 2018. Pg-6.

[5] Lilley, H. "Kneehigh's Retellings", Reilly, K (ed). *Contemporary Approaches to Adaptation in Theatre*, Palgrave Macmillan, 2018. Pg-6.

[6] Radosavljevic, Duska. "Chapter 4 Kneehigh Theatre", ed. Tomlin, Liz. *British Theatre Companies 1995 - 2014*, Bloomsbury, 2015. Pg-160.

[7] Marmion, P. *Kneehigh Archive*, "A local play, for local people…", 2005.

[8] Marmion, P. *Kneehigh Archive*, "A local play, for local people...", 2005.

[9] Gatti, T. "Where theatres wild things are", *The Times*, published 24th July 2010. Pg-1.

[10] Bettelheim, B. *The Uses of Enchantment - the meaning and importance of fairy tales,* Penguin Books, UK, 1976. Pg-6.

[11] Blackmore Vale Magazine, "Wolf, Kneehigh Theatre on tour", 2001.

[12] Dorney, Kate. "Chapter 5 - Touring and the Regional Repertoire: Cheek By Jowl, Complicite, Kneehigh and Eastern Angles", ed. Dorney, Kate & Merkin, Ros. *The Glory of the Garden English Regional Theatre and The Arts Council 1984 - 2009,* Cambridge Scholars Publishing, 2010. Pg-118.

[13] Klein, Naomi. *No Logo*, Fourth Estate, 2010. Pg-146.

[14] Gillinson, M. "Punchdrunk's Sleep No More: is this a sell-out which I see before me?", *The Guardian,* 2012.

[15] Rebellato, Dan. *Theatre and Globalisation*, Palgrave MacMillan: Hampshire, UK. 2009. Pg-87.

[16] Harvie, J. & Rebellato, D. *Contemporary Theatre Review,* "Editorial", 2006, 16:01, 3-6, Pg-4.

[17] Nield, Sophie. *Contemporary Theatre Review,* "There is another world: Space, theatre and anti-capitalism, 16:01, 51-61, 2006. Pg-53.

[18] Barnett, David. "Political theatre in a shrinking world: René Pollesch's postdramatic practices on paper and on stage", *Contemporary Theatre Review,* 16:01, 31-40, 2006. Pg-32.

[19] Giannachi, Gabiella. *Contemporary Theatre Review*, "Exposing globalisation: Biopolitics in the work of critical art ensemble", 16:01, 41-50, 2006. Pg-45.

[20] Giannachi, Gabiella. *Contemporary Theatre Review*, "Exposing globalisation: Biopolitics in the work of critical art ensemble", 16:01, 41-50, 2006. Pg-45.

[21] Rae, P. *Contemporary Theatre Review,* "Where is the cosmopolitan stage?", 16:01, 8-22, 2006. Pg-9.

[22] Gilbert H. & Tompkins, J. *Post-Colonial Drama – Theory, Practice, Politics*, Routledge, UK. 2002. Pg-7.

[23] Gilbert H. & Tompkins, J. *Post-Colonial Drama – Theory, Practice, Politics*, Routledge, UK. 2002. Pg-110.

[24] Legrain, Phillipe. *Open World: The Truth About Globalisation,* Abacus, 2007. Pg-119.

[25] Legrain, Phillipe. *Open World: The Truth About Globalisation,* Abacus, 2007. Pg-120.

[26] Legrain, Phillipe. *Open World: The Truth About Globalisation,* Abacus, 2007. Pg-123.

[27] Gillespie, K. & Hennessey H.D. *Global Marketing*, South-Western, Cengage Learning, Third Edition, UK, 2011, Pg-294.

[28] Legrain, Phillipe. *Open World: The Truth About Globalisation,* Abacus, 2007. Pg-123.

[29] Gardner, L. "We like our plays to be foolish", *The Guardian,* published 2005.

[30] Cavendish, D. *The Telegraph*, "The short hop from old barn to Broadway", V&A Theatre Archive, Published 2nd August 2010.

[31] Legrain, Phillipe. *Open World: The Truth About Globalisation,* Abacus, 2007. Pg-129.

[32] Welton, M. *Emma Rice of Kneehigh Theatre in Conversation with Martin Welton 9th October 2012,* Queen Mary University of London.

[33] Welton, M. *Emma Rice of Kneehigh Theatre in Conversation with Martin Welton 9th October 2012,* Queen Mary University of London.

[34] Legrain, Phillipe. *Open World: The Truth About Globalisation,* Abacus, 2007. Pg-118.

[35] Parker, S. *The Western Morning News,* "Play tells fishy story of a boy who wouldn't fit in", Published 25th September 2001.

[36] *The Kneehigh Plan 1999-2001 Appendices,* Kneehigh Theatre. Pg-8.

[37] *The Kneehigh Plan 1999-2001 Appendices,* Kneehigh Theatre. Pg-8.

[38] *The Kneehigh Plan 1999-2001 Appendices,* Kneehigh Theatre. Pg-9.

[39] Legrain, Phillipe. *Open World: The Truth About Globalisation,* Abacus, 2007. Pg-129.

[40] Steger, M.B. *Globalisation - A Very Short Introduction,* Oxford University Press, Oxford. 2009. Pg-77.

[41] *The Arts Council Consultation Paper* 2011-12, Kneehigh Theatre.

[42] *The Arts Council Consultation Paper* 2011-12, Kneehigh Theatre.

[43] Cornwall County Council Application 1996-97

[44] Govan, E., Nicholson, H. and Normington, K. *Making a Performance – Devising Histories and Contemporary Practices,* Routledge, Abingdon UK. 2007. Pg-138.

[45] Legrain, Phillipe. *Open World: The Truth About Globalisation,* Abacus, 2007. Pg-4.

[46] Burke, Peter. *Cultural Hybridity,* Policy Press, Cambridge, UK. 2009. Pg-94

[47] Steger, M.B. *Globalisation - A Very Short Introduction,* Oxford University Press, Oxford. 2009. Pg-77.

[48] Dorney, Kate. "Chapter 5 - Touring and the Regional Repertoire: Cheek By Jowl, Complicite, Kneehigh and Eastern Angles", ed. Dorney, Kate & Merkin, Ros. *The Glory of the Garden English Regional Theatre and The Arts Council 1984 - 2009,* Cambridge Scholars Publishing, 2010. Pg-111.

[49] Dorney, Kate. "Chapter 5 - Touring and the Regional Repertoire: Cheek By Jowl, Complicite, Kneehigh and Eastern Angles", ed. Dorney, Kate & Merkin, Ros. *The Glory of the Garden English Regional Theatre and The Arts Council 1984 - 2009,* Cambridge Scholars Publishing, 2010. Pg-119.

[50] Dorney, Kate. "Chapter 5 - Touring and the Regional Repertoire: Cheek By Jowl, Complicite, Kneehigh and Eastern Angles", ed. Dorney, Kate & Merkin, Ros. *The Glory of the Garden English Regional Theatre and The Arts Council 1984 - 2009,* Cambridge Scholars Publishing, 2010. Pg-119.

[51] Dorney, Kate. "Chapter 5 - Touring and the Regional Repertoire: Cheek By Jowl, Complicite, Kneehigh and Eastern Angles", ed. Dorney, Kate & Merkin, Ros. *The Glory of the Garden English Regional Theatre and The Arts Council 1984 - 2009,* Cambridge Scholars Publishing, 2010. Pg-119.

[52] Dorney, Kate. "Chapter 5 - Touring and the Regional Repertoire: Cheek By Jowl, Complicite, Kneehigh and Eastern Angles", ed. Dorney, Kate & Merkin, Ros. *The

Glory of the Garden English Regional Theatre and The Arts Council 1984 - 2009, Cambridge Scholars Publishing, 2010. Pg-122.
[53] Inside Cornwall. "Crazy like a wolf", *Insider Info*, Dec/Jan 2001.

CHAPTER TWO

ARCHIVE AND ASYLUM

The previous chapter has discussed theories of globalisation in conjunction with the Kneehigh brand. It has highlighted the key productions to be examined as case studies, documenting the evolution of 'Brand Kneehigh'. This chapter will discuss the methodology used in this book comprising the following two main components; research into the Kneehigh archive, attendance at Kneehigh's Asylum and other performances. Research within the Kneehigh archive will investigate documents about performance in the form of production reports and theatrical reviews. Furthermore, interviews with company members past and present will also be examined.

My performance research will include productions seen at the Asylum; productions seen at venues other than the Asylum, experiences of entertainment events and mementoes. In consideration of the materials encountered in the archive and Asylum, I was aware that spectatorship and my own experiences of being an audience member were paramount in the 'reading' of this theatre company. Attendance at the Asylum was a fundamental component in my methodology, providing an experience of their theatrical style, but also the entertainment experience containing products, mementoes and events in addition to the main production.

In conjunction with the research on globalisation examined in Chapter 1, this chapter will explore other theoretical approaches on archives and archival research and spectatorship. As will be discussed, the theorists considered in this study have been influential in an appreciation of archival research and spectatorship; whilst signposting a range of responses to resources encountered, developing approaches to spectatorship of performance and archive. Exploring different theorists and their systems of spectatorship and reading theatrical performance, provided the theoretical tools to develop an individual response specific to the demands of the Asylum and Kneehigh archive, considering performance from a globalised 'branded' lens. The system described in this text parallels other theorists discussed, but also includes mementoes, reviews and experiences pre and post-show. Most of these productions have been seen live in performance, whilst other productions utilise elements of an 'experiential archive' to piece together fragments of the performance and production experience. For further reference, a production list has been included in Appendix C, signposting changes in artistic direction and reprisals of productions.

Experiential Archive

The 'experiential archive' is a label given to the research model of this book, which encompasses a range of elements used for performance analysis, with a specific slant towards a branded performance experience. It contains the following elements in this study: performance, event 'experience', mementoes, press and performance reviews, interviews, and production reports and evaluations. It combines material from both the Kneehigh archive and the Asylum to analyse the theatrical style and brand identity of Kneehigh, whilst also observing a range of influences through cultural sharing. Due to the range of materials contained within this research model, both a traditional document-based archive and performance are considered in this holistic approach.

Kneehigh originally stored the archive at their office in Truro but have since moved it to Falmouth University in 2010. It contained ninety-three boxes of material, varied in content and form, spanning the entire career of the company since 1980, until the production *Brief Encounter* in 2009. During my research, I examined the entire archive over four consecutive summers from 2010 to 2013. The archive included production reports and evaluations, audience surveys, press cuttings, correspondence, programmes, DVDs, CDs, and video tapes, amongst other documentation saved by the company. The material discovered within the archive presented the evolution of Kneehigh from a local company to an ensemble in demand globally. The archival narrative revealed Kneehigh's own engagement with this local/global dichotomy and their attempts to resolve issues encountered. It should be observed, that even with an archive consisting of 93 boxes, singular and biased limitations are still experienced in using the company's own archive. Despite a lack of extensive academic critique within the archive, alternative perspectives and critical discourses have been provided through journalist interviews and theatrical reviews. This has been included in an attempt to balance any potential singular and biased perspective, offering a broader discourse.

As a researcher in an archive with extensive materials, I was able to select and utilise a number of key documents pertinent to my subject field. Kneehigh's many *Feasibility Reports* and business plans ranging from 1984 to 2002 were extremely useful in providing evidence of a company dealing with globalisation. These reports portrayed a company wishing to engage with global business models as a way to expand and create stability. These also displayed an ongoing debate for the company in shaping their brand identity. Material found within these documents displayed many qualities relating to theories on globalisation and cultural exchange (analysed in the previous chapter). There was also transparency in the work, illustrating an ambition for economic growth, facilitated by their broadening appeal from local to global arenas.

Archival materials relating to some of Kneehigh's productions were quite extensive: The Three Islands Project (2003-2005), featuring the production *The Very Old Man With Enormous Wings* being one such example. Twelve boxes of material based on this project were stored within the entire archive, displaying the breadth of documentation available. The resulting investigation and analysis of this material supported a view of the global nature of the company. Participation surveys included a commentary on the benefits of cultural exchange as did press cuttings, highlighting the blending of cultures and languages to create a show which performed on all three islands; Cyprus, Malta and in the UK (Cornwall). These surveys also communicated the opportunity to share and develop artistic practice, with participants taking on and experimenting with artistic roles; actors became set designers and musicians learned dance routines etc. Likewise, cultural differences between participants were embraced and integrated to create a blend of material evidenced in performance, crossing geographical and cultural boundaries. A box list (with materials included) was provided by Falmouth University, and illustrates the breadth of material contained for some productions within the archive: this has been placed in Appendix B.

Press reviews in the form of document-based archival material were important in constructing definitions of Kneehigh's theatrical style. This supported my spectatorship of performance, reinforcing qualities perceived in the performance work. In some instances, theatre reviewers commented on the Kneehigh branded experience, describing pre and post-show experiences and evaluating mementoes received. Reviews for *Quicksilver* (2002) offered a detailed description of the 'goody bag' given to audience members at the Acorn Theatre in Cornwall. In the absence of attending this performance and receiving the 'goody bag', the description provided valid information to use for reflection in this study. Mementoes found within the archive provided a tangible opportunity to explore elements of Kneehigh's productions. Mementoes including; gifts, objects, programmes, flyers, etc., triggered images and associations, contributing to a wider notion of spectatorship. It continued the branded experience described by Pine and Gilmore, with the experience 'living on' for me as a spectator.[1]

Although there were other materials used within this archive, the ones cited below were key research components; with reports documenting the Three Islands Project and interviews with different company members being extensive. Kneehigh's financial reports established the economic struggles the company faced. This particular archival narrative was revealed in the *Trustees Reports and Financial Statements* from 1999 to 2000 onwards, portraying the near closure of the company. The *Trustees Reports* explained the company's artistic dilemma between their devotion to create work for their locality and a global 'pull' to perform elsewhere. Additionally, a variety of journalistic interviews and transcripts, found within the archive, have been referenced. Some of these interviews were conducted before my research began in 2010. Additionally, I conducted an interview with Andrea Perez-Lyons (a former actor and collaborator with Kneehigh in 2012) and engaged with her in a debate focused on the subject of artistic cultural exchange. In conjunction with reports on productions, Asylum designs and proposals found within the *Mobile Touring Structures Feasibility Reports* offered detail on the development and artistic ambitions for the Asylum. The report also included Kneehigh's assertions of this venue as the solution to their artistic dilemmas.

My spectatorship of performance by Kneehigh has spanned over 15 years of productions, starting with *The Wooden Frock* (2004) at the Battersea Arts Centre London, and has included productions at the MAC, Birmingham Rep, Little Angel Theatre, Islington and performances in the Asylum in Cornwall. My attendance at various performances allowed for an experience of Kneehigh's theatrical style and provided evidence of Kneehigh's ongoing debate on Cornish cultural identity. Attendance at Asylum has provided the opportunity to conduct an extended analysis of an evolving company brand and entertainment experience. During this time observations of performance have acknowledged modifications in dramatic style, shifting interests in stimuli for devising and adaptation, artistic and economic partnerships, and changing of core members.

My trips to the Asylum ran between July 2010 – August 2016, contributing an important component of my examination of this company in their 'home' environment. The Asylum, a multi-functioning rehearsal and performance venue, opened in the Summer of 2010. It is a portable canvas venue based in three areas of Cornwall: in Blackwater near Truro in 2010-2012, in the Cornish tourist attraction The Lost Gardens of Heligan near Mevagissey since 2012-18, and more recently in Carlyon Beach in 2019. In describing the venue, a dedicated page on the company website stated the following about the Asylum:

> The Asylum is our long-awaited, much dreamed about, jaw-dropping, spirit-
> lifting nomadic theatre space. A place of fun, playfulness and sanctuary, The
> Asylum is a purpose-built tent, a home and a place - as described by The
> Guardian as 'a place predisposed to magic'. For the last two years, The
> Asylum has taken up a temporary home at Tywarnhayle Farm, Blackwater.[2]

In the description of this venue, the emphasis is on fun and entertainment,
with its quality of creative exploration in keeping with a 'fun palace'.
English director Joan Littlewood and architect Cedric Price developed the
concept of a 'fun palace' in 1961, as a 'laboratory of fun', a place lending
itself to artistic experimentation and enjoyment.[3]   The Asylum was
designated as a 'fun palace' in 2014 as part of a national campaign led by
The Albany, Paul Hamlyn Foundation, and Wellcome. Over 100 'palaces'
appeared around the UK, celebrating Littlewood and Price's artistic vision.
With Littlewood and Price's original utopian ethos of 'artwork for all', these
recent 'palaces' aimed to offer culture and science for all to consume. Since
2014, 362 fun palaces have been designated in the UK alone, with more
palaces planned from 2018 onwards.[4] The Asylum has been a 'longed for'
platform for Kneehigh to display their creativity, and as stated by Kneehigh
(and analysed within this book), with it they aimed to resolve their
local/global dichotomy, providing a place for creative autonomy.

Attendance at the Asylum provided an experience of 'Brand Kneehigh'
in its home venue, encompassing pre and post-show entertainment, food and
drink, merchandise, and art exhibitions. The range of events at this venue,
including gigs and a symposium, displayed diversification and variety, and
a willingness to engage in a debate concerning the company's and
Cornwall's place within the world. The Asylum offered the brand in its most
complete form of entertainment, immersed within a 'world' shaped by
Kneehigh.

Performances at other venues not only portrayed the development of
Kneehigh's performance style, but over several years, also illustrated a shift
in the selection of stimuli. The company received criticism for their move
away from fairy tales, myths and legends, to instead focusing on adapting
famous literary works and films. This was reiterated in press reviews and
interviews. However, my spectatorship allowed individual reflections on
this work, explored within the production case studies. Some of the venues
did allow for experiences beyond the performance area, contributing to a
branded entertainment experience, but not as fully formed as the branded
experience within the Asylum. The production *Brief Encounter* is a clear
example of this, with a decorated foyer area, cream teas on sale, and 1940s
usherettes extending the work of the play and entertainment experience.

The combination of materials addressed two areas of research, archival and performance/spectatorship. It was important to consider these two areas as they supported one another in generating a depth of analysis. The material available offered multifaceted descriptions and perceptions of the company and production work.

Theoretical Approaches: Use of Archive

The materials found in the archive displayed in detail, Kneehigh's plans for their brand, processes of cultural exchange, and the formation of their home venue. With regards to document-based evidence for cultural sharing; commentary was framed in either future tenses as aspirational, or in evaluative past tenses after the project had occurred. In contrast, the Asylum (performance) allowed for an immediate physical experience of the brand (in the present), their theatrical style and cultural exchange in production. I would also add that the performance experience allowed for pre and post show analysis. If I was to be guided by Legrain's, Klein's, and Pine and Gilmore's ideas of branding and brand experience, I needed to go through the Kneehigh entertainment process.

The use of an archive instigated comparative explorations into other researchers and scholars, considering their ideas on archival research within traditional document-based parameters, and also performance. It was important to discover the limitations and the strengths encountered by other scholars along their journey of using archives. With this knowledge, I was able to reflect on my experiences, consider approaches and perceptions of the archive to support my methodology and assist in making sense of the range of material available. It provided a theoretical basis to situate Kneehigh's archive and Asylum, particularly when dealing with live performance material witnessed in contrast to 'traditional' literary archive documentation. As a starting point, the work of Michel Foucault and Jacques Derrida gave a theoretical background on archival philosophy. In their considered responses, the complexities of archival research were described, provoking comparison with my experiences and how this contrasted to performance and spectatorship. Research into traditional archives provided a platform to consider the notions of a performance as archive, described by Diana Taylor.[5] The debate on how performance can be 'fully' documented is still ongoing, and provoked research into spectatorship.

Exploring the above theorists triggered reflections on my experience as a researcher; some in keeping with a traditional document-based archive, whilst others are participatory and experiential. Taylor supports the idea that performance, which she describes as 'repertoire', is archival material. Taylor's repertoire validates my notion of the experiential archive, defining performance studies as 'vital acts of transfer, transmitting social knowledge, memory, and a sense of identity'.[6] Taylor's theory on repertoire affirms performance and other oratory forms of information considered as ephemeral, as 'embodied memory', available for transfer and interpretation.[7] This stance of performance or repertoire as archive enjoys equal emphasis afforded to the traditional documents-based archive described by Derrida and Foucault.[8]

Foucault's work on the nature of a traditional document-based archive provided observations on the difficult and somewhat elusive process of organising and interpreting information, some of which may be clearer and more accessible than others. In the case of Kneehigh, production reports, theatrical reviews and my spectatorial viewings were often based on a range of different performances of the same production and different dates. This is not uncommon within theatre research, however the spectatorship of performance dates matching those of theatrical reviews has not been used in the methodology of my research. In some production case studies, matching the performance dates would have been impossible. Likewise, there are instances in which I refer to different versions or rather reprisals of the same production spanning a number of years. As already indicated, Kneehigh often reprises popular shows for tour in different venues nationally and internationally. Such reprisals have been acknowledged within the case studies where appropriate; informed either by my spectatorship of multiple performances or through documents encountered in the archive.

Dorney describes the romanticised notion of discovering a narrative and using archival research as 'a continual quest for treasure' in 'Archives'.[9] During this discovery process, gathering and selection of resources provides an opportunity to re-contextualise this material at a later stage. Reexamining this material again may provide surprising discoveries on what is useful and what can be abandoned. This process should ideally be conducted with an openness to allow its 'narrative' to emerge. In contrast, the material encountered can also be manipulated to fit a specific narrative. Paul Allain suggests that 'an archive is never neutral or passive' [10]and is in a malleable state:

> We should approach them [archives] with caution and always be prepared, for an archive is to some extent only as good as what it is used for, ultimately reflecting the abilities of its explorer. [11]

Of course, the material is only as useful as deemed by the 'explorer' and is 'passive' or dormant until used by the researcher to form a narrative. Pearson and Shanks draw parallels with archaeology and manipulations of material to reinforce a narrative.

> What archaeologists do is work with material traces, with evidence, in order to create something - a meaning, a narrative, an image - which stands for the past in the present. Archaeologists craft the past. [12]

As suggested by Pearson and Shanks, this archaeological analysis rather than being 'a reconstruction of the past from its surging remains' is a re-contextualisation.[13] Re-contextualisation and 'crafting of the past' allow for interpretation and selection of relevant sources, as a way of making sense of the archive. The emergence of 'a narrative, an image', as stated by Pearson and Shanks, reinforced the inherent globalism within Kneehigh's work. It also confirmed its localism, whilst portraying the changing shape of the Kneehigh brand.

Although an archaeologist may look in a specific area intending to find evidence they predict to come across, they must acknowledge any discoveries allowing new material to shape their narrative. Pearson and Shanks make valid connections between the limits and possibilities of archaeology, applicable to the documenting of theatre. They present its importance and relevance, embracing the gaps in information and experiences.

> The special practice that is performance operates in a liminal space or heterotopia. Archaeology too is at the edge and in the gaps, working on discard and decay, entropy and loss. Its topic of the material and ineffable immediacy of the past has given it a special place in a construction of personal and cultural identity. [14]

This proved useful as a reminder to be responsive to the transitional state of gaining information: aware that further information may confirm or contradict lines of enquiry. Shanks and Pearson also communicated the liminal state of documenting performance, greatly affected by the decay and entropy due to its immediacy. This was evident within the lack of video recording of performances within the Kneehigh archive, some of which were corrupted through damage to videotapes and their inaccessibility to playback through digital platforms replacing analogue video machines.

Music theorist, R. Wayne Shoaf, offered commentary on the immense capacity of archives, and the potential complexities of archival research and retrieval of material. Shoaf perceives difficulty in the use of storage systems, making it difficult to uncover resources, stored away, never seen again.

> 'The sheer quantity of material stored for future use can be large, as dramatically exemplified in the closing scene of Steven Spielberg's *Raiders of the Lost Ark* in which the Ark of the Covenant is wheeled into a vast government warehouse filled with crates of multitudinous size, probably never to be found again.' [15]

These were concerns shared whilst working through the Kneehigh Archive: dealing with the sheer volume contained within it (despite materials being box listed with brief descriptions). There was the additional factor of the potential material found within, contributing or detracting from the research narrative: provoking my manipulation of the resources for the narrative.

An archive (and the artefacts found within) can create a story and can be manipulated to support a narrative. Installation artist, Susan Hiller in *Working Through Objects* (1994), commented on the ambiguous nature of configuring or grouping objects into an archive.

> I take it that any conscious configuration of objects tells a story. In fact, this is something I've believed for a very long time. In the early seventies I made a collection piece called enquiries/inquiries, which revealed quite explicitly, although drily, in the style of the seventies, that any collection of objects was an ambiguously bounded unit that told a particular story, and it was by setting the boundaries that the story was told. [16]

Hiller describes the 'ambiguity' of a collection of resources that can be manipulated through selection to support a story which the user wishes to tell, strengthening an argument. Unlike Hiller's assertion that any collection of objects can be 'ambiguously bounded' to form a story, my search of the available material sought to investigate Kneehigh's branding ambitions. There were very little resources found that contradicted this stance, but instead contributed to stages in development and evolution – like many other global brands. Although there are parallels with the objects Hiller alludes to, it is important to remember that Hiller is an artist working towards a very different outcome and end 'product'.

A story or 'narrative' can emerge from exploring an archive, superseding original lines of enquiry. Such a description highlighted potential encounters when working on an archive, proposing a duality between working with a research agenda, whilst allowing the materials to suggest an emerging narrative. Due to the size of the Kneehigh archive, a myriad of stories presented themselves. Whilst I acknowledged their potential, focus remained on the scope of global theatrical research and the case studies examined. Displayed in the archive, supporting a globalised narrative for Kneehigh, was a duality in their approach to work incorporating both local and global concerns and artistic ambitions. The company report *The Kneehigh Plan* provided a detailed account of their strategies for developing Cornish tours in village halls, schools and the landscape in cliff walks. Also listed was their ambitions for national touring and international projects, whilst considering their marketing to embrace this transition beyond the Cornish county. This was not a narrative that needed to be elicited or expanded on but referred to by company members themselves in several interviews in the archive. Shepherd has provided his stance on the importance of portraying a Cornish voice in the company's storytelling, whilst at the same time addressing the ambition for Kneehigh to have an international reputation for making theatre.

Archives can support a narrative, as illustrated above. However, the material found can be problematic due to archive instability, affected by changes and additions. Observations on archival storage considers how archives can store and retrieve materials effectively. There is the potential for archival materials to be changeable and transitional, offering different information through re-visitation. Taylor questions the validity and immovable state of other more traditional forms of archive, suggesting that these sources are as changeable as performance.

> 'Archival' memory exists as documents, maps, literary texts, letters, archaeological remains, bones, videos, films, CDs, all those items supposedly resistant to change... Archival memory works across distance, over time and space; investigators can go back to re-examine an ancient manuscript, letters find their addresses through time and place, and computer discs at times cough up lost files with the right software. [17]

Archival materials can offer new information at different times and through re-visitation. Initial explorations of show programmes and other promotional materials within the Kneehigh archive provided evidence of both a local and global slant in their work. The shifting emphasis between local and global areas of interest was revealed in Kneehigh's production mission statements made by Mike Shepherd or Emma Rice. As research into globalisation evolved, materials were perceived in a new light - as part of the overall experience and building towards the experiential archive. In this capacity, it was useful to keep hold of these artefacts (even when they contained no written references to globalisation and cultural exchange).

Through re-analysis, these resources developed a new significance, offering elements as fragmentary parts of the experience of the event. They were the physical embodiment of globalisation, allowing the consumer to continue to 'experience' the main brand product long after the original event has ceased to exist. A toy motorbike within a gift box, given to audience members for the production *Cymbeline*, is a strong example of this process (provided in greater analysis as part of the production case study in Chapter 5). This item went through a transitional state of interpretation and documentation. Unable to take this object outside of the archive, physical analysis and the experience with this gift was conducted on-site. Later, interpretation was conducted on my memory of the experience, photography documentation, and notes made at the time of inspection.

Limitations are encountered because an archive is permeable, changeable and unstable: 'Nowhere is this more the case than in performance studies, which grapples to find appropriate styles in which to catalogue and shelve its ghosts'[18]. Iball highlights the ever-changing state of the archive within performance, illustrating its vulnerability and ephemerality. Despite these complexities, the potential for creativity emerges within the archive itself. Archival research (compared with archaeology by Pearson) is a creative process which may generate different outcomes.

> Nor is there a single way to do archaeology: different things can be made from the same traces and fragments. People may work on the same material and produce different outcomes. [19]

Derrida suggests that the process of archiving is also creation: 'The archivization produces as much as it records the event'.[20] Archiving can also influence the shape of the archived content:

> ...the technical structure of the archiving archive also determines the structure of the archivable content, even in its very coming into existence and in its relationship to the future. [21]

This quality of creativity within the archive confirms its instability and ever-evolving status, whilst establishing the archive's ability to expand and continue to develop.

As outlined by Taylor, repertoire can provide connections between different viewpoints and arguments, facilitating a review on cultural practices: 'The repertoire allows for an alternative perspective on historical processes of transnational contact'.[22] Performance is multi-layered in communicating cultural/social facets, triggering different associations within the spectator.

Embodied performance, then, makes visible an entire spectrum of attitudes and values. The multicodedness of these practices transmits as many layers of meaning as there are spectators, participants, and witnesses. [23]

Layers of meaning can be encountered during the immediacy of the live performance, unpacked further through re-analysis post-event. This can also occur within the archive, with immediate responses made on-site, reinterpreted later through a review of notes made or other forms of documentation. I found the process of using both archive and 'repertoire' mutually informative and reflective of one another. Material discovered in both archive and repertoire culminated in a range of evidence for production case studies. Experiences of performance; productions reports, press reviews, interviews, and in some instances a memento, provided a breadth of resources. They also offered a range of voices and perspectives for reflection and critique: some of which are Kneehigh's (including Artistic Directors and company members); some from press reviewers, and some from my own spectatorship.

During archival use of recorded performance within archives, complexities and critiques relating to the recording of performances were explored. The critique on fully documenting performance was encountered during visits to the National Theatre Archive and the V&A Archive, both containing recordings of Kneehigh's productions. The V&A, during their induction to the recorded resources in their archive, explained the reasons behind various recordings of the same show. Some recordings featured a single shot encompassing the whole stage, whilst other recordings featured multiple shots and close-ups. What is implicit in these varied recordings is the inability to document the experience and atmosphere of the live production. The cinematic, multiple shot recording takes control away from the viewer, focusing on aspects of the production that the live viewer may not wish a close up of, while other moments are lost. Likewise, the single shot encompassing the whole stage recording, can appear somewhat uneventful and mundane in its translation in form and media from a live event to a recorded artefact. The National Theatre Archive described a similar approach in multiple recordings of productions, commenting on the recent successes enjoyed through their National Theatre Live productions being aired in cinemas across the country. The National Theatre Live uses a different shooting style from the V&A and their own Archive, with its purpose being a viable form of entertainment at the cinema, rather than a form of archival material. Ongoing debates are still taking place relating to recorded live performances, particularly during the Covid-19 pandemic lockdown in 2020 spanning theatres around the world. As commented by an editorial in *The Guardian,* there is an 'irony' observed in the amount of theatre work available online during this pandemic, which highlights the qualities of live performance lost in its recorded translation.[24] Notably, Rice's production *Wise Children* is included in the range of 'exuberant' and creative work available online.

Dan and Kiraly argue that 'people retain a strong distrust of technical reproductions, and a fanaticism about the uniqueness of the art piece'.[25] Taylor also touches on the difficulties of recording these experiences. Considering the transitory nature of the repertoire and the difficulty of maintaining performance:

> Performance's only life is in the present. Performance cannot be saved, recorded, documented or otherwise participate in the circulation of representations of representation. [26]

Phelan indicates a viewpoint agreeing with Dan and Kiraly's observations, objecting to the reproduction of performance through recording, highlighting the immediacy of the art form. These perspectives are part of a complex debate on performance documentation in contrast to the immediacy of a live performance. I acknowledge them within my methodology, ensuring these perspectives did not dominate my use of performance and experience. My use of the 'experiential archive' to observe some of the spectatorial practices used by Skantze, Knowles, and Pearson, worked towards resolving this conflict within my own research.

Use of Spectatorship and Performance

Spectatorship of performance has been fundamental to the research in this book, as a core component and supportive of material encountered in the archive. Consideration of other researcher's experiences and models of spectatorship has provided insight into my own practice; providing comparison and contrast. Some researchers have included descriptions of their pre and post show reflections, whilst other scholars acknowledged cultural semiotics with historical, political and social connections being formed. Exploring their models of research allowed for comparison with how they used marketing, production reports, and reviews in conjunction with performance experience. This research has also assisted in my conceptualisation of the 'experiential archive', helping me identify and combine a number of components together and generating a label to concisely describe my individual research model.

P.A. Skantze's text *Itinerant Spectator (2013)* has been influential in shaping my response to performance in a holistic sense. Skantze, like other theorists commenting on spectatorship, challenged notions of the audience's experiences of a production. The methodology cited by Ric Knowles in *Reading the Material Theatre (2004)* offered useful strategies for considering the immediate conditions of a performance (both culturally and theatrically), whilst also observing how performances are produced and received. My spectatorship of *Blast* (2010) provided strong examples of Kneehigh's debate on cultural (Cornish) identity and globalisation; it also triggered historical connections with the demise of the clay and tin industries. These triggers were reinforced by visits to the Eden Project, Tintagel and Boscastle. The immensity of the loss of these industries, as described by historian, R.M. Barton, took on new significance when performed in the locations where these historical events took place when examined and referred to in *Blast.* This is a historical context I acknowledge in Chapter 3 in reference to *Quicksilver, Blast* and *Tristan and Yseult.*

Helen Freshwater states the British political scene has informed her responses to performance and is interested in examining the connections between 'collective experience, audience participation, political agency'.[27] Elements of Freshwater's 'collective experience' and 'political agency' mirror observations within the case studies for the productions *Blast* and *Global Cornwall.* Arguably, both events had an explicit political agenda, Cornish political assertions are discussed in the case study for *Tristan and Yseult.* In the case of *Tristan and Yseult,* Cornish political references drew attention to issues Kneehigh wished to communicate; generated comedy within the performance, and reinforced elements of the theatrical brand. I share a similar methodological process as Mike Pearson in *Mickery Theater: An Imperfect Archaeology (2014)*, using company reports, reviews and company evaluations to reflect on theatre and performance. Pearson acknowledges the 'incompleteness' of his approach; whilst highlighting the potential for varied archival elements to contribute towards performance research.[28] Comparatively, Pearson's work also portrays a research journey that is responsive and descriptive of the materials encountered. Pearson, like Skantze, includes accounts of encounters with a range of material, offering a personal narrative and context.

Using experiences of live performances, in addition to the examination of documents and mementoes found in the Kneehigh Archive, provided a varied and extensive amount of material for consideration. Utilising definitions and experiences of spectatorship outlined by Skantze and Knowles, and mementoes as a way of building brand association and repeat custom by Gilmore and Pine, offered varied perspectives to consider the production case studies in this book. The use of these 'varied perspectives' enabled me to consider extensive evidence over a number of years. My combination of researching; archive, performance, spectatorship and mementoes/artefacts, offered a holistic (yet 'imperfect') way to examine Kneehigh's work. Whilst Skanzte and Knowles discussed their spectatorial experiences of live productions, Pearson considered company documents and reviews of performances seen. I have found both these processes helpful and incorporated them into my working methods in conjunction with production mementoes for performances I have seen (and those I have not experienced live).

The use of mementoes within my research contributed physical, tangible evidence as a 'product', reinforcing the 'branded' gaze applied to my research. Of course, performance and literary based archival evidence are also physical. However, mementoes themselves have a different function, created to form associative semiotics of memory, evoking the original performance or experience. Mementoes are used for brand association and identification, functioning as marketing tools to demonstrate brand. As a 'product' they are part of an economic transaction, whilst encouraging further consumerism. The inclusion of performance mementoes provided an additional source for examination, whilst considering the branded ambitions of Kneehigh.

Skantze's ideas of spectatorship have reinforced my own observations of performance, as well as extending the parameters for what can be included within the experience. According to Skantze, performance experiences are driven by a divergent range of elements, some starting long before the performance occurs. They begin from marketing campaigns to promote the show, designed to develop expectations of the performance. Expectations continue to grow with the journey to the venue. By embracing Skantze's acknowledgement of marketing as: 'the imaginative process of spectating'[29], spectatorial experience begins with encountering promotional material. Likewise, this encounter also reinforces consumerism as described in Pine and Gilmore's theories on the 'experience economy'. Each year, my spectatorship was shaped, not just by the varied Kneehigh performances at the Asylum, but by my journey/trip as a whole. My first year was influenced by my solo travel to Cornwall and visiting the archive at the University.

Skantze's notion of spectatorship as a shared cultural memory formed by watching a performance with other audience members illuminated my appraisal of *Blast*, illustrating how we (the audience) are a product of our past and present. Reinforced through the experience of the production, the ramifications of political, historical, social and cultural events provide additional layers of interpretation and meaning, as do our own personal experiences. Commenting on the nature of itinerant spectatorship Skantze states:

The method has the effect of providing textual 3-D glasses, a kind of looking at sees the historical dimensions, often flattened when one looks without such an aid, with the added volumes made by memory and interpretation. [30]

Skantze shared her own examples and responses to spectatorship, detailing how these intersect and provoke memories and perceptions relating to her political, historical, social, racial and gender experiences. I have been conscious of this in my responses to the live Kneehigh productions encountered.

My perceptions of Skantze's writing, when describing performance, was reminiscent of a stream of consciousness, with associations being formed and shared in retrospect. Whilst liberating when reflecting on my own experiences, I found it to be quite disjointed with its introduction of new ideas and associations, and at times quite hard to follow. However, as a responsive and immediate spectatorial response, Skantze's observations display an honest and 'spontaneous' reaction to performance, with fluctuating narratives influenced by pre and post show observations. Structurally, Skantze has engaged in sectioning her examples of spectatorship through the senses. I have not followed this particular structure, but like Skantze, I have included responses to performances during and post the event. Diverging from Skantze, I have not considered in great detail pre-show implications. Although pre-show anticipation can be informed by brand associations, I have focused on considerations during and after the performance. Just as Pearson has analysed performances after the event, through reviews and company reports, I have utilised this same methodology. The senses are discussed in case studies, referring to the production aesthetics, triggering 'material semiotics' and other cultural associations.

The examples of productions as case studies are structured according to their significance for localism, cultural exchange, and national and international collaborations. The sensory experiences described by Skantze, Knowles and Pearson, have been a useful guide in considering specific qualities of the work. As outlined earlier, case studies will consider theatrical elements of the Kneehigh brand, in conjunction with the social, political, historical and cultural semiotics inherently displayed within the productions. Additionally, the process of adaptation will be discussed, particularly in reference to Kneehigh versions of popular cultural works.

The methodology cited by Ric Knowles in *Reading the Material (2004)* offered useful strategies for considering the immediate conditions of a performance (both culturally and theatrically), whilst also observing how performances are produced and received:

One corner, 'performance', refers to the raw theatrical event shared by practitioners and audiences, what is traditionally thought of as the performance 'itself'. The other two corners refer to the open 'material conditions' that shape both what appears on stage and how it is read or understood - what has traditionally been understood to be the 'context' within which the performance happens. [31]

Tensions can be felt between production communication and audience reception; opening a debate within theatrical spectatorship and more directly to this text, reactions to participation. Production evaluations for the Three Islands Project, in conjunction with collated press reviews, offered 'second-hand' spectatorship together with observations on the performance by those working on the project. The latter ranged from stallholders in the marketplace, musicians, performers, and work experience volunteers, sharing ideas and opinions on the cultural exchanges achieved within the project. As indicated by Knowles's research, these observations illustrated the 'context' the Three Islands Project was developed in and 'read' by a divergent cohort. There is an affinity with Knowles' reference to 'materialist semiotics' (and my own research) underpinning the cultural and globalist impact of production work. Knowles defines materialist semiotics in the following terms:

> ...as a materialist approach to viewing performance: The goal is to articulate and apply a method for achieving a more precise and more fully contextualised and politicised understanding of how meaning is produced in the theatre.[32]

Arguably, Knowles's reading of the material mirrored elements of Skanze's 'itinerant spectator' and shares commonalities with my own 'experiential archive'. This includes an appreciation of the location/neighbourhood/ environment of the performance, programmes, reviews of the performance, in addition to mementoes/products for sale:

> And, of course, all of these conditions function within larger social, cultural, and historical contexts, as meaning is shaped directly, performance by performance, by local regional, national and global events of the moment. [33]

In using 'materialist semiotics' to examine and redefine performance, Knowles acknowledged the influence of 'cultural materialism'. Cultural materialism is defined as a combination of cultural aspects within society, viewed in conjunction with a materialist lens, and embraces the influence of 'material forces' in shaping a production.[34]

The research on *The Umbrellas of Cherbourg* (2011) is 'read' within a culturally materialist framework in Chapter 5, discussing the pressures felt by Emma Rice using the Kneehigh brand name, and her own reputation as director. Rice and Kneehigh were approached by the original filmmaker, Michel Legrand, to provide the theatrical qualities of Brand Kneehigh and Rice's directorial style. Although this chapter does establish how the production fulfilled 'cultural materialist' definitions, it does consider the critique encountered on its reception, affected by these parameters. The methodology for this production includes spectatorship of live performance, production reviews, and my own responses. Where I deviate from Knowles' spectatorship is in the use of production reviews when I had not experienced the live production. Knowles limited his examinations to performances he had seen live, whereas my engagement with an 'experiential archive' assisted my 'reading' of a performance in a range of ways through mementoes and artefacts. Knowles does state, however, that his exploration of similar artefacts contributed to the examination of specific case studies supporting his lens of 'materialist semiotics' and triggered the exploration of associations with a wider social, cultural, political and historical context.

Knowles reflected on the impact of the overall theatrical space, including the entrance and foyer area, suggesting that it is governed by the 'architecture and geographic frames that serve to shape their meanings'.[35] This 'architecture' conditions the perception and emotional tone of the performance, and influences the psychology of the spectator, encouraging repeat custom and providing semiotics to decode:

> The entire theatre, its audience arrangements, its other public spaces, its physical appearance, even its location within a city, are all important elements of the process by which an audience makes meaning of its experience. [36]

Knowles highlighted through his definitions of 'spaces of reception', the importance of the entire auditorium and its impact on the audience in 'framing and preparing audience horizons of expectations'. A similar use of space in reference to *Brief Encounter* (2008), is discussed in Chapter 5. This production premiered in a cinema (transformed into a theatre space), reinforced the world of a 1930s cinema which is one of the play's key locations. Knowles observed that production associated merchandise such as souvenir stands, food and drink, reinforce the 'material semiotics' of the performance, and can 'either reinforce, modify, or undercut artistic intent'.[37] In the case of Kneehigh, such merchandise reinforced the 'world' created in *Brief Encounter,* whilst also supporting the branded world of the Asylum. Likewise, Skantze observed the relationship between auditorium, stage and audience, as does Knowles who commented on this unique combination, open to a myriad of interpretations: 'Each space - auditorium and stage - has its own semiotic significance and ideological import'.[38] Knowles also broadened his scope of spectatorship to include the location of the theatre and the journey to get there:

> The geographical location of theatres is significant both of the ways in which it is 'read' and for the experience of the spectator in getting there. This has to do with factors that include the degree of physical or psychological difficulty involved in traversing familiar or unfamiliar, comfortable or uncomfortable districts, the distance between the theatre and its community (Or 'target audience'), the proximity and cost of public transportation or parking, and so on. [39]

The reflections of performances included in this study will embrace this notion of spectatorship, and will include references to the theatre locations, and if applicable the journey to those venues.

Helen Freshwater outlined an engagement with the senses as a way to structure responses to performances, recognising that 'many practitioners and scholars consider the bodily engagement as something to explore, exploit and celebrate'[40]. Alison Oddey and Christine White in *Modes of Spectating (2009)* considered the factors affecting an audience member, suggesting spectatorship goes further than sensory perception and encompassing 'the subjective capabilities of their own body and nervous system'.[41] Oddey and White suggested an audience already considers performance with a diagnostic gaze arguing that 'an act of viewing or spectating will involve the spectator making sense of the viewed object, and this will happen at both a conscious and unconscious level'.[42] This search for meaning of course happens automatically as the human body constantly processes and attempts to interpret a range of stimuli at any given time. In contrast, Jacques Ranciere seeks to move beyond a 'passive' variant of spectatorship, calling for a more 'conscious' audience who exercises agency in response to sensory stimuli:

> She observes, selects, compares, interprets. She links what she sees to a host of other things that she has seen on other stages, in other kinds of place. She composes her own poem with elements of the poem before her.[43]

Ranciere's statement offers insight into the structure of Skantze and Pearson's work. As I have done within my own research, these scholars have 'observed, selected and compared' material they have encountered and interpreted. Spectatorship on a micro-level is personal and unique. This is appreciated by Oddey and White's 'diagnostic gaze', embracing the conscious and unconscious. A collective response can be gathered through audience surveys, which may potentially lack the detail afforded individual study and theatrical reviews (which are personal responses). Theatrical reviews and my own spectatorial responses to performance have been used in my research to gain a broad appraisal within each production case study.

Helen Freshwater states that the British political scene had informed her responses to performance, examining the connections between 'collective experience, audience participation, [and] political agency'.[44] Freshwater also acknowledges the broad demographic of the audience, highlighting individualism and the potential for this to shape reception of the performance:

> So it is important to remember each audience is made up of individuals who bring their own cultural reference points, political beliefs, sexual preferences, personal histories, and immediate preoccupations to their interpretation of a production. [45]

The biography of the audience member is more explicitly considered by Freshwater, in contrast to my own work, and that of the other theorists discussing spectatorship and audience. Interpretations developed by the audience are embraced and acknowledged: hypothesising how 'their understanding of the meaning of individual text is dependent upon a broader 'intertextual' network'.[46] The individualism inherent in spectator case studies are of course more apparent within the live productions attended and performance mementoes considered, and less explicit in production case studies based on company reports, production evaluations and journalistic theatrical reviews.

Freshwater refers to Susan Bennett's theory of 'interpretative communities', discussing the temporal audience appreciation of a performance, due to changes in social, cultural and political values over time. This book incorporates the voices of other audiences, in addition to my own spectatorship, and 'interpretive communities' in response to the production *Cymbeline* (2006). This included theatre reviewers who gave polarised views of the production. I refer to 'interpretive communities' in my examination of the Three Islands Projects, relying on audience and participant surveys. However, my spectatorship of *A Very Old Man with Enormous Wings* (2012) at the Little Angel Theatre, Islington, contributes to the experiential archive and analysis in this production case study. Freshwater offers validity in individual accounts of spectatorship, underpinning the importance of personal response.

> ... individual experience of spectatorship, rather than mass audience response, and provides a valuable reminder that emotional and embodied responses have a significant and legitimate role in the analysis of performance. [47]

Developing this argument further, Freshwater suggested that theatrical analysis cannot provide what an audience 'felt' or understood, rather it provides 'evidence of meaning and responses that specific performances in particular locations made available'.[48] I would add that this specificity lends itself to the individual, and their experiences leading up to the event. The contributions to knowledge made within this study, work within this premise of specificity, offering individual performance responses.

Evaluation of Archive/Asylum Research Experience

During my time using both 'Archive' and 'Asylum', exploring the vast amount of archival and performance material over several years, a number of issues presented themselves. The use of global theories as a 'lens' to explore Kneehigh was important; but could not fully appreciate the entirety of their brand. In fact, other qualities involving company member's artistic aspirations, values and performance style were valid elements, and could not be considered using global business theories alone. Pine and Gilmore and their ideas of 'experience' embraced the theoretical discussions of globalisation, combining them with the 'theatricality' of consumerism assisted in creating balance. Experience within performance can also be appreciated, helping me to build a link between globalism and 'branded' theatre performance.

The potential for 'archive fatigue', overwhelmed by the amount of material in the archive, was described by a number of theorists as a potential factor. Maintaining a specific focus prevented 'archive fatigue. Additionally, my framework of exploring the archive during the summer months of attending the Asylum offered a specified period, allowing time for a reflection of the material discovered at other points. I should add that a time goal with which to look through the archive was not explicitly set and the aim of looking at its entire contents was important to achieve and is represented in the range of sources referenced.

The organisation of material and how it was presented needed careful consideration. It was important to present the research findings in a way that communicated the multifaceted nature of Kneehigh's work, establishing localism, Cornish identity, cultural exchange and brand development. It became apparent that an analysis of their production work could display this trajectory, portraying shifting focuses and interests. The organisation of the productions included case studies based on a timeline of earlier work and progressing through to recent productions. The earliest production referred to in this study is *Quicksilver* in 2002. Kneehigh had been running since the 1980s. However, archival material was much more limited for production work in the 80s and 90s. In this capacity, the study is limited to work between 2002-2020, but still covers an extensive period of nearly two decades for the company. I felt much more confident in covering material from this period due to my spectatorship since 2004 but also given the access to material for productions from 2000 onwards. The combination of archive and performance through the experiential archive provides an opportunity to be responsive in different ways to each production analysed, based on the available resources.

The ethical responsibility of using an archive as a researcher is more acute given your relationship with the subjects of the archive, and the holders of the archive itself. I would like to state that there were no external influences affecting my archival use. Of course, this may not be the case with projects in which the parties involved influence the researcher to manipulate the archive and generate a particular 'story'. Kneehigh, although interested in this research, had no control or vested interests in this book being developed. Likewise, Falmouth University as holders of this archive were supportive in allowing access to the archive but did not exert control over its subject matter.

The ideas of Skantze, Knowles and Pearson were useful to me in supporting my experiences in spectatorship performance. These scholars drew my attention to the range of experiences quantified as performance. These included: marketing pre-show encounters, triggers and associations made during the performance, the performance itself, post show reflections, and production merchandise. In the case of Pearson and my own research, production reports, reviews, and programmes were also part of the performance experience. It was important to be aware of other researchers within this specified performance/spectatorship field, considering what they regarded as performance in relation to my own ideas. As well as acknowledging my own experiences, it provided the opportunity to build on these elements: introducing mementoes to the collection of performance experience in the form of the 'experiential archive'. I also assert that these materials within the experiential archive contribute towards an analysis of a performance experience not seen live. This was the case in my analysis of the production *Quicksilver*. Admittedly, while there are limitations with the incompleteness of the performance experience, I was still able to conduct a detailed analysis of this production in response to the research questions posed. All aspects of material found can be useful for interpretation, despite the fragmentary nature of these resources. In fact, all materials are fragmentary yet still beneficial for interpretation, reflection and critique.

Research using the experiential archive engaged with a range of experiences and interactions, beyond the world of the play and within a designed environment. Linda Stoian, a spatial artist and theorist, stated that even in the digital age, we do not have the means to record the full sensory experience of a performance which 'continues to resist being represented in the archive'.[49] Stoian reports that the perfect performance archive 'would need to be a kind of time machine'.[50] Stoian's article mirrored my own feelings towards 'repertoire', and although a full sensory experience is elusive to recording, fragments of that experience can be combined. Just as forensic science assists the police in reconstructing a crime scene, I use these fragments of materials from my own experiential archive. Despite its fragmentary nature, the progression of the Kneehigh brand and its performance style in each production case study can still be charted. This form of archive is also 'imperfect', and although I have applied some form of standardisation of the material examined, it is not precise due to variation: performance itself is an imperfect art form and field of study. One performance in contrast to another varies considerably within the same production. However, the inclusivity of this archive facilitates this analysis through a broad inclusion of resources, subject to availability and specific to each production.

This chapter has provided an overview of archival research, and performance spectatorship. The comparative research exploring ideas on traditional archives and performance as archive by performance scholars and creative practitioners, assisted in shaping the research framework used. Theoretical works on spectatorship offered the examination of production case studies as a way to expand ideas, whilst also charting the writer's own spectatorial experiences. I use a similar strategy, sharing personal accounts of production experience in addition to archive documents such as production reports and reviews.

Analysis within a traditional 'document based' archive was effective in communicating brand evolution. It was also able to portray cultural exchange, detailing the company's commitment to local interests in addition to international pursuits. Archival documentation offered detail and complexity, with performance experience and spectatorship illustrating them in practice. The next chapter will explore the selected case studies in more detail, considering the 'local' components of the company and their work. This chapter will consider Kneehigh's work as a way to communicate their Cornish identity and heritage, presenting 'forgotten' stories and political contexts.

Notes

[1] Gilmore, J.H. & Pine, B.J. *Authenticity what consumers really want*, Havard Business Press, USA. 1-191. 2007. Pg-57.

[2] Shepherd, M. and Rice, E. *Kneehigh Theatre The Asylum Summer Season 2010*, Kneehigh Archive Falmouth University. 2010.

[3] http://funpalaces.co.uk

[4] http://funpalaces.co.uk

[5] Taylor, Diana. *The Archive and the Repertoire: Performing cultural memory in The* Americas, Duke University, 2003. Pg-49.

[6] Taylor, Diana. *The Archive and the Repertoire: Performing cultural memory in The* Americas, Duke University, 2003. Pg-2.

[7] Taylor, Diana. *The Archive and the Repertoire: Performing cultural memory in The* Americas, Duke University, 2003. Pg-20.

[8] Taylor, Diana. *The Archive and the Repertoire: Performing cultural memory in The* Americas, Duke University, 2003. Pg-16.

[9] Dorney, Kate. "Archives", *Contemporary Theatre Review,* 23:1, 8-10, 2013. Pg-9.

[10] Allain, Paul. "The Archive", *Contemporary Theatre Review,* 25:1, 32-35, 2015. Pg-33.

[11] Allain, Paul. "The Archive", *Contemporary Theatre Review,* 25:1, 32-35, 2015. Pg-35.

[12] Pearson, Mike. and Shanks, Michael. *Theatre/Archaeology,* Routledge, London, 2001. Xiv – 54. Pg-11.

[13] Pearson, Mike. and Shanks, Michael. *Theatre/Archaeology,* Routledge, London, 2001. Xiv – 54. Pg-11.

[14] Pearson, Mike. and Shanks, Michael. *Theatre/Archaeology,* Routledge, London, 2001. Xiv – 54. Pg-54.

[15] Shoaf, R.W. "Notes", *Second Series,* Vol. 56, No. 3, Mar 2000: 648-654. Pg-649.

[16] Hiller, Susan. "Working Through Objects." *The Archive*. Ed. Charles Merewether. Whitechapel Gallery Ventures: London, UK, 2006. Pg-42.

[17] Taylor, Diana. *The Archive and the Repertoire: Performing cultural memory in The* Americas, Duke University, 2003. Pg-19.

[18] Iball, Helen. "Dusting Ourselves Down." *Performance Research: On Archives and Archiving.* Ed. Gough, Richard. & Roms, Heike. *Vol 7. No.*4, Routledge, Dec 2002. Pg-59.

[19] Pearson, Mike. and Shanks, Michael. *Theatre/Archaeology,* Routledge, London, 2001. Pg-11.

[20] Derrida, Jacques. *Archive Fever - A Freudian Impression*, The University of Chicago Press: Chicago, USA, 1996. Pg-17.

[21] Derrida, Jacques. *Archive Fever - A Freudian Impression*, The University of Chicago Press: Chicago, USA, 1996. Pg-17.

[22] Taylor, Diana. *The Archive and the Repertoire: Performing cultural memory in The* Americas, Duke University, 2003. Pg-20.

[23] Taylor, Diana. *The Archive and the Repertoire: Performing cultural memory in The* Americas, Duke University, 2003. Pg-49.

[24] Editorial, *The Guardian,* "The Guardian view on UK theatre: on the brink", published 20.05.2020. Pg-1.

[25] Dan, Catlin. & Kiraly, Josef. "Politics of Cultural History." *The Archive.* Ed. Charles Merewether. Whitechapel Gallery Ventures: London, UK, 2006. Pg-115.

[26] Phelan, Peggy. *Unmarked the Politics of Performance,* E Library, Routledge, 2005. Pg-142.

[27] Freshwater, H. *Theatre and Audience*, Palgrave MacMillan, UK, 2009. Pg-5.

[28] Pearson, M. *Mickery Theater - an imperfect archaeology,* Amsterdam University Press, 2014. Pg-29.

[29] Skantze, P.A. *Itinerant Spectator*, Punctum Books, New York, 2013. Pg-12.

[30] Skantze, P.A. *Itinerant Spectator*, Punctum Books, New York, 2013. Pg-8.

[31] Knowles, R. *Reading the Material Theatre*, Cambridge University Press, 2004. Pg-3.

[32] Knowles, R. *Reading the Material Theatre*, Cambridge University Press, 2004. Pg-9.

[33] Knowles, R. *Reading the Material Theatre*, Cambridge University Press, 2004. Pg-11.

[34] Knowles, R. *Reading the Material Theatre*, Cambridge University Press, 2004. Pg-12.

[35] Knowles, R. *Reading the Material Theatre*, Cambridge University Press, 2004. Pg-66.

[36] Knowles, R. *Reading the Material Theatre*, Cambridge University Press, 2004. Pg-67.

[37] Knowles, R. *Reading the Material Theatre*, Cambridge University Press, 2004. Pg-74.

[38] Knowles, R. *Reading the Material Theatre*, Cambridge University Press, 2004. Pg-74.

[39] Knowles, R. *Reading the Material Theatre*, Cambridge University Press, 2004. Pg-80.

[40] Freshwater, H. *Theatre and Audience*, Palgrave MacMillan, UK, 2009. Pg-19.

[41] Oddey, A. and White, C. *Modes of Spectating*, Intellect, Uni of Chicago Press. 2009. Pg-8.

[42] Oddey, A. and White, C. *Modes of Spectating*, Intellect, Uni of Chicago Press. 2009. Pg-126.

[43] Ranciere, J. *The Emancipated Spectator*, Verso, UK, 2011. Pg-13.

[44] Freshwater, H. *Theatre and Audience*, Palgrave MacMillan, UK, 2009. Pg-5.

[45] Freshwater, H. *Theatre and Audience*, Palgrave MacMillan, UK, 2009. Pg-6.

[46] Freshwater, H. *Theatre and Audience*, Palgrave MacMillan, UK, 2009. Pg-12.

[47] Freshwater, H. *Theatre and Audience*, Palgrave MacMillan, UK, 2009. Pg-25.

[48] Freshwater, H. *Theatre and Audience*, Palgrave MacMillan, UK, 2009. Pg-33.

[49] Stoian, Linda. "Archive Review: Learning performance by archiving Performance." *Performance Research: On Archives and Archiving.* Ed. Gough, Richard. & Roms, Heike. *Vol 7. No.*4, Routledge, Dec 2002. Pg-128.

[50] Stoian, Linda. "Archive Review: Learning performance by archiving Performance." *Performance Research: On Archives and Archiving.* Ed. Gough, Richard. & Roms, Heike. *Vol 7. No.*4, Routledge, Dec 2002. Pg-128.

CHAPTER THREE

THE 'LOCAL'

This chapter explores the 'local' components influencing and affecting Kneehigh Theatre Company by considering the productions: *Quicksilver* (2002) directed by Bill Mitchell, *Tristan and Yseult* (2005) directed by Emma Rice, and *Blast* (2010) directed by Mike Shepherd. It draws local components from a range of elements, including Cornish location, history, community and cultural influences. Using the theoretical lenses of globalisation, cultural exchange and spectatorship, the above productions will be reviewed considering Kneehigh's focus on Cornish cultural identity. By referring to experiences of seeing these productions, alongside research material from the Kneehigh archive, the concept of the experiential archive (defined in Chapter 2) will be used to conduct performance analysis. This analysis will consider Kneehigh's artistic aims to create work for Cornwall, and their positionality when considering cultural identity. Research within this chapter will also include references and critical reflection on funding, creation and reception of the above production work.

Notions of the 'Local'

Opinions of the frequently used term 'the local' are often diverse, making the term difficult to determine definitively. The ways in which definitions of 'the local' are often in opposition to each other requires the term to be carefully considered and clearly delineated. Ruediger Korff offered a commentary on the complexity of defining what is 'local', he himself asserted that it is difficult to pinpoint.

> It seems as if, as a legacy from the classical period, it is assumed that everybody knows what local is, and thus there is no need for further elaboration. This can be taken as one reason why the current literature dealing with 'local', is not at all explicit about what is meant by it. [1]

Much of the research encountered for this book regards the 'local' as describing social groupings, ethnicities, as well as specific regional areas, without providing 'further elaboration' as alluded to by Korff. However, just as globalisation encompasses local elements through cultural exchange, ideas of 'the local' have been influenced by global factors, offering qualities and descriptors towards defining localism. According to Korff, defining 'the local' as isolated and cut off from the rest of the world is no longer applicable in a modern, global age: 'The local, is a point of articulation of diverse cultural/social, economic and political impacts reaching from neighbours via the state to the global level'[2]. Korf's description of the 'local' includes cultural exchange, and as discovered through research into localism and globalism, is intrinsic in descriptions within theories relating to locality and globality.

Stuart Hall cited the return to 'the local' as a response to globalisation, suggesting this occurs when the individual is 'confronted' by a globalised form of modernity.[3] Inherent in Hall's definition, is a critique of globalism, with localisation providing a sanctuary or 'safe place' to retreat to. The ongoing situation of Brexit illustrates Hall's descriptions of withdrawing to a 'safe place' and can be viewed in the context of the UK's retreat from the EU affecting the Cornish county and Kneehigh. In fact, this retreat from globalisation is at odds with Kneehigh's perceptions of Cornish cultural identity and the company's global business model. Although this subject is pertinent to localism, I will address Kneehigh's stance on the referendum in the concluding chapter, addressing developments for the company post-2016 onwards.

The work of David B. Knight on the 'local' described many of the ideas and ambitions implicit in company reports for Kneehigh, discovered within the archive. One such example presents Knight's hypothesis on areas of 'local interest': 'The reconstruction of 'local' has been used to entice visitors to the 'treasured place' – for the village's economic advantage'.[4] This is highly pertinent in describing Kneehigh's venue. My perception of the Asylum as Knight's 'treasured place' is strengthened through its associations with other notable tourist and cultural venues, such as The Lost Gardens of Heligan, and the Cornwall Coliseum. These locations have been home to the Asylum in previous summer seasons and will be explored in further detail in Chapter 6.

Many theorists explored in this chapter, including Knight, indicated that the local is an integral part of globalisation, as essentially people live in 'the local' combined with varying degrees of globalisation. Catherine Kingfisher extends the local and global further by citing a duality between them: 'The global, in other words, is always already local, and the local is, perhaps, always global: each is implicated in, and constitutive of, the other'[5]. In this philosophy, there is an interconnectedness that resonates with cultural exchange, underlining the parity between the local and global within Kneehigh's work and business strategy. Kingfisher supported a description that unifies the local and global, illustrating its complexities.

> In discussions of globalisation, the global is often taken to be 'out there', as opposed to the 'in here' of the local. The concept of glocalization attempts to move beyond this binary by recognising the dialectical nature of the so-called global and local. [6]

In this chapter, the phrase 'the local' is used in relation to globalisation and the view that 'the local' is a specific (and in connection to Kneehigh and the Asylum) 'treasured' place, with shared ideals of location, social and cultural groupings. Links between the local and global are acknowledged and used in connection with each other. As highlighted by Kingfisher, they are often used when describing each other and are not mutually exclusive.

Kneehigh and Cornwall

Kneehigh has maintained its commitment to their home and its history. This includes a cultural, social, historical and political legacy of the county which Kneehigh embraces: 'Cornwall is our physical and spiritual home. We draw inspiration from the landscapes, history, people and culture'.[7] The term 'Cornish County', embraces the 'macro' concept of Cornwall as a locality, contrasting with the national and international factors influencing the company's work. In contrast, the 'micro' elements of this place are not discussed within this chapter, choosing to focus on a broader perception of Cornish identity. Cornwall and the Cornish landscape provide a central focus that informs Kneehigh's work by providing the stimuli for their performances, and by affecting the company members' experiences during rehearsal and devising.

In an interview with a former company member, Andrea Pelaez Lyons described the playful nature of the creative process, as a direct influence from the 'relaxed beauty' of the environment. In other interviews conducted by Cornish author Maurice Smelt, Artistic Directors Emma Rice, Mike Shepherd, and Bill Mitchell discussed the routine of rehearsal. During Smelt's interview, Rice, Shepherd and Mitchell discussed how Kneehigh used the outdoor location to their advantage, to create a close-knit community or a family unit.[8] From a creative standpoint, Mitchell commented on the power of the landscape to act as a stimulus and influence the 'narrative line' in the audience interactive based works, produced by WildWorks.[9] Mike Shepherd indicated why the company feel it is important to work on their productions at their rehearsal base in Cornwall: 'The company doesn't work here full time, but almost all its shows start life here'.[10]

The Kneehigh rehearsal barns at Gorran Haven were the place all Kneehigh shows begin. The barns and surrounding landscape, including a garden with flowers, benches, and a wooden shed filled with costumes and props, provide their creative 'home' for working on and developing all productions. Gorran Haven is a tiny village on the Cornish South-West Coast: the barns are 10-minutes away from the centre of the village, uphill along a coastal path near to the beach. Those working on a production would work within this environment for an intensive two-week 'retreat'. Within the barns, a varied devising and adaptation process takes place. This involves the use of music, poetry and props (before introducing text) in a playful form of improvisation. Research and development are highlighted by Rice as a way of constructing a map or plan, charting how the piece will start and end.

> We always do research and development, even before the show is programmed, and that's where I start to explore the ideas that I've had, and decide, as a company, whether it's going to work. [11]

Communicated in Rice's statement is a collaborative creative journey, co-authored by the members of the company and inspired by research and ideas shared in the rehearsal barns.

In conversation with Martin Welton, Rice described the positive aspects of working at the barns: 'They're fantastic, beautiful... I think that is absolutely key to what we do. When we're at the barns nobody's telling us off; there's no boundaries really. It's idyllic, but we've fought really hard for it'.[12] Everyone working on the production takes turns with kitchen responsibilities, with the entire company sharing meals together to reinforce the bonding process as an ensemble. Rice reflected on a comparison between working at the barns with Kneehigh and her former training with Gardzienice Theatre in her 20s. Rice acknowledged her sense of ensemble was formed during her time with the company, instilled by night runs in the forest as a core part of her training.[13] This tradition was continued at Kneehigh rehearsals with morning jogs along the coast at Gorran Haven.

Lilley, whilst participating in a Kneehigh workshop with the company at the Little Angel Theatre in Islington, refers to the creative ethos or 'energy' generated at Gorran Haven, which is instilled in other rehearsal locations: 'Kneehigh's devising exercises focused not only on retelling the story, but also on exploring the cast's personal connections to it through their collective artistic skills'[14]. The focus is a localisation of personal experiences which can contribute to the devising and rehearsal process. It is reinforced and inspired by the Cornish location of the barns, but also established in other rehearsal environments.

Smelt's second interview with the company allowed former company member, Sue Hill, the opportunity to comment on the benefits that the Cornish community can receive by presenting the positive aspects of living in Cornwall. This is something the company expressed the responsibility to promote: 'And the message – such as it was – was that this is a great place to live, and you are sharing it with great people, and this place has got a future'[15]. Hill stressed how important it was for the Cornish community to know Kneehigh are proud to be Cornish, and to display their national identity 'and wave that flag and wear that badge'.[16] Other core members of Kneehigh within this interview considered the multi-skilled nature of the company representing qualities attributed to Cornish values, something they perceived makes the company unique. Cornish values, as with other notions of cultural identity, are extremely hard to pin down and define. Despite this complexity, Kneehigh have shared their perceptions of Cornish identity and values within their productions and press interviews. One such trait perceived by the company is being outward looking towards the rest of the world, rather than parochial. This 'outward looking' approach is maintained whilst having a pride in the beauty of the Cornish land and its people.

Former artistic director Bill Mitchell expands on this multi-faceted view of Cornish identity by stating: 'this is how you survive in Cornwall, I think it's how it works in Cornwall' [17]Both Mitchell and Hill argue that Cornwall and Cornish identity are unifying factors, illustrating there are: 'strong feelings which runs through all the work'[18], with the central theme of community recurring again and again.

> If you look at almost any of the shows that theme will crop up or will be a foundation stone, and that originates in the fact that Kneehigh is a community; but also we live in Cornwall and have a sense of location and place – more than if we were jobbing actors and therefore going round where the work was taking us. (*BM*: I think we're not only a community, we're a family.) Yes, true – family or community…(*BM*: …or tribes.) [19]

Mitchell and Hill concurred that Cornwall provided them with a 'great deal' of material but conceded that the stimuli did not have to be Cornish, and were open to using stories from around the world. However, Kneehigh has used performances and celebrations in village halls to celebrate local community and Cornish heritage.

> Since 1989 Kneehigh has been generating Pride of Place projects in Cornwall; local carnival projects, lantern processions, Feast Days and anniversaries, with the aim of achieving cultural regeneration and

encouraging local people from all sections of the community to take pride
in the places they live in and their communities. [20]

These events are underpinned by a celebratory sharing of experiences, in
addition to their participation with 'cultural regeneration', allowing for
creativity between local parties. As indicated by this report, the National
Lottery has involved Kneehigh with the above listed events for several
years. This has been conducted to support their local community, but also
as this document suggests, in evaluation of National Lottery funds, to gain
funding.

   Placing Cornwall at the centre of Kneehigh's work is a core aim of the
company, by developing Landscape Theatre as a new art form within their
practice. The company perceive it as '... a unique outdoor experience of
mobile theatre in Cornwall, telling powerful resonant stories in
unconventional ways, moving objects and people through the landscape and
where the audience is mobile and participates in the story'[21]. Landscape
Theatre is as an art form integral to the company's aims, listed in several of
their production reports, including the *Hevva! Report (1999)* and *Trustee's
Report and Accounts (2001).* Kneehigh defined Landscape theatre in the
following terms:

> Landscape Theatre mixes theatrical disciplines and turns theatrical
> conventions upside down. We tell powerful resonant stories in
> unconventional ways. The form is an unusual hybrid of film grammar,
> operatic scale and sculptural skills, moving objects and people through a
> land and seascape to unfold a narrative. The audience too is mobile and
> participates in the story. Artistically, we feel we have just scratched the
> surface. [22]

There is a freedom of creativity afforded to them because of the Cornish
location and environment, suggesting that it is a place where 'you can make
things happen'.[23] Likewise, Susannah Clapp commented on Kneehigh's
brand associations with Cornwall, stating that Kneehigh has a reputation for
making theatre out of 'seascapes and landscapes' in addition to offering a
fusion of styles by incorporating music hall, cabaret and 'hurdy-gurdy
boisterousness'.[24]

   Kneehigh communicated their ambitions to raise 'the profile and status
of the performing arts in Cornwall' [25]and landscape theatre by securing
funding within the *Trustee's Report and Accounts* report. It is debatable
whether this was achieved nationally, with advertisements for *WildWalks[1]*

---

[1] A Kneehigh project in which audience members are told stories, hear poetry and
see performances whilst working through the Cornish landscape and coastline. In

tours based within Cornwall during the summer months in the UK. However, this form of landscape theatre has only been maintained outside of Cornwall on the Three Islands Project (which will be discussed in more detail in the next chapter). Most productions on tour nationally and internationally are performed in more traditional theatre and performance venues. Conversely, Kneehigh's specific notion of landscape theatre is unique to the Cornish coast and their brand. From this standpoint, there is no requirement (apart from the case of the Three Islands Project) to create landscape theatre in other locations. In the case of the Three Islands Project, the UK component was performed in the town of Hayle, in Cornwall.

Cornwall's long history of trade, travel and exchange with other countries underpins the company's ethos, establishing Kneehigh's role within this historical framework.

> Cornwall has a long and lively history of international trade and cultural exchange. For a county so distant from the capital it boasts remarkably cosmopolitan and global influences and culture. We are proud to be an active part of this tradition. Our European touring has influenced our work enormously through contact with Spanish, Portuguese, Russian, Polish, Dutch and South American theatre and music. We recognise strong resonances in our work of Spanish and Portuguese companies. [26]

As indicated above, Kneehigh affirm the impact touring has had on their work through cultural exchange and developing international connections. However, cultural exchange can be a complex and difficult process. Kneehigh both explored and reinforced Cornish cultural heritage, displaying an openness and pragmatism to the tensions preventing them from working in their home environment. The tensions experienced by Kneehigh did not lie in their ability (or lack of) to combine local and global influences in an artistic product enjoyed by local, national and international audiences. It initially resided in the difficulties of performing in Cornwall due to economic factors that impeded the company from performing to their local target audience. Kneehigh wanted to perform in Cornwall, and their local audience and fan base wished them to perform there too, but during the late 90s, neither Kneehigh nor their audience could financially support the company to enable them to base their work solely in Cornwall.

Shepherd and Rice have communicated in interviews that coming from Cornwall makes them predisposed to be global, stating that 'we always wanted to be world citizens'.[27] Rice suggested cultural exchange is inherent

---

recent years a smartphone app has been developed, offering another format to enjoy this experience.

in Cornish identity, due to Cornwall's location near the sea. Shepherd and Rice argue that this international connectedness is 'a fundamental thing about being in Cornwall'[28], although such claims raise questions why Rice and Shepherd appeared to take great pains in underlining their globalism. Other communities can lay claim to globalisation being fundamental to their heritage, with cities such as London and Birmingham experiencing successive periods of immigration during the 50s and 60s. These and other such communities developed through varying degrees of cultural exchange, incorporating local and national differences, creating a new independent identity. Most people may not associate this globalism with Cornwall, when local history and facts, according to Shepherd in his interview with Dominic Cavendish for *The Daily Telegraph*, are suppressed by 'English' variations of history.

Regarding stereotypes of Cornish identity, Kneehigh perceives a misunderstanding and misrepresentation of Cornish identity and community as harmful to the community, the arts in Cornwall and the company itself. Shepherd in *The Guardian* again voiced Kneehigh's ambitions to be a global and popularist product. He expressed the company's evolution of producing work outside Cornwall, arguing against parochial perceptions, stating that 'we're too ambitious for that. We want to travel the world'.[29] In presenting this viewpoint, Shepherd and Rice offered a more diverse and complex variant of Cornish identity. However, Kneehigh has used stereotypical Cornish characters as a source of comedy within their productions, reinforcing them and offering opportunities to question and subvert these characteristics, providing depth and layers of meaning for consideration.

Cornish myths and legends have been used by Kneehigh as principal stimuli for devising. Likewise, the company have adapted fairy tales with a Cornish slant, creating additional Cornish characters placed within famous stories. This can be seen in the Kneehigh production *Cymbeline* (2008). *The Telegraph* observed the Cornish character Joan Futtock, as a narrator figure, providing Cornish connections to the show[30]. The review for bbc.co.uk agreed that using this narrator figure, underlined Cornish links, making 'a complicated plot more accessible'[31]. The company does not assert a definitive Cornish role, rather they offer ideas and shared experiences that build towards common factors, contributing towards a continually developing notion of identity.

Emma Rice has described feelings of being ostracised as symptomatic of coming from Cornwall and of Cornish identity, attracting other communities and people to the company: 'And how do their Chinese or Syrian audiences respond? How can they relate to Kneehigh's Cornishness?

'It's to do with being an outsider,' says Emma Rice.[32] Feelings of being ostracised are also found within counter-arguments against globalisation. Naomi Klein described anti-globalist groups, who share many of the same attributes described by Rice. Klein in *No Logo* described feelings of being on the outside socially and culturally, with local culture squeezed out by more dominant and global strands. Kneehigh wished to draw attention to the diversity within Cornwall, presenting feelings expressed by Cornish inhabitants, of being subjugated to English and London-centric narratives. Rice and Kneehigh sought to re-address the portrayal of Cornish culture, noting that other cultures share similar feelings and experiences. Govan et al. suggest that communities and national/cultural identities are symbolic constructions, based on stories told from different viewpoints. Theatre practitioners are sought after to tell these stories, using performance to construct a robust sense of community. Changing the conceptions of community and narrative enables the acknowledgement of the complexities of identification, allowing members the choice to form multiple forms of identity. Kneehigh has revisited Cornish cultural identity in their productions, presenting a range of multi-dimensional characters, questioning their own heritage and values.

Quicksilver (2002)

The productions *Quicksilver* (2002) and *Blast* (2010) addressed Cornish identity, its economy and the decline of the once all-powerful mining industries. Whilst *Blast* considered the impact felt by the county in the twenty-first century, *Quicksilver* explored the formative history of the mining industries. The term 'quicksilver' refers to the liquid qualities of mercury (a metal also mined) and also describes the elusive and difficult nature of mining for precious resources. The term grew in popularity in the 1800s during a growth period for the industry, particularly in North America. Kneehigh's exploration into Cornwall's history of mining and its eventual dwindling economy provided an opportunity to revisit and reexamine this period in history, rewriting it, forging new associations with popular culture and western iconography. Laera offers definitions relating to theatrical adaptations, providing the opportunity for a historical and cultural examination, re-examination and re-definition:

> As a memory machine, theatre is the site for the recollection, re-elaboration and contestation of readily available cultural material, and for the production of new, and newly adaptable ideas out of established ones. [33]

The production *Quicksilver* (directed by Bill Mitchell) displayed creative processes for recollection and re-elaboration as cited by Laera, building new connections with the economic and social history of Cornwall. This was a story the company wished to express, developed through devising and improvisation and formalised through the script written by Carl Grose.

The collapse of the mining industry in the late 1800s defined Cornwall's economic power and shaped the Cornish landscape. R.M. Barton, a noted historian and archivist, recorded the experiences of the Cornish Industries before and during the industrial revolution. His research outlined the connections made with pottery businesses in Staffordshire in exporting clay from Cornwall, because of the dwindling supplies of raw materials for the expanding industries in Staffordshire. The term 'The Cornish Adventurers' described those (from 1820 to 1860) who sought partnerships with potters in Scotland, Wales and the Midlands. However, closer inspection depicts the inter-war slump and closure of most clay pits, together with the losses the Cornish community experienced when a thriving industry, exporting materials globally for one hundred years, closes down after two world wars. Interestingly, Barton highlighted another facet to the stereotypically held view of Cornish people being insular and reluctant to venture beyond their county or share their 'raw materials' with the rest of the world. Migration or 'the great migration of the nineteenth century' saw up to half a million people move away from Cornwall because of the collapse of the mining community[34]. This became part of Cornish culture with descriptions of families migrating overseas to earn enough money to return home. Garry Tregida and Kayleigh Milden described the ways in which migrants maintained their cultural identities overseas by creating 'little Cornwalls'. By recreating elements of the county, descendants embraced this Cornish identity even if they were not born in Cornwall, nor had seen the place themselves: 'Celtic festivals and Cornish tartans have been co-opted as cultural icons of Cornish societies from Australia to the United States of America'.[35]

Kneehigh explored 'the great Cornish migration' in the production *Quicksilver* (2002). The play followed the 'adventures' of Cornish Miners leaving the county to earn a living in unfamiliar parts of the world. There is a local and global narrative (seen through the historical source material and the plot), highlighting the influence of globalisation on the Cornish community in the 1800s. Likewise, there is a blend of local and global cultural signifiers in presenting the tale of Cornish miners emigrating to America, combined with Country and Western music and iconic imagery, blending integral elements of the story with popularist and international components. 'The main character is a miner and mining is what he does, but it is also a Western so certain elements have to be included.', said Carl [Grose] [36]. Production reviews and press interviews found within the Kneehigh archive, revealed the Western elements Grose alludes to above. Photographs included in these press releases showed Grose, in the title role, dressed as a sheriff holding a gun, reminiscent of a character from the Wild West.

Associations are immediately drawn from the semiotics established with this imagery and the production title. The context drawn from the photograph of Grose as a sheriff, provoked social, historical and political connections linking Cornwall with America in the 1800s. Further connotations are made with popularist culture and the Wild West. Historical elements from this time period have developed iconic status through popular culture, emerging from the American film and TV industry in the 50s and 60s. 'Westerns', a term describing films and TV shows based on the Wild West, was a hugely successful and profitable genre. Hundreds of films and TV shows were made as 'Westerns', filtering down to merchandise such as clothing and toys[2]. American [Wild] Western culture has been highly influential in music and fashion, particularly in the 1950s and 60s, with elements of this genre still prevalent in the twenty-first century. Through the development of *Quicksilver* as a Western, Kneehigh has aligned themselves with this popularist genre. Arguably they have done so from a place of historical 'authenticity', utilising the aesthetics of the era to inform choices in set, costume, music, props, etc. In terms of the mechanics involved in adaptation, Laera described a transposition of a source or stimuli into a new 'form'. Adaptation can also seek 'matches' for 'certain features' or 'mismatches' between the original source material and the adapted work[37]. Grose and Kneehigh have formed links with Western culture and the historical context of the Cornish migration.

An added component of 'authenticity' is established through the selection of the performance venue by hosting this production at Carnglaze Caverns. There is a historical relevance in performing this production at Carnglaze Caverns during the tour schedule. Carnglaze was an open quarry, developed into three man-made caverns as a consequence of mining slate over 300 years ago. A press release from Kneehigh advertising place this as a 'special' performance highlights the historical legacy of the cavern, promoting the unique opportunity to witness the performance within its original historical environment. The location worked as both a marketing strategy for the company and the production to generate sales, while staying

---

[2] The *Toy Story* series by Disney features Woody and Jessie – western inspired toys from the 50s, acknowledging how influential this genre was during the time period.

true to the company's artistic notions of landscape theatre. The quarry acted as a mirror for the environment of the lead character, a tin miner, supplying realistic historical connotations and atmosphere and offering an experience not possible in a more traditional theatrical location.

At a performance of *Quicksilver* (at another theatrical venue), a 'gift' was given to audience members. During the show at the Acorn Theatre in Cornwall, audience members received free merchandise, drawing attention to the historical elements of the production. This was particularly relevant in performances outside of Carnglaze Caverns, evoking some (if not all) of the experiences generated by the landscape venue. As described by a review in *The Cornishman:*

> Members of the audience at the panto will have the chance to win a special piece of Cornish history – as each week throughout its tour one of the company's famous 'goody-bag' style programmes will contain a piece of hand-crafted jewellery made from the last tin to be mined in Cornwall. The Jewellery – which includes miniature mining tools, pasty lapel badges and pendants – has been donated by the South Crofty Collection. [38]

This article confirmed Kneehigh's reputation for creating 'goody bag' style programmes, mirroring my discovery within the archive of the present containing a toy motorbike promoting *Cymbeline*. Likewise, this article reinforced observations of Kneehigh's brand awareness, creating mementoes to promote the show and the company once the tour has concluded. The 'material semiotics' within the goody bag exercised commercial agency and acted to encourage repeat custom, while at the same time maintaining powerful connections with their Cornish heritage. The merchandise promoted the company and their work and educated audience members on elements of Cornish history pivotal to the plot of the play. Local press reviewing this production stated that *Quicksilver* is a 'requiem for the souls of all the Cornish' who left home to venture further afield. In my view, the performance conjures up images of an act of remembrance, a token or gesture, or a religious ceremony, underpinned by music. The language used in the review supports Shepherd's ideas that the production provides a platform to express a Cornish 'voice' and share 'forgotten' stories and histories. Kneehigh's use of humour to portray more serious issues of nineteenth-century Cornish diaspora was established through their creation of a character called: He Who Talks With Half-Eaten Pasty. As indicated by Ruhrmund's review, this comically invented name displayed a playful reference to Cornish stereotypes, whilst reinforcing them. [39]

Tregida and Milden argue that it has only been in recent decades that an interest in Cornish dispersion or the effects of global migration has developed. This may be symptomatic of the global age of the twentieth and twenty-first centuries, with a desire, to re-discover Cornish roots, and Cornish identity. In summary of Tregida and Milden's observations; when researchers tried to quantify cultural identity, they encountered limitations through participants' vague descriptions of feelings and instincts as a way of defining the qualities of being Cornish. There is a disconnect from one's ancestral heritage and cultural identity when you move away from your 'homeland', even if only a short distance away.

> [An individual has] An inability to connect the present to an identifiable ancestral past, because of the dislocation from the 'homeland'. Ethnicity can only be expressed in such terms such as 'it's just a feeling' or 'something that is just there'. The past can only be reconstructed through artificial language with words such as 'roots', 'heritage' or 'belonging'. [40]

The fragile nature of national/cultural identity eroded by familial migration is perceived by Tregida and Milden. Likewise, the inability to describe cultural identity in more concrete terms other than feelings, instincts or half-remembered stories from previous generations is also observed. It is understandable why the Cornish community and Kneehigh protect their cultural identity.

Storytelling and sharing the histories from previous generations is a key element in maintaining cultural identity and a sense of belonging. Kneehigh have a duty/role in this, coming from (or being based in) Cornwall, they have a shared sense of responsibility to pass down Cornish stories and heritage. Through their global creative endeavours, they have reached out to a global Cornish community. This is a community that has relocated from Cornwall, with previous generations forced to migrate due to the socio-economic collapse of the tin and clay industries. Migrated generations may feel more disconnected from their cultural identities and in search of what it means to be Cornish. Globalisation, caused by the economic marketplace, is a prime factor which has damaged the sense of cultural identity and familial belonging. Therefore, tensions are experienced, not only with globalisation and local community but also with globalisation and the notion of family.

Quicksilver offered an entertaining way to engage with a lesser-known narrative of Cornish globalisation, using popular culture and landscape theatre to create an experience of historical authenticity. Performances within the Carnglaze Caverns offered a spectator the opportunity to experience the historical legacy and relevance of this environment in an immersive site-specific event. The location, the historical subject matter of the performance, and the 'goody bag' mementoes, combined to offer a multi-layered interpretation. The cultural symbolism within *Quicksilver* communicated globalisation and diaspora, western culture and the history of mining in the 1800s. Kneehigh's marketing strategy with 'goody bags' to establish their brand provided an authenticity of experience through historical location, and landscape theatre as part of 'Brand Kneehigh'. Arguably, other performances discussed within this study could be described as offering a multi-layered context. The work of Skantze and Knowles illustrated this point through their descriptions of productions with the social, historical, political associations generated in their spectatorship. Yet despite this being the only show (or variation of) included in this book that I have not seen 'live', I have been able to use other materials in the experiential archive. *Quicksilver* is an important production in the formation of 'Brand Kneehigh'. Analysis of this production displayed elements integral to the brand, including popular culture and entertainment, Cornish focus, branded products/mementoes, landscape theatre and a branded 'environment/world'.

Tristan and Yseult (2005)

The production (directed by Emma Rice) was based on the Celtic myth *Tristan and Isolde,* concerning a tragic love story induced by a love potion. King Mark instructs Tristan to accompany Isolde (King Mark's intended bride) on a journey back to Cornwall. It is during this trip that Tristan and Isolde accidentally drink a love potion and become 'locked' together in an adulterous romantic relationship. I attended a performance of *Tristan and Yseult* at the Cottesloe in the National Theatre in 2005, with my experiences of this production starting pre-show. Through association from my first Kneehigh performance, my expectations were set to see a re-telling of a classic story, using humour balanced by an underpinning of darker themes. Based on my first performance encounter, I expected to see a use of multi-media and projection, reconfigured props and physical theatre. These elements contributed to my growing perceptions of their theatrical brand.

The performance venue at the National Theatre also elevated these expectations. I assumed Kneehigh was a company with growing national success to warrant inclusion within the 2005 summer season at the National Theatre. Theatre venues, as well as theatre companies, enjoy a notable USP. For example, the Battersea Arts Centre, venue to *The Wooden Frock,* has a reputation for showcasing new, experimental performance and Fringe Theatre. Kneehigh's earlier appearance at the BAC shaped my pre-show perceptions of this company as 'an emerging' theatre troupe at *The Wooden Frock*. A year later, with the performance venue at the National Theatre, new opinions of the company were being forged. Although this venue also had a reputation for showing new work, it has an added prestige from its title and artistic legacy from its inception in the 1960s. My connections between Kneehigh and the National Theatre were that the company had developed a strong enough reputation and audience base to warrant their performance at the National Theatre, having become a noted part of the contemporary British theatre scene.

In examining *Tristan and Yseult*, I used my experiential archive, including my spectatorship as an audience member, reading of programmes, reviews and mementoes. The combination of the above elements built towards a multi layered experience of the performance. American visual artist and composer, Arnold Dreyblatt, considers the nature of performance, hinting at its limitations and possibilities for recording:

> One might understand the performance as presentation of a process which has been developed and stored in the past. On the other hand, a performance, an event, exists only as a fleeting ephemeral moment before disappearance. An archive is a representation of mankind's endless battle against the disappearance of information from the past; an attempt to freeze and keep forever. The archive is utopian in character. Perhaps one could create a concept of ritual, which might bridge this gap. Ritual, which involves a kind of performance of repetition, has often served as a temporal and oral means of passing on cultural knowledge. [41]

It is interesting that Dreyblatt described the archive as 'utopian' indicating idealistic attempts to document and record, again limited in its attempt for perfection, characteristics attributed to utopia. I would add that the utopian view of an archive is limited in its attempt of completion or being 'complete' as opposed to perfection. An archive can never be complete, as there will always be materials missing or omitted. However, elements from the performance can provide an experiential impression, irrespective of its 'completeness'. In this capacity, the experiential archive proposed does not achieve Dreyblatt's utopia but is more positive in embracing the fragmented nature of a performance archive. It acknowledges 'gaps' of information and the impossibility of documenting a 'complete' experience, whilst proposing the potential for varied fragmented elements to form an archive. Mike Pearson developed his own 'imperfect archaeology' to document Mickery Theatre, with commonalities experienced in his use of archive and performance and the experiential archive: 'There is no claim to completeness: fragments of differing types are assembled to create a partial picture, a glimpse of creative aspirations'.[42]

From the very beginning, the performance established its connections with Cornish heritage, supported with contemporary visual aesthetics. As discussed earlier, Kneehigh associates themselves with Cornwall and its cultural/national identity, and this was very much the case with Cornish references to the Celtic legend, Tristan and Isolde. References were made during the show for comedic effect, reinforced by the presentation of a map of Cornwall to the audience during King Mark's monologue, in the style of a history lesson:

> KING MARK: Now picture this country etched on a map.
> *FROCIN produces a map.*
> Then regard what you see as nothing but crap.
> Forget what you've been taught or think you know:
> The centre of everything's here - Kernow.
> We don't look inland, there's not much point
> Let Rome rule the Anglos, their foreheads anoint.
> No, outward lies the way!
> Inland there's little to write home about and much less to say. [43]

King Mark's monologue mirrored Shepherd's statements over the 'English' dominance of Cornish history. The speech signposts the significance of Cornwall within this Celtic tale, portraying the county as superior to all other parts of Britain: 'The centre of everything's here – Kernow'. Patrick Marmion in his review of *Tristan and Yseult* (2005), argued that Kneehigh has reclaimed the original Cornish story: 'So the doomed saga of Tristan and Yseult is snatched from Teutonic legend and gleefully returned to its native Cornwall'[44]. This assertive stance established by Marmion's description of Kneehigh's reclamation of this story for Cornish Identity was mirrored by the 'history lesson' scene included in the show. Shepherd described Kneehigh's ability through performance to provide a Cornish 'lens' to historical events, myths and legends. King Mark's statement 'Forget what you've been taught or think you know' mirrors Shepherd's call to re-contextualise history to include this forgotten and displaced narrative. As a spectator, I noticed this stance through the inclusion of this scene early on in the production. The style of direct address to the audience took the format of a lecture, didactically informing the spectator of Cornwall's positionality within this folk tale.

Kneehigh brand is not synonymous with political activism. However, there was a cultural agenda evident in asserting Cornwall's place in history within this play. During the show, and with more consideration post-show, there were connotations with other minority groups and a retelling of history. Movements such as Black History month seek similar redress, offering a post-colonial narrative. Kneehigh's production work does intersect with post-colonial theatre (although this subject will not be considered in depth within this study). In the accompanying programme to the production, Kneehigh highlighted the historical connections of Cornwall and the story. Coleman argued that through this production, Kneehigh are reclaiming Cornish territory: 'Here, in Tristan and Yseult we have an archetypal epic with an ancient Cornish provenance. Who better to make a new map and reclaim this venerable territory than our own champion cartographers of the Cornish cosmography, Kneehigh Theatre?'[45]. Steve Wright in his article 'Cornish Past', is keen to establish links between the origins of the story and Kneehigh's cultural identity, describing the company's work on cliff tops and landscapes around the county as being suited to dealing with the origins of this 'centuries old Cornish love story'[46].

Marmion (in his review of the production) summarises Kneehigh's theatricality: identifiable by its creative qualities as well as the influence of Cornish heritage. Marmion's viewpoint gives a perceived fusion of classic works combined with modern aesthetics as Kneehigh's theatrical style. On describing the creativity and originality in Kneehigh's contemporary revision of *Tristan and Yseult (2005)* with references to popular culture, Marmion stated that the company has taken a classic story and embedded it with 'freshness and charm'.[47] Setting the production in modern times by portraying male characters as gangsters reminiscent of a Quentin Tarantino or Guy Ritchie film provided contemporary film connotations. This modern presentation underscored the darker qualities of the legend and harnessed global components, including references to contemporary cinema and use of a multi-national cast to appeal to an international and multi-cultural audience. Contemporary costume provoked my semiotic reading of the production, forming associations with modern cinema: contemporary suits and sunglasses, replacing medieval armour.

In addition, the physicality of the actors representing the battle between Ireland and Cornwall was staged using the same cinematic qualities: knives and guns replaced swords. Contemporary stage combat was reminiscent of gangster brawls common in Tarantino and Richie fight sequences. The cultural materialism observed in this production indicated a willingness to align with a popularist but also a violent brand of contemporary cinema. In doing so, it illustrated the danger and violence inherent within the tale, whilst also being subversive towards the royal and aristocratic characters – likening them to modern-day gangsters jostling for power. Likewise, branded associations with contemporary cinema can encourage additional clientele to attend more Kneehigh performances. An ambition to broaden the audience demographic through the adaptation of popular works can be seen in Kneehigh's theatrical treatment of cinematic classics *A Matter of Life and Death* (2007) and *Brief Encounter* (2008), literary works *Nights at the Circus (2006)* and *Rebecca (2015)*, and television show *Steptoe and Son*

(2013). The adaptation of these works encourages new spectatorship from the fan base of the original source. This is a strategy used by other theatre companies: but can trigger criticism and unfavourable comparison.

Kneehigh's ability to reinvent a story, using popular and entertaining contemporary association and incorporate localism within a global product are core components to 'Brand Kneehigh'. Marmion observes a 'blended international performance style' which is ingrained with localism. By providing comical stereotypes of British culture, alongside other international cultural examples [including American 'gangster' cinema and 1950s rock-and-roll iconography], Kneehigh is successful in merging these influences together. According to Marmion, the local content of the work (in this case presented as British rather than Cornish) is at the 'heart' of the global collection of styles and influences. In fact, how local is 'local' when compared to the company's international work? Local can refer to Kneehigh's Cornish base, in contrast to their national work, but is problematic when referring to Kneehigh as a British company in contrast to the rest of the world. From my experience of the production at the Cottesloe in 2005, I was clear in differentiating between the local [Cornish] components of the story and its place within national culture. This production can be both local and national, and as a spectator, I found that both were clearly communicated. The 'history' lesson Kneehigh provided in *Tristan and Yseult* allowed for clarity in the distinction between local and national, and the venue of the National Theatre underscored the national and international relevance of the story and of Kneehigh Theatre Company. However, Kneehigh's inclusion of this history lesson would assist audience members from different parts of the world, unfamiliar with the UK's geography and cultural borders.

Wright (as well as other authors whose articles were contained within the Kneehigh Archive) supported the idea that the company created a recognisable brand with Cornish associations; qualities that can be embedded into a range of projects. Wright observed that Kneehigh 'have put their own stamp on the story' and given *Tristan and Yseult* a 'robust updating'[48]. My own recollections of this production concurred with Wright's observations. In addition to associations with the cinematic gangster genre, other imagery was equally powerful. Costumes, music and rock-and-roll inspired dance routines displayed influences from the 1950s, with elements of 'rockabilly'[3] culture embedded throughout. The 50s was identified as a time in which the very first notions of the 'modern teenager'

---

[3] Rockabilly culture is perceived as one of the earliest styles of rock and roll music, dating back to the 1950s in the United States.

were constructed. This cultural shift in perceiving young adults as having their own identity saw the simultaneous growth of rock music and the birth of modern popular culture. Rock music targeted teenage audiences, expressing the concerns of this teenage demographic: focusing on love (both true love and unrequited). This imagery was extremely powerful in updating the story for a modern audience whilst underpinning the naïve and also 'fated' elements to the story. The subject of love is perceived by Kneehigh as an experience felt universally, signposted at the very beginning: 'So, I welcome you to our story: We're all in it...all of us.'[49]. Other tragic love stories also share similar cultural and contextual reinventions. For example, *West Side Story* was effectively a modernised version of *Romeo and Juliet.* It is fitting that Kneehigh not only developed the story using their own branded theatrical elements but also reconfigured the story into a modern incarnation with Cornish cultural foundations.

The initial tensions, experienced in defining and using terms of locality, mirrored the complexities of Kneehigh's own experiences in negotiating between local and global cultural identities. Although the company emphasised the Cornish component of this Celtic tale, they combined many other cultural influences and associations. The renaming of the lead character, Yseult, rather than Isolde displayed a keenness to marry more global cultures with the original Celtic version of the tale, allowing for a multi-cultural cast and audience. This global cultural exchange was established within the title and instigated questions within the pre-show spectator experience: why Yseult and not Iseult or Isolde? On further investigation, the name has French and German origins, widening the international scope for this Arthurian story. It also underpinned the global casting of the production in 2005, with Eva Magyar, a Hungarian actress, cast in the role of Yseult, opposite Cornish actor Tristan Sturrock as Tristan. Referring to Lilley's observations of the company; 'the casts personal connections' are explored within the devising and adaptation process as a form of creative individuation.[50]

My experience of the show and the associative branding of Kneehigh continued post show and related to a former production of *Tristan and Yseult* (2004) at the Minack Theatre in Cornwall[4]. Many of the other audience members I encountered (some at international conferences discussing my research on Kneehigh), had seen the production at the Minack in 2004. Within their appraisal of seeing this show, was an account of the uniqueness of seeing this story played in the Cornish landscape. This is part of the unique qualities of the Minack: an outdoor theatre, built into

---

[4] *Tristan and Yseult* has since returned to the Minack in 2017.

the Cornish cliffs, looking out onto the sea. This choice of location helped to reinforce the romanticism of the legend, mirroring the romantic qualities specific to the theatre location itself. It also illustrated the strength of Kneehigh's branding of landscape theatre: the production is a physical and extremely popular realisation of this theatrical style. The production has been performed twice at this venue, ideally suited to the location of the story, demonstrating Daniel Schulze's ideas on authenticity in contemporary theatre. Schulze indicated a modern pre-occupation with authenticity, partially in light of an age 'marked by social media, global interconnection'.[51] Schulze asserted his study revealed that audience and consumers alike are 'in pursuit of the real and authenticity (instigated by medialisation)'[52]. Although I do not wish to focus on the 'medialisation' of this particular production, the idea of authenticity in conjunction with witnessing this production at the Minack opens an interesting debate.

Those who had seen the production at the Minack described their experiences indirectly in terms of authenticity. Their commentary on the venue reinforced elements of Cornish heritage and Cornish cultural references in the play. This proved to be highly memorable with extremely positive recollections. The venue and the specifics of location offered those spectators the 'pursuit of the real'. However, rather than encouraging repeat custom for when the production was reprised in national tours in 2005 and 2017, former audience members expressed their concern that the experience was too unique [to the Minack] to repeat elsewhere. The Minack Theatre production enjoyed a highly revered reputation, and in my response to queries relating to whether I had seen this incarnation of the production, I felt almost apologetic that I had seen it at the National Theatre a year later. I experienced spectatorial remorse, lacking in the authenticity communicated by those that had witnessed it in the Minack. Unintentionally, those questioned sounded disappointed I could not mirror their experiences. However, despite their responses, I still value the experience at the National Theatre.

As part of my experiential archive, I can appreciate the qualities specific to the production at the Minack, not just for the authenticity of experience offered, but for the time period this represented for the company within landscape theatre. This production was made during the three-year time span of the Three Islands Project, whilst Bill Mitchell was the artistic director. Mitchell's influence on the production is cited on the Minack website in the synopsis of past productions, despite Emma Rice being listed as Director. Mitchell eventually left Kneehigh as Artistic Director to focus on WildWorks, a company created specifically to develop site-specific (landscape) theatre. His departure enabled him to pursue his interests in this area, continuing to explore and develop landscape theatre. *Tristan and Yseult* represents the last show developed with Mitchell in post, and the quality of work observed on landscape theatre provided the platform for Kneehigh to progress to prestigious and mainstream venues like the National Theatre a year later.

Blast (2010)

The production *Blast* (directed by Mike Shepherd) explores the impact of the collapse of the mining industry in contemporary Cornwall. Shepherd has commented on the once global importance of the Cornish mining industry, which he now perceived as being forgotten, suggesting 'English' history lessons had overlooked the history of Cornwall and its people: 'It was because I was taught the English version of events'.[53] In making these statements, Shepherd argued that a 'London-centric' dominance had overridden local diversity. Here he underlines the negative outcomes of globalisation, considered by global sceptics as all-pervading and homogenous. Shepherd considered this factor had pushed Cornish history to the side-lines, whilst local events and records had been dominated by more 'London-centric' English culture. Like other minorities, Cornish communities can feel under-represented and misunderstood by other groups. Shepherd considered *Blast* (2010) as a way of addressing this balance and drawing focus back to local people and events. Emma Rice added further support to this statement, suggesting that the work is important and is 'a moment in our shared history'[54]. Both artistic directors of Kneehigh displayed an awareness of the potentially damaging effects on local diversity and cultural history caused by a more globally known heritage. Shepherd and Rice commented that *Blast* was made for: 'Cornish village halls to spark interest in some of these people and events which have led to life in Cornwall today'.[55] As observed by Lee Trewhela for the local press: 'This is a sly and prescient look at Cornish nationalism that is more about raising laughs than flags'[56]. In terms of their theatrical style, *Blast* exposed these very issues with an exploration into Cornish cultural identity, use of comedy, and a 'Brechtian' influenced direct address to the audience.

The plot of the play centred on a pair of Cornish terrorists, hijacking the performance venue as an act of political protest to communicate tensions felt personally by themselves and 'on behalf' of the Cornish community. The lead protagonists state this is because of the collapse of the mining industries, globalisation and the implications of tourism. The characters assert that unless we hear their stories, they will detonate the bombs they have planted on themselves and around the auditorium. However, it is clear from their ineptitude that these terrorists posed no genuine threat with comedy generated from their haphazard political provocations. *Blast* provided the Cornish community with a public voice to express their fears about this economic disaster, critiquing the latest industries that have now replaced mining: tourism and property ownership. The theme of land being bought and sold is key as it points to the negative aspects of outside owners buying holiday homes, while local inhabitants are out-priced.

Despite the above factors having a negative impact on the Cornish community, *Blast* displayed a willingness to share family stories. These stories exposed the difficulties experienced through the generations, whilst still encouraging pride (within the audience members present) in being Cornish, regardless of these struggles. In fact, the play established the difficulties brought into Cornwall by 'outsiders', acting as a catalyst to unify the Cornish community. 'Family' has been at odds with the modern incarnations of globalisation since the nineteenth century, causing a disconnection between current generations and knowledge of their family stories through earlier centuries. This awareness is evident in a growing desire to explore an individual's cultural heritage from the rising popularity of TV programmes such as *Who do you think you are?* (in the UK, USA and Australia), and genealogy websites. Psychologist Bruno Bettelheim (quoted by Kneehigh in production literature to support the modern-day relevance of fairytales) suggested that the act of storytelling allows for a reflection on wider issues beyond home and family life:

> Myths and fairy stories both answer eternal questions: What is the world really like? How am I to live in it? How can I truly be myself? [57]

Through globalisation, we lose our connection with our ancestral past, making us question who we are and where we are from: making our dependence on or search for cultural identity even more important.

The accompanying programme to the Asylum summer season (and this production) and my experiential archive, built towards the spectatorship of this performance. In contrast with Skantze's 'itinerant spectator', my spectatorship started with seeing the programme advertising the Asylum, and a leaflet promoting the Archive (including my first solo trip to visit both in Cornwall). I associate my memories of the opening season of the Asylum and seeing *Blast* and the *Red Shoes* with the pre-show environment created. Kneehigh associate photographer Steve Tanner displayed photographic exhibitions in this first summer season of the Asylum. Additionally, Tanner set up an enclosure for audience members to have their own photographs taken to be part of the online component of the exhibit. Sculptural 3D art decorated areas of the Asylum. One such artistic piece was a wooden puppet version of Cinderella in a wooden dress, triggering my memories of *The Wooden Frock*. The display took on significant relevance for me, provoking memories of the first Kneehigh production I had attended at the Battersea Arts Centre.

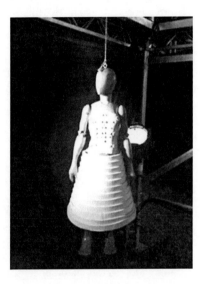

Fig. 3-1. *The Wooden Frock*, C.Trenchfield (2010)

Elsewhere, a boat with oars was displayed in reference to the production *Brief Encounter*. For myself (and those familiar with the show), a particularly romantic and pivotal scene between the main protagonists was recalled. Stalls with merchandise were set alongside these pieces of artwork, and a patchwork quilt acknowledging key contributors to the *Friends of Kneehigh Scheme* was also displayed. The patchwork quilt triggered memories of *Cymbeline*, used in the production to announce the ending of the show. The context of this item communicated the rustic and homely descriptors of Kneehigh's style of theatre, whilst also underpinning the economic factors supporting the company. Using the quilt as an artistic display to name and celebrate individuals and companies that had made the biggest financial contributions to Kneehigh, underlined the importance of these contributions to the company. As a spectator, I am reminded that Kneehigh is a company governed by financial considerations, as well as artistic ambitions.

Food and drink communicated contrasting symbolism within this event. Local Cornish companies were used to sell refreshments, ranging from health food to traditional Cornish fare. These companies contributed to the complete entertainment product described in the Asylum programme, whilst ironically creating sensory elements within the world of the play. The 'terrorist' characters in *Blast* satirised the tourism and food industry of Cornwall, creating a juxtaposed tension by this neoliberalist critique between the performance and the locally branded food available. As a spectator, I felt this tension and had figuratively 'consumed' it by purchasing the locally sourced food before the performance. At this moment within the performance, I felt conflicted: was I contributing to the tensions of globalisation in Cornwall by purchasing merchandise that reinforces Cornish tourism (viewed with cynicism by the playwright Carl Grose and Kneehigh)? Or was I supporting 'Brand Kneehigh' and local trade? My first reaction (during the show) was the former. However, it is possible to perceive both outcomes. It is understandable why Kneehigh provided a modern commentary on the longstanding influence experienced by the collapse of the mining industries. These industries, in a historical sense, have only just ended in the 1930s and 40s. Those born during this time (including founding members of Kneehigh), would have grown up under the shadow of the collapse of a once strong global industry.

The performance itself displayed Kneehigh's performance traits formulating their theatrical style including; comedy underpinned with darker emotions, Brechtian address to the audience, use of miniature props to represent much larger objects, environments, music and movement. A debate on Cornish heritage and identity was at the forefront, with the performance style evocative of pantomime and comedic fringe theatre. The performance was clearly developed with a local audience in mind: with references to feeling like an 'outsider' as part of the established Cornish cultural identity. Interestingly, the production satirised the notions of 'local' and authenticity, through a discussion on which area of the South West could be classed as Cornish in contrast to communities who would like to be associated as Cornish, but in fact, were not considered in such terms. For example, residents of Plymouth are referred to in this capacity with comedic effect.

Financial Difficulties

Although Kneehigh was inspired by their Cornish identity, financial difficulties have had a seismic impact on their artistic outlook and business model. As a result, the company engaged with global business models in response to these difficulties. Kneehigh encountered a potentially ruinous situation in the early 90s, with the company facing closure because of lack of funding and financial revenue. As observed by Graham Saunders, many companies like Kneehigh found it increasingly difficult to function, given the reduction of arts funding:

> British theatre after 1979 was dominated by companies struggling to survive through a miasma of steadily increasing financial hardship, going precariously from project to project, many being dissolved by the end of the decade. [58]

In light of the cuts to Arts Council funding, the concomitant crisis and closure of a range of theatre companies and producing houses, Dorney and Merkin considered the challenging homogeneous impact of globalisation, stating that 'the local matters':

> The danger of this in theatrical terms is self-evident - as citizens of nowhere with 'the same chains in every high street; the same bricks in every new housing estate...the same menu in every pub' we are also to have the same shows in all our theatres. This tide of McDonaldisation is something that regional theatres can stand out against. [59]

Dorney and Merkin raised a pertinent issue with the growing globalised business demands encountered by regional theatre companies using 'commercial terminology' which 'overwhelmed subsidised theatre'[60]. *The Glory of the Garden (1984)* Arts Council Report encouraged a focus away from London, with funding offered to regional theatre companies. This report cited an inequality between London and other regions. However, according to Ros Merkin, the ambitions of this report were never fully realised (and by 1986 were obsolete). They ushered an era 'dominated by the business of assessment' with fourteen criteria in *The Glory of the Garden* report[61]. In fact, according to *The Cork Report (1986)*, this report made the situation financially worse for regional theatre companies than they were before, providing a grim political and economic background for Kneehigh to continue to work and devise theatre[62].

In an interview with *The West Britton,* Kneehigh expressed their realistic concerns that without the financial backing given by the Arts Council, the company could no longer meet their creative commitments for the coming year. This was a situation that Kneehigh wanted to take control of through incorporation of alternative business models to generate financial security. There are few contemporary theatre companies that run without some form of funding from the Arts Council or additional income from local council authorities. Many successful companies use funding opportunities from partnerships with charities and other theatre companies/ producing houses[5].

Local press, the company themselves and the MP Matthew Taylor produced a series of articles flagging up the dire straits the company was in, highlighting the important work Kneehigh generated for the county. Cornwall County Council pledged their full support. Kneehigh in response via letter on 28th February 1991, stated that they welcomed this news and expressed their appreciation[63]. Mike Shepherd's response was that the £30,000 funding from the Arts Council was of benefit, however because of the 'one-off' nature of the subsidy, they needed more to place the company in a stable financial situation. Through changes in their business strategy, Kneehigh ensured that the work 'flies the flag' for Cornwall and is both global and popular in appeal sufficiently to generate enough income to prevent potential closure. If globalisation is pervasive socially and economically, 'going global' provides a way to survive and generate relevance and longevity. MP Matthew Taylor, in communications with the local press, expressed his concerns that viable community projects are no longer available to the Cornish community. He also indicated that Cornwall is under-represented in the arts and in obtaining funding: 'The truth is that theatre and the arts in general in Cornwall do not get a representative proportion of national expenditure on the arts'[64]. Taylor's comments mirrored descriptions of Arts Council England funding provided by Saunders, indicating that despite the increase of funding (by 20% from 1990-1993), very little money reached individual and independent theatre companies, with most going to high profile and well-established companies like the RSC.[65]

The article, 'Kneehigh Theatre on point of cruel collapse', offered further support for the continued running of the company. This article highlighted the paradoxical and ironic situation of the company facing grant cutbacks on the back of an acclaimed and successful tour of *The Tinder Box* (1991) playing to full houses throughout the South West[66]. With a growing demand for Kneehigh, both locally, nationally and internationally, the diversification into other audience communities provoked adaptations to their product and consequently generated enough funds for the company to survive. It was these difficulties that encouraged Kneehigh to incorporate global business models (supported by Arts Council policy) and to become more financially successful and survive.

---

[5] In addition to receiving funding from the Arts Council, has partnership with the Birmingham Repertory Theatre and Berkley Repertory Theatre (www.kneehigh.co.uk).

Arts Council policy had grown through global business models to demand applicants display potential income and partnerships. The application process required a display of financial gains and products produced, with an emphasis on gaining maximum exposure. In response, Kneehigh became adaptive to these requirements, with the following stipulations listed in the Arts Council website: 'Does the application demonstrate that the activity is attracting income from other sources?' [67]'Does the application make a strong case for public engagement with the activity?'[68]. By becoming a company that embraced global influences, embedding them in their work through cultural exchange, they have interwoven these global components whilst addressing local concerns; successfully maintaining artistic integrity and ownership of their work.

Commentary within the *Trustees' Reports and Accounts* (2001) acknowledged financial factors, besides the cultural and artistic ones affecting the running of Kneehigh, resulting in a loss of £33,508 in 200[69]1. The trustees stated that the company could not afford to make a loss on any upcoming project in the near future and should be 'clawing back money' to place into the reserves[70]. In response, Kneehigh indicated the financial loss had allowed for creative and artistic explorations but argued that this could not be incurred again in the next financial year. There is an awareness within the report that a review is needed to explore ways of 'running things more economically', moving towards global business models to realise ambitions for success and financial growth[71]. Two years later in the *Trust Limited Trustee's Report and Accounts for the year ended 31st March 2003,* the company had reviewed their achievements, highlighting local, national and international activities. The report communicated the range of work produced by the company including Cornish village hall tours, landscape theatre, international tours in China, Hungary and Lebanon, and an award-winning national tour of *The Red Shoes*[72]. However, comments in the report also highlighted the tensions experienced by the company in wishing to develop work they have an engagement with, in contrast to work that is more successful but less inspiring. Arguably the work listed above helped generate attention, reinforcing their reputation as theatrical innovators. The repertoire of work demonstrates an achievement in seeking balance within their artistic pursuits: performing in 'Cornish village halls' whilst also performing and touring in national and international theatres.

Kneehigh has been transparent about the 'global pull' away from creating work for Cornwall, due to the weakness of the Cornish economy and its ability to fund community arts projects being a primary factor. By being in demand at European theatre festivals, Kneehigh can command high fees. Areas such as London, the Midlands and Wales, have stronger economies and can afford to pay them 'realistic rates for our touring work', taking the company away from Cornwall for longer periods of time[73]. There is a transparency and pragmatism in this statement behind the development of the Kneehigh brand. Cornwall is an economically deprived area but also appears to be an area that Kneehigh is proud of both in terms of its location and identity. As this chapter has explored, the company conceded a dilemma in its devotion to creating work in an environment it is inspired by, versus a drive to produce work elsewhere to survive. In maintaining its community work and by building on successes nationally and internationally, the company is developing its ability to provide work in both local and global arenas. Diversification of their brand, rather than being viewed cynically from the global sceptic's standpoint as a way of filtering down artistic integrity to gain capital and wider audience appeal, is a way of allowing more local and artistically exclusive work to exist alongside productions with a wider ranging appeal.

The next chapter will look specifically at Kneehigh's adaptation through cultural exchange. It will discuss how this was achieved with the *Three Islands Project*: a unique collaboration between theatre organisations in Malta, Cyprus and the UK (Cornwall). It will analyse this collaboration and the resulting production *A Very Old Man with Enormous Wings* in-depth, considering adaptation, cultural exchange and the impact this had on Kneehigh's inspiration: Cornish cultural identity.

Notes

[1] Korff, Ruediger. "Encloses of Globalisation: The Power of Locality", *Dialectical Anthropology*, Vol. 27, No. 1, 2003, Pg-4.

[2] Korff, Ruediger. "Encloses of Globalisation: The Power of Locality", *Dialectical Anthropology*, Vol. 27, No. 1, 2003, Pg-7.

[3] Hall, Stuart. "The Local and The Global: Globalization and Ethnicity", *Culture, Globalization, and the World-System – Contemporary Conditions for the Representation of Identity*, editor Anthony D. King, University of Minnesota Press, 1997. Pg-33.

[4] Knight, David, B. "Extending the Local: The small town and globalization", *GeoJournal*, Vol. 45, No. ½, *Globalisation and Geography,* 1998, Pg-147.

[5] Kingfisher, Catherine. "Globalisation as Hybridity", *Globalisation and Women's Poverty*, editor Catherine Kingfisher, University of Pennsylvania Press, 2002. Pg-50.

[6] Kingfisher, Catherine. "Globalisation as Hybridity", *Globalisation and Women's Poverty*, editor Catherine Kingfisher, University of Pennsylvania Press, 2002. Pg-52.

[7] www.kneehigh.co.uk/*history*

[8] Smelt, M. *Interview with Mike Shepherd and Maurice Smelt*, Kneehigh Archive, Recorded at Morrab Library, published 21st March 2000.

[9] Smelt, M. *Interview with Mike Shepherd and Maurice Smelt*, Kneehigh Archive, Recorded at Morrab Library, published 21st March 2000, Pg-14.

[10] Costa, M. *The Guardian G2,* "Arts: Theatre: Troupe therapy: Kneehigh", Published 2008.

[11] Laera, M. *Theatre and Adaptation: return, rewrite, repeat,* Bloomsbury, 2014, Pg-231.

[12] Welton, M. *Emma Rice of Kneehigh Theatre in Conversation with Martin Welton 9th October 2012,* Queen Mary University of London.

[13] Staniewski, W. with Hodge, A. *Hidden Territories – the theatre of Gardzienice,* Routledge, London. 2004.

[14] Lilley, H. "Kneehigh's Retellings", Reilly, K (ed). *Contemporary Approaches to Adaptation in Theatre,* Palgrave Macmillan, 2018. Pg-20.

[15] Smelt, M. *Interview with Sue Hill, Bill Mitchell and Maurice Smelt*, Recorded at 42 Weeth Lane, Camborne, 28th April 2000.

[16] Smelt, M. *Interview with Sue Hill, Bill Mitchell and Maurice Smelt*, Recorded at 42 Weeth Lane, Camborne, 28th April 2000.

[17] Smelt, M. *Interview with Sue Hill, Bill Mitchell and Maurice Smelt*, Recorded at 42 Weeth Lane, Camborne, 28th April 2000, Pg-5.

[18] Smelt, M. *Interview with Sue Hill, Bill Mitchell and Maurice Smelt*, Recorded at 42 Weeth Lane, Camborne, 28th April 2000, Pg-23.

[19] Smelt, M. *Interview with Sue Hill, Bill Mitchell and Maurice Smelt*, Recorded at 42 Weeth Lane, Camborne, 28th April 2000, Pg-23.

[20] Kneehigh Theatre. *Kneehigh Theatre Application to the Arts Council of England National Lottery Funding Capital Programme for Equipment October 1998 Reference 98-642*, Kneehigh Theatre.

[21] (Kneehigh Theatre. *Kneehigh Theatre Application to the Arts Council of England National Lottery Funding Capital Programme for Equipment October 1998 Reference 98-642*, Kneehigh Theatre, Section 4.

[22] *Hevva! Project Report: Additionality Landscape Theatre,* Kneehigh Theatre, 1999.

[23] Costa, M. *The Guardian G2,* "Arts: Theatre: Troupe therapy: Kneehigh", Published 2008.

[24] Clapp, S. "Coming to a clay-pit near you", *The Guardian,* 2001. Pg-2.

[25] *Kneehigh Theatre Trust Limited 2001. Pg-3.*

[26] *The Kneehigh Plan 1997-2000*, Kneehigh Theatre. Pg-20.

[27] Cavendish, D. *The Telegraph*, "The short hop from old barn to Broadway", V&A Theatre Archive, Published 2nd August 2010.

[28] Cavendish, D. *The Telegraph*, "The short hop from old barn to Broadway", V&A Theatre Archive, Published 2nd August 2010.

[29] Costa, M. *The Guardian G2,* "Arts: Theatre: Troupe therapy: Kneehigh", Published 2008.

[30] Sierz, "Cymbeline", *The Telegraph,*2008.

[31] Markwell, R. *Cymbeline Review,* BBC.CO.UK.

[32] Kneehigh Archive Press Cuttings 2012.

[33] Laera, M. *Theatre and Adaptation: return, rewrite, repeat,* Bloomsbury, 2014. Pg-3.

[34] Tregida & Milden. "Before My Time: Recreating Cornwall's Past through Ancestral Memory" Oral History, Vol. 36, No.1, Spring 2008, 23-32 Oral History Society

[35] Tregida & Milden. "Before My Time: Recreating Cornwall's Past through Ancestral Memory" Oral History, Vol. 36, No.1, Spring 2008, 23-32 Oral History Society. Pg-27.

[36] Parker, S. *Western Morning News,* "Yee-ha! Roll up for a real wild west panto", Published 26th November 2002.

[37] Laera, M. *Theatre and Adaptation: return, rewrite, repeat,* Bloomsbury, 2014. Pg-4.

[38] *The Cornishman.* "Panto Sold Out", Published 19/12/2002.

[39] Ruhrmund, F. "Kneehigh's quickdraw 'pantomine' is full of laughs", *Western Morning News,* Published 24/12/02.

[40] Tregida & Milden. "Before My Time: Recreating Cornwall's Past through Ancestral Memory" Oral History, Vol. 36, No.1, Spring 2008, 23-32 Oral History Society. Pg-30.

[41] Dreyblatt, Arnold. "Questionnaire 2." *Performance Research: On Archives and Archiving.* Ed. Gough, Richard. & Roms, Heike. *Vol 7. No.*4, Routledge, Dec 2002. Pg-49.

[42] Pearson, M. *Mickery Theater - an imperfect archaeology,* Amsterdam University Press, 2014. Pg-31.

[43] Grose, C. *Tristan and Yseult,* Oberon Modern Plays. UK. 2005. Pg-25.

[44] Marmion, P. *Kneehigh Archive,* "A local play, for local people...", 2005.

[45] Coleman 2005, *Tristan and Yseult* Programme.

[46] Wright, S. *Performance,* "Cornish Past", Published 9th September 2005. Pg-15.

[47] Marmion, P. *Kneehigh Archive,* "A local play, for local people...", 2005.

[48] Wright, S. *Performance,* "Cornish Past", Published 9th September 2005.

[49] Grose, C. *Tristan and Yseult,* Oberon Modern Plays. UK. 2005. Pg-23.

[50] Lilley, H. "Kneehigh's Retellings", Reilly, K (ed). *Contemporary Approaches to Adaptation in Theatre,* Palgrave Macmillan, 2018. Pg-20.

[51] Schulze, *Daniel. Authenticity in Contemporary Theatre*, Bloomsbury Publishing, 2016. Pg-6.

[52] Schulze, *Daniel. Authenticity in Contemporary Theatre*, Bloomsbury Publishing, 2016. Pg-36.

[53] Shepherd, M. and Rice, E. *Kneehigh Theatre The Asylum Summer Season 2010,* Kneehigh Archive Falmouth University. 2010. Pg-4.

[54] Shepherd, M. and Rice, E. *Kneehigh Theatre The Asylum Summer Season 2010,* Kneehigh Archive Falmouth University. 2010. Pg-5.

[55] Shepherd, M. and Rice, E. *Kneehigh Theatre The Asylum Summer Season 2010,* Kneehigh Archive Falmouth University. 2010. Pg-4.

[56] Trewhela, L. "It's back to Cornish roots for masters of surprise", *The West Briton Redruth, Camborne & Hayle Edition,* Published 11th November 2007. Pg-2.

[57] Bettelheim, B. *The Uses of Enchantment - the meaning and importance of fairy tales,* Penguin Books, UK, 1976. Pg-45.

[58] Saunders, G. *British Theatre Companies 1980-1994*, Bloomsbury Methuen Drama, 2015. Pg-50.

[59] Dorney, Kate. "Chapter 5 - Touring and the Regional Repertoire: Cheek By Jowl, Complicite, Kneehigh and Eastern Angles", ed. Dorney, Kate & Merkin, Ros. *The Glory of the Garden English Regional Theatre and The Arts Council 1984 - 2009*, Cambridge Scholars Publishing, 2010. Pg-2.

[60] Dorney, Kate. "Chapter 5 - Touring and the Regional Repertoire: Cheek By Jowl, Complicite, Kneehigh and Eastern Angles", ed. Dorney, Kate & Merkin, Ros. *The Glory of the Garden English Regional Theatre and The Arts Council 1984 - 2009*, Cambridge Scholars Publishing, 2010. Pg-5.

[61] Dorney, Kate. "Chapter 5 - Touring and the Regional Repertoire: Cheek By Jowl, Complicite, Kneehigh and Eastern Angles", ed. Dorney, Kate & Merkin, Ros. *The Glory of the Garden English Regional Theatre and The Arts Council 1984 - 2009*, Cambridge Scholars Publishing, 2010. Pg-80.

[62] Dorney, Kate. "Chapter 5 - Touring and the Regional Repertoire: Cheek By Jowl, Complicite, Kneehigh and Eastern Angles", ed. Dorney, Kate & Merkin, Ros. *The Glory of the Garden English Regional Theatre and The Arts Council 1984 - 2009*, Cambridge Scholars Publishing, 2010. Pg-83.

[63] Kneehigh Archive Press Cuttings 2012.

[64] Kneehigh Archive Press Cuttings 2012.

[65] Saunders, G. *British Theatre Companies 1980-1994*, Bloomsbury Methuen Drama, 2015. Pg-50.

[66] Kneehigh Archive Press Cuttings 2012.

[67] Arts Council England, *Appraisal process for Grants for the Arts,* information sheet, Appraisal 7.

[68] Arts Council England, *Appraisal process for Grants for the Arts,* information sheet, Appraisal 6)

[69] *Kneehigh Theatre Trust Limited 2001,* Kneehigh Theatre, 2001. Pg-13.

[70] *Kneehigh Theatre Trust Limited 2001,* Kneehigh Theatre, 2001. Pg-13.

[71] *Kneehigh Theatre Trust Limited 2001,* Kneehigh Theatre, 2001. Pg-13.

[72] *Trust Limited Trustee's Report and Accounts for the year ended 31st March 2003*, Kneehigh Theatre. Pg-2.

[73] *Hevva! Project Report,* Kneehigh Theatre, 1999. Pg-5.

CHAPTER FOUR

THREE ISLANDS PROJECT AND CULTURAL EXCHANGE

This chapter looks solely at the Three Islands Project, as the strongest example within Kneehigh's work of cultural exchange. The breadth of research covered indicates the extensive amount of material discovered within the Kneehigh Archive; allowing for critical analysis, and contribution to the experiential archive proposed in Chapter 2. Within this chapter, issues of community, cultural identity, funding, adaptation, and cultural practices will be examined.

About the Three Islands Project

The Three Islands Project was a 'trans-national theatrical collaboration' between Kneehigh, WildWorks Theatre, St. James Cavalier Centre for Creativity Malta and the Cyprus Theatre Organisation: comprising three separate stages in Malta 2003, Cyprus 2004 and Cornwall in 2005'[1]. Bill Mitchell led the project in his capacity as artistic director for Kneehigh and WildWorks. Using a Spanish folktale as source material, the devised play *A Very Old Man with Enormous Wings* was formed, using participants from Malta, Cyprus and Cornwall. Participants were derived from a range of backgrounds, occupations and ages. Some worked professionally as performers while others worked in professions indigenous to the locations for each performance such as fishing, basket weaving, etc.

The narrative explored the story of a man with wings falling to earth, who is first looked after by a boy and his family, then exploited as a spectacle by the entire town. The 'winged' man escapes, leaving the townsfolk behind to reflect on their greedy, capitalist and exploitative behaviou

r. The town described in the story is reminiscent of many towns within the Cornish locality, whilst also resonating with other small localities around the world.

> The town, once a thriving fishing port and important engineering centre, now has a derelict heart owing to the non-development of its old harbour site, where the production would take place. [2]

The production was particularly relevant to the Cornish community, underlining economic and social factors mirrored in the collapse of the mining and fishing industries discussed in Chapter 3. In each version its 'derelict heart' provided the emotional and historical core, connecting it specifically to the place and its people. Elaborating on the aims of the project, each venue wished to 'develop artistic and cultural links between Malta, Cyprus and Cornwall, honouring ancient trading routes and forging new collaborations'[3]. The project aimed to integrate local elements specific to each island, embracing the globalism inherent within their shared histories and cultural identities.

This collaborative project had further reaching ambitions. Through the physical construction of a life-sized fishing village set, performers and crew were able to live in this environment for the duration of the project. Cast and crew developed a community bond through working, eating, drinking and socialising together, with the emphasis on forging a safe space for creative and cultural sharing and experimentation. Within their evaluative responses, Kneehigh stressed the cultural benefits of 'embedding' the artists in the locality of this performance environment to aid their creativity:

> It is impossible to overestimate the critical importance of embedding a team into an environment to gain a sense of place. This was a particular success of this project. [4]

A sense of place is described, offering a unique experience. This is specific to localism and location, encountering and incorporating elements of cultural identification. This specifically created village was also a physical, tangible platform for cultural exchange to take place. Likewise, the opportunity to conduct varied work during the rehearsal period was encouraged, with participants taking on different roles to gain experience in a variety of different disciplines, from set builders to performers. In this capacity, cultural exchange occurred between different countries, but also between different facets of work within the production[5]. Erika Fischer-Lichte debated that theatre is implicitly a product of cultural exchange, instigating a spectator's own semiotics and meaning in a range of paradigms:

> The productivity of the theatrical space seems, in this way, almost limitless. Although it is spatial relations that are presented, these spatial relations prove to be, at the same time, political and anthropological, interpersonal

and introspective, mythical and historical, grammatical, syntactic, or semantical: indeed, relations of [different] kinds can be wholly externalised in the performance area as spatial relations. True, the spectator may often put together a whole chain of such relations even before the actor has created, revealed, or even suggested specific relations through change of position and action. [6]

The uniqueness and specificity posed by this project, in the way it was performed and reconfigured, offered a range of evolving semiotics, some of these featured linguistic adaptations, whilst others represented changes and 'exchanges' between people and places. The multi-faceted nature of the environment, containing set, living quarters, and marketplace provided 'materialist semiotics' and 'itinerant spectatorship' in line with Knowles and Skanzte's concepts of spectatorship and the totality of the production.

This chapter uses the evaluative documentation compiled by Kneehigh, with support from collaborative partners and external artistic agencies. This material was used to form the *Three Islands Project 'A Very Old Man with Enormous Wings' Report 2003* and *Three Islands Project Evaluation Report 2005* used extensively throughout this section of the book. Both reports were generated with different intentions and perspectives pre and post-project. Kneehigh, like other producing theatre companies and receiving venues, used monitoring and data collection activities (such as audience and client surveys, production reports), to gain knowledge about their audience in response to this project. The generation of statistical evidence was a requirement by the funding bodies concerned in evaluating 'successes' and outcomes. This material, contained within the Kneehigh Archive, provided an opportunity to chart Kneehigh's own assessment measures. It also supported an archival 'narrative' of a company seeking cultural exchange, willing to experiment in doing business with local, national and international partners.

The feedback involved company members, business partners, and audiences from a range of performances for the duration of the project. Evaluation sheets were placed in Appendix 5 of the *Three Islands Evaluation Report* (2005) with a total of thirty-five evaluations included in this section. The majority of the forms were completed by participants living in Cornwall (with some inclusions from those living in other parts of the country and Europe). There is a slight gender bias: with nineteen evaluations completed by women, and sixteen completed by men[1]. Defining the

---

[1] Twelve participants expressed an interest in devising theatre but gave no indications of their professions. Ten participants discussed their contributions to

participants' professions was more difficult to decipher, as this was not always noted down. The statistical data represented only a small cohort working on the project, with the majority from Cornwall, supporting a local theatre company. An age median for these evaluations has not been determined conclusively, as this information was not requested. However, the youngest participant completing an evaluation form was aged eleven years, and from there, the age range continues upwards. Likewise, there was a lack of clarification whether these are the only feedback sheets produced for this production or selected for inclusion within the project reports.

My spectatorial experience of *A Very Old Man with Enormous Wings* (2011) in London was a very different incarnation to the Three Islands Project. Mirroring the cyclical theories of adaptation described by Laera, Kneehigh reprise and revise their own productions including *Tristan and Yseult* in 2005 and 2017, *Brief Encounter* in 2007 and 2013, and *Dead Dog in a Suitcase and other love songs* in 2014 and 2020. The performance at the Little Angel Theatre in Islington in North London, is an example of such a reprise and has since been performed again in 2016/17. The 2011 production was a product of a newly formed creative relationship between Kneehigh and The Little Angel Theatre, renowned for their work in puppetry and children's theatre. In this adaptation, the production was geared towards children, with the focus on puppetry (supported by performers/puppeteers). The festival environment and purpose-built set of the Three Islands Project were replaced with a traditional theatre location. Also gone was the Esperanto 'style' language (a combination of English, Maltese and Cypriot Greek), replaced with English and a few scattered words of Kernow (an archaic Cornish language) for comic effect. Kneehigh marketed the performance as a children's show, utilising the Little Angel branding as a children's puppet theatre.

The anti-global context, formerly established in the Three Islands Project was still prevalent, illustrating the negative impact of globalisation and capitalism. In this version, a party to celebrate the financial growth of the town (due to the exploitation of the 'winged' man) was evocatively presented through puppetry and props. An excessive amount of food and drink filled the stage whilst the puppet townsfolk consumed and cavorted. Imagery of the celebratory bunting and cakes: traditionally representing stereotypical English afternoon tea, now took on new meaning.

As the celebration became more 'Dionysian', the bunting, cakes and drink became associated with excess. Using an anti-global standpoint, the reading

---

music in the production or worked in the music industry, five participants were in some form of education, five described themselves as 'actors', and three as 'artists'.

of this scene establishes critique against capitalism and globalisation. In order for this wealth and materialism to continue, the townsfolk actively encouraged more tourism: irrespective of the detriment to the community or exploitation of their human 'exhibit'. Illustrating the tensions of global tourism, a coachload of tourists arrived in the village, took photos without consent, consumed vast amounts of food and drink, quickly exiting while leaving their refuse behind them. This was effectively communicated with comedic effect within a matter of seconds - establishing a range of complex issues.

Spectatorial connections with ethics, globalisation, tourism and human rights were indicated within this scene, forming new associations and arguments. The presentation of these subjects displayed a negative bias. However, this was already inherent within the original narrative. The fears over the loss of individualism by global factors are examined but are not resolved. Instead, the winged man escapes, leaving behind his only friend (a small boy) to witness his departure. This is his only option, to reclaim agency in light of extremely dominating and de-humanising capitalist hegemony. The play ends with the suggestion that the townsfolk will reflect on their behaviour and their place within a globalised world. I felt there was an indication of the town retreating to a more localised state, reconnecting with 'self' and a more humanised, ethical standpoint. As a spectator, I could perceive these observations as simplistic: that globalisation has negative connotations, in contrast to positive associations of localism. The debate is more complex, but in terms of layers of thoughts, layers of meaning, the consideration of dichotomy was activated in my spectatorship. Optimistically, the solitary boy watching the winged man fly away (allowing him to escape without opposition) introduced hope for the future, for the evolution and resolution of these arguments. This debate was, however, replaced with a magical, ephemeral sight of a sky filled with angels, hinting that this winged man belonged to a higher, more celestial realm – too good for the capitalist machinations of the village he was leaving behind.

Community, Cornish Identity and Funding

Although the project was developed with three very different locations and cultures, Kneehigh placed Cornish community and Cornish identity at its core. Rather than being parochial towards the Cornish community, Kneehigh defined and refined identity and community, seeking to engage with other cultures and global influences. Despite Cornish community being central to their theatrical brand: Kneehigh is outward looking. Maurice

Smelt outlined this philosophy in an interview in 2000, in which members of Kneehigh including Bill Mitchell and Sue Hill commented on the internationality of their members harmoniously co-existing with the company's Cornish identity:

> It's not a nationalistic thing: there are members of the company who are Scots and Catalans, and it's not to do with Cornish ancestry, it's to do with actually a commitment to making this place work. And it's not to do with being insular, as well. One of the wonderful things about growing up in Cornwall and returning to it is recognising that it isn't [withdrawn], we have this tremendous tradition – inherited – which is outward-looking, [enriched by] emigration. [7]

Kneehigh's ambition towards working with a cast that has an international cultural background presented the potential growth through globalism. Part of Cornish identity and ancestry has involved cultural exchange through the collapse of the clay and tin mining economy, causing many Cornish inhabitants to migrate to unfamiliar parts of the world to gain work. Kneehigh and their notion of the Cornish community have progressed and are still progressing. This is achieved through cultural homogenisation; polarisation with individuals and groups pulling away asserting local/individual influences, and acceptance of these changes through convergence. In this capacity, they are working towards cultural acceptance involving a hybridisation of cultures: 'Cultures do not collide but borrow from each other and adapt in different ways'.[8]

As mentioned earlier, two reports were produced on this project, with different objectives and intentions. The initial report, written in 2003 using references to notable artists in advocacy of the company (to support Kneehigh), was developed as a proposal for the project. The poet Charles Causley 'champions' the company, describing Kneehigh as Cornwall's National Theatre. His admiration going beyond the borders of the county uses the metaphor that Kneehigh is 'one of the brightest jewels in Cornwall's crown'[9]. Causley had been a long-time supporter of the company, born and living in Launceston, Cornwall for most of his life, writing the play *Tinderbox* in 1990. In affirming Kneehigh's ability to work beyond the Cornish county, Causley highlighted the propensity for cultural exchange in their work. Globalism through cultural exchange reinforces Cornish identity, bringing favourable appeal by association. Likewise, Trevor Nunn supported Kneehigh's claims of being engaged in community work and shared experiences, suggesting 'they are themselves a community of shared experience and passionate commitment'[10]. The validation offered by Causley and Nunn underpinned Kneehigh's abilities for creative collaborations. Their affirmations were important in the application for funding. They were used at the start of the report to strengthen their case for funding by illustrating the project's potential to meet specific criteria. The second report is an evaluative document, post-project. It offered reflections and elements of evidence and data to consolidate the achievements of the project: a requirement by the funding and creative partners involved.

Arts Policy and Funding

Arts Policy and funding have been pivotal in the artistic journey of Kneehigh Theatre, influencing the company to follow global business models. It is this funding landscape which has had far-reaching impacts on many theatre companies within the UK. Changes made to government arts policy from the late 70s and 80s has continued to have a strong influence on funding in the 90s and 00s. This economic narrative has run concurrently with the chronology of Kneehigh, with shifting objectives being incorporated within the company strategy. As described by Deirdre Heddon and Jane Milling, because of a reduction of Arts Council funding in 1979 (at the time of Thatcher coming to power, cutting the budget by £1.1 million), funding schemes encouraged theatre companies to seek match-funding, seeking private sponsorship. Heddon and Milling note that the preferred conservative Arts Council structure was that of 'a limited company with an artistic director, a structure which emulated private businesses, but diametrically opposed to the practices and ideals of many non-hierarchical collectives'[11]. The influence of government, filtering down to council policy, has encouraged theatre companies to 'embrace the forces of the market' and seek sponsorship or investment, rather than funding. According to Heddon and Milling, theatre and arts organisations were encouraged to use business 'rhetoric' and develop 'efficient management of their brand'[12]. This is a paradigm that Kneehigh has been encouraged to use, influencing how they have perceived and organised themselves as a company and brand.

In contrast, Heddon and Milling highlight the emergence of devising companies from the 60s and 70s, developing an anti-establishment and anti-hierarchy ethos. Kneehigh continued this tradition in the 80s, with a desire to work with non-trained performers, allowing for freedom of creativity and expression. Although Kneehigh establishes hierarchical structures through a core team led by artistic directors, the use of non-trained and trained performers mirrored elements of the aforementioned anti-establishment ethos whilst providing opportunities for greater community participation. Graham Saunders described the political climate impacting British theatre in the 80s affected by funding cuts. Theatre is broadly perceived as experiencing a time of 'crisis and retreat', with many companies struggling to survive in a new economic climate.[13]

The 1980s began with a 2.9% cut in arts funding and ended with a further 4.8% (Saunders 33). This was the first time this had occurred in the 35-year history of the Arts Council, which had previously worked on the capitalist ideology of exponential growth. During this time Arts Minister Norman St John-Stevas introduced the policy which required artists to gain private sponsorship to make up for any shortfall in Arts Council funding (Saunders 34). The reality of attracting sponsorship from high profile businesses only transpired for major national companies like the RSC or the National Theatre (Saunders 35). Likewise, the development of the application process necessitated the recruitment of an administrator to maintain funding applications.

> Arguably, the Arts Council's insistence on professional administration allowed artists to concentrate on creative work, but it also produced a culture that seemed increasingly to look towards financial accountability and organisational skills as key factors in assessing the health and viability of a company. (Saunders 37)

Although Saunders work discusses arts funding within the 80s, the ideology of financial accountability and an encouragement to seek additional private funding was very much in place during Kneehigh's work on this project. The two reports based on the Three Islands Project mirrored the described financial accountability, aiming to underpin its viability and display 'success' and 'value' in the work created. Some elements of 'success' and 'value' would include; involvement of the community, reaching as broad an audience base as possible, and encourage tourism within the respective landscapes performed.

The *Creative Objectives* set out by the Arts Council England, South West as part of their 'Locality Plan', are quoted within the 2003 project report, with Kneehigh stating that the project was created with these objectives in mind in order to secure financial backing[2]. The *Creative Objectives* are as follows:

---

[2] The Arts Council has the following strategies as per their guidelines for 2020: Goal 1: Excellence is thriving and celebrated in the arts, museums and libraries. Goal 2: Everyone has the opportunity to experience and to be inspired by the arts, museums and libraries. Goal 3: The arts, museums and libraries are resilient and environmentally sustainable. Goal 4: The leadership and workforce in the arts, museums and libraries are diverse and appropriately skilled. Goal 5: Every child and

- Nurture existing and potential companies, production resources and networks to encourage and sustain the widest possible range of work.
- Encourage initiatives that enhance the quality and broaden the artistic range of produced work.
- Encourage the use of exciting and significant indoor and outdoor spaces in the county.
- Research and develop opportunities for the promotion and development of large-scale outdoor work and festivals within the existing and developing cultural and social landscape. [14]

The company acknowledged the necessity to apply for government funding, arguing that the South West enjoy far less funding and support for the arts in comparison with other areas of the country[15]. Likewise, Kneehigh indicated that the work produced would meet all the objectives and criteria stipulated by the Arts Council England and Objective One. Implicit within this objective is the creation of 'cultural excellence' within the arts and making the arts 'available to all'. Kneehigh justified that allowing the work to continue (through the Creative Skills initiative and proposed Summer School) would be of benefit to those in the community developing their skills with the company. The 'skills' alluded to would include working with Kneehigh and exploring the working processes of the company in the Summer School. Outreach work connected to the show would allow different members of the community the opportunity to work on the stalls and sideshows contributing to the festival: 'This work can be in a multitude of forms – film, music, theatre, puppetry, storytelling etc. All ages could be involved.[16] The Summer School activity mirrored Saunders observations of theatre companies required by the Arts Council, to demonstrate a social or educational function to secure funding, whereas previously artistic merit alone had been the most important factor.

References are made again to the Arts Council England, South West's 'locality plan' for theatre in Cornwall, highlighted artistic and cultural objectives applicable to Kneehigh's work. As mentioned above, included in these objectives was the policy to nurture 'production resources and networks to encourage and sustain the widest possible range of work'[17]. The Arts Council aimed to promote and develop large scale outdoor work and festivals within the existing and developing cultural/social environment. In response, Kneehigh stated that within the 'spirit' of these objectives, the company created a *Very Old Man with Enormous Wings* (2003). In support of the above 'locality plan', an additional driver for the project, was

---

young person has the opportunity to experience the richness of the arts, museums and libraries. (Arts Council 2020)

spearheaded by Cornwall Arts Marketing: to raise the local and global profile of Cornwall's artistic and cultural life and promote Cornwall as a key location of the 'cultural tourist'[18].

Kneehigh's role in raising the profile of Cornwall has been discussed in greater depth in Chapter 3. The company has 'wrestled' with the title of being the 'National Theatre of Cornwall' and working with the Arts Council, South West to generate and support tourism. Causley's and Nunn's positive descriptions of Kneehigh reinforced the notion of the 'cultural tourist', intersecting other cultures and international communities through the cultural exchange: inherent within the Three Islands Project. In terms of associative branding, Kneehigh aligned their brand to incorporate Cornish tourism.

Kneehigh, in their evaluation report for the *Three Islands Project* (2005), explained their use of UNESCO's four major programmes in 'intangible' cultural heritage. This statement underpinned the relevance of cultural heritage within their work and illustrated the place of 'the arts' in continuing this tradition:

> The 'intangible cultural heritage' means the practices, representations, expressions, knowledge, skills – as well as the instruments, objects, artefacts and cultural spaces associated therewith – that communities, groups and, in some cases, individuals recognise as part of their cultural heritage. This intangible cultural heritage, transmitted from generation to generation, is constantly recreated by communities and groups in response to their environment, their interaction with nature and their history, and provides them with a sense of identity and continuity, thus promoting respect for cultural diversity and human creativity. [19]

By incorporating a 'sense of identity' and developing cultural diversity in collaboration with contributors from Cyprus and Malta, Kneehigh created *A Very Old Man with Enormous Wings*. The whole process of creation was founded on cultural exchange. The company negotiated UNESCO and Arts Council England (ACE) external frameworks, which impacted on the creative autonomy of their work. However, Kneehigh successfully integrated the requirements. All ACE targets had been achieved, as set out within the eight objectives by the National Policy for Theatre in England, as recorded in the *Three Islands Project Evaluation Report (2005)*. Focusing on the devising process created to meet these objectives, Kneehigh reflected that this style of creativity has universal resonance:

> We are nurturing a new process, which is authentic and truthful, producing work with real meaning; work that is specific for the site and community, but which has universal resonance. [20]

The statement illustrated the project's wider appeal, utilising the 'site and community' created by a 'new creative process'. I would argue that this process is part of 'Brand Kneehigh', as it featured elements of their branded theatricality, using site and community, engaging with 'universal' subject matter.

Adaptation and Cultural Identity

Kneehigh's theatrical brand encompasses adaptation, with associative characteristics recognised in their work. Theories of adaptation highlight the power adaptation has in reinventing work, ultimately 'adapting' this new adaptation in a continued creative cycle: 'Theatre, one could say, never stops adapting its features to the world and the world to its features'.[21] Adaptation lends itself to globalisation, with changes made in the process of generating broader appeal. According to Laera, adaptation through repetition is key within cultural exchange, with a significant role in the formation of culture:

> The production of community, therefore is rooted in the repetition of cultural units of meaning through the rituals of sociality and belonging, otherwise known as 'tradition'. [22]

Through repetition and adaptation, culture is exchanged, and community is formed. Kneehigh commented on the material used to inspire their creativity, which they concluded dealt with the theme of community, in addition to humanistic 'universal' issues.[23] It is this central theme that allowed for and encouraged interaction between Kneehigh and the community. This interaction was achieved by utilising their devising process to develop a collective creativity, blending influences from the participants involved. Heddon and Milling described the tradition of devising companies in the 60s and 70s drawing on pre-existing forms of entertainment (such as clowning, Commedia and vaudeville) which 'already carried a popular, political weight'[24]. Heddon and Milling observed that companies like Footsbarn (a Cornish theatre company which formed ten years before Kneehigh), presented stock characters with actors 'representing' them onstage, as opposed to embodying predetermined characters. Kneehigh utilised similar techniques, with actors exaggerating stereotypes for comedic effect. However, the company also encourage awareness and sharing of backgrounds, responding to the actor's cultural identities and artistic/performance skills.

Bill Mitchell wished to pioneer an alternative way of working in his overview of the project, encouraging both community and cultural exchange[3]. Mitchell intended the Three Islands Project to incorporate the local diversity of the audience, creating a production that had global appeal, with key aspects specific to the local audience.

> We target people and communities we want to work with. We lead the process, giving a strong framework for people to work within, but we are very accepting of 'offers' from the community – if gardening is strong locally, then there will be flowers, produce or gardeners in the show. [25]

By responding to local communities whilst considering a broader demographic, Kneehigh displayed elements of 'McDonaldization'. The devising material is 'de-culturalised' to be more universal but is culturalised or 're-culturalised' by incorporating local variation to make this a more local and thereby personal performance product. What are Mitchell's intentions by 'targeting' people and communities they wish to work with? Are the changes that the company makes nominal gestures of incorporating local interests, or is this an exploitative use of local issues and concerns to integrate themselves into the community and secure a wider audience? These are questions pertinent to any company blending local and global influences together. However, evidence within the archive illustrated a genuine commitment to incorporate local elements with equal respect and sensitivity. The act of adaptation presented specificity and uniqueness to each island. The same show was repeated, with vital changes needed and arguably occurring naturally through the changing and evolving components: from location, personnel, to the creative choices made.

Bettelheim observed that the re-telling of stories is reshaped and reinvented, generating de-hybridisation and re-hybridisation, a philosophy shared by Kneehigh's development of fairy tales, legends, etc:

> The folk fairy tale, as distinct from more recently invented fairy tales, is the result of a story being shaped and reshaped by being told millions of times, by different adults to all kinds of other adults and children. Each narrator, as

---

[3] Identified in the Three Islands Project report is the potential for brand diversification, stating that one of the significant outcomes of the project is the development of Wildworks. They describe this as a new Cornish based company created by Kneehigh's former artistic director Bill Mitchell. Although the company enjoys its own identity, they keep links and associations with Kneehigh, constructing what they term a landscape production – work produced 'outside conventional theatre spaces' (Kneehigh Theatre, Three Islands Project Evaluation Report 3). Established within the report is Kneehigh's diversification into other products, offering a range of opportunities under the umbrella of the 'Kneehigh' identity.

he told the story, dropped and added elements to make it more meaningful
to himself and to the listeners, whom he knew well. [26]

Bettelheim supported this adaptation, stating that 'slavishly sticking to the
way a fairy story is printed robs it of much of its value'.[27]

Peter Boyden, in his foreword to the *Three Islands Project Evaluation
Report (2005)*, observed the storytelling processes inherent in Kneehigh's
work as integral to our analysis of the world. It is through the telling of
stories we codify and make sense of our cultural identity:

> Through them we make sense of a threatening world of fragmented
> communities and isolated individuals. The arc of narrative retains a visceral
> power to make us think differently about the impact of our actions and the
> choices we make as citizens. [28]

Laera also questioned the role theatre and adaptation have in the formation
and deconstruction of culture and identity.[29] Kneehigh not only served this
purpose of storytelling and cultural analysis but also provided an active
engagement and celebration of its Cornish identity:

> [It has taken] Kneehigh Theatre over more than two decades to bring them
> together in a rich and potent theatrical brew. Through the empathetic trust
> of a long-term ensemble, their Cornish identity has been repeatedly
> celebrated in a heady combination of creative energy, emotional
> intelligence, high seriousness and physical knockabout. [30]

Many of Kneehigh's shows were formed in the Cornish landscape, using
Cornish folklore and stories, playing to the immediate community.
Performers and devisers recognised and used the notion that people can
have emotional attachments/belongings to more than one place.

> Contemporary devisers have sought to develop performance practices that
> invite the audience to re-envision and re-imagining familiar places and
> recognise the multiplicity of meaning they carry. [31]

In this capacity, contemporary devisers share an important role in
contributing to the debate challenging preconceptions of communities being
bound by place. It is something that Kneehigh explored through global
collaborations and their outward-looking notion of community. In this
capacity, theatre can transcend geographical barriers, configuring new
boundaries.

Govan et al. underlined that people are identified by cultural and
ancestral roots, but also by the journeys and routes they have embarked on.

This notion of identity embraces both the local and global complexities interwoven into people's lives:

> The image of life as a trail or path accounts for both the specificity and porousness of cultural memory and suggests how multiple attachments to different places are part of the process of personal change and development.[32]

The metaphor of 'journey' to connect people to places is apt when navigating cultural exchange, allowing for additions and adaptations to identity. Govan et al. shared comparisons between Kneehigh Theatre and another Cornish tourist attraction: The Eden Project, citing it as an example of an 'ecological journey' and as a 'living theatre of plants and people'[33]. Its vision was to connect the local and the global through environmental change.[34] Rather than evoking nostalgia for past communities, the Eden Project sought to represent futures. It compressed global time and space through the different biodomes and environmental landscapes created.

> The aesthetics of space at the Eden Project troubles oppositions between the local and the global, between the natural and the artificial, art and science and encourages visitors to take an imaginative journey to an ethical place of possibilities. [35]

Kneehigh, through their willingness to engage with other cultures displayed a forward-thinking grasp on this notion of 'community' and cultural identity, recognising that their Cornish identity is limiting and hard to define. By reconfiguring and re-drawing the lines (de-culturalisation and re-culturalisation) around their own theatre community and Cornish identity, they have included distinct people, cultures, locations etc. to enrich the material in each production. In doing so, the company raised questions rather than offering definitive answers. However, this model of community and cultural identity supports the suggestion, outlined by Govan et al., that 'identity' can be seen as a journey that records and incorporates both elements of the local and global in our lives.

Cultural exchange is a complex balancing act between various parties engaged. Culturalisation establishes these changes in the re-configuration of local and global culture to generate a balance between these two components to ensure the maximum appeal of the product. The Three Islands Project not only displayed a production international and global in scope but mirrored some of the ideologies of Wang and Yeh in its 'culturalisation' and 'de-culturalisation' of a performance product to meet the needs of the audience. Wang and Yeh reflect on 'de-culturalisation' and 're-culturalisation' and propose that 'de-localisation' describes a process which minimises a product's local elements for a larger and more diversified audience. 'Re-localisation' concerns the 'incorporation of local elements into transnational products'[36]. They proposed cultural exchange as a way of breaking down cultural boundaries and egocentrism for an individual's socio/cultural background.

> It unsettles the introverted concept of culture, a concept that underlines ideologies such as romantic nationalism, racism and cultural essentialism. It helps to release us from the boundaries of nation, community, ethnicity, or class, while presenting a 'kaleidoscope' of collective experience in motion.[37]

Thorough culturalisation and de-culturalisation, a fine balance must be realised, even if de-culturalisation is required to engage with globalisation.

> Although de-culturalisation maybe the key to entering the global market, it's 'a-cultural' outlook may in fact be deceptive, as storytelling cannot be accomplished without touching on beliefs, attitudes, values and behavioural patterns. [38]

Laera highlighted several types of adaptation, engaging with Wang and Yeh's 'global market', dependant on the nature of the adapted work, the nature of engagement, and the resulting product:

> In this intertextual sense, the process of adaptation implies negotiations of numerous kinds, such as interlingual, intercultural, intersemiotic, intermedial, but also ideological, ethical, aesthetic and political. [39]

Butler in the review 'Plunge into show's heart' (about *A Very Old Man with Enormous Wings*) commented on both the fusion of language, adapting the story through an 'interlingual' cultural exchange (as stated by Laera) to make the product global. De-culturalisation occurs by using languages to form a new hybrid variant in keeping with the world invented by the play. This de-culturalisation is then culturalised or 're-culturalised' and reconfigured by the audience through the duration of the production, with audience members being able to learn this new hybrid language through well-placed visual cues.

> The tale, adapted from a short story by Gabriel Garcia Marquez, is told in a universal hybrid language combining elements from Maltese, English, Spanish, Italian, Greek, Cypriot and even Cornish dialect – 'dreckly' could be picked out a few times – which becomes understandable amid strong visual signals. [40]

In an interview with Emma Clayton, Shepherd discussed the challenges posed by performing internationally: 'We often play to non-English-speaking audiences in some parts of the world so visual imagery plays a big part. Wherever we perform the challenge is to create intimate, engaging theatre with a sense of fun, adventure and visual ingenuity'.[41] This mirrored the experiences of Butler with 'strong visual signals' constructed through Kneehigh's artistic ambitions to create 'visual ingenuity'.

A review by the BBC local website page commented on the newly created language, stating that despite the audiences difficultly in following this fusion of languages, 'your ears adjust and you just go with it and 'get the gist' throughout the performance'.[42] Likewise, *The Guardian's* review of the production suggested that the town represented in the show is both everywhere and nowhere, is both culturalised and de-culturalised in a form of inclusive globalisation that allowed the audience to connect with the similarities and recognise the differences evidenced.

> To make the point that Maha-le is both nowhere and everywhere, the village has its own language: a composite of Romance languages, Japanese, English and made up words. [43]

Mahoney described critical commentary on the loss of cultural identity induced by the effects of globalisation with the above fusion of languages as a byproduct. As I have discussed within my own spectatorial experience, the capitalist competitiveness of neoliberalism is a key component of the plot of this production.

> Unsure whether he is a fraud or a miracle, an angel of death or life, the villagers greedily lap up the Euros that his fame brings. Transformed by electricity, running water, plasma television and broadband, the place loses its sense of self, and the celebration turns to tragedy. [44]

The Independent is less enthusiastic about the fusion of languages in the performance. Although the review highlights the comic potential of this 'Esperanto', it describes its inability to convey the plot:

> The actors are a buoyant international troupe (the show having also played in Malta and Cyprus), speaking a kind of comical Esperanto ('homo sapiens, flappy wangs' 'tutti populi totally at a lost'). The storytelling doesn't always run smooth, there are slack patches and the conclusion is decidedly bleak. [45]

Bassett raised an important critical point in the potential confusion experienced by this adaptation. How 'successfully' was the intended meaning conveyed through an unfamiliar language? As discussed by

Skantze and Knowles, a spectator can interpret performance semiotics from a range of experiences, specific to the individual. Skantze gave one such example when watching a performance in Italian, a language she is not fluent in but willing to 'surrender' to the possibility of non-comprehension. In light of the use of subtitles, Skantze suggested an induced passivity in contrast to emancipation: 'A mix then of the active spectator who reads and interprets and the habits of dependence that lead to passivity'.[46] This 'passivity' can occur when the spectator knows the story well, but relies on subtitles, 'forgetting' their own ability to decipher the text. Skantze queried whether refusing the aid of subtitles makes for a more authentic spectatorship of the performance in progress.[47] As described by Skantze, while elements of the dialogue lack textual clarity, the sound of the dialogue in terms of its quality (rather than its literal meaning), become the primal focus. Butler above indicated that despite potential misinterpretation, the plot becomes understandable through strong visual cues, with a global language forming through cultural exchange and adaptation.

For the production to survive in its third and final island location, Kneehigh integrated material both global and local, with aspects benefitting the wider community to secure funding. The work is deconstructed for wider appeal and viability, then re-constructed to create inter-connecting products as an offshoot from the main product. This shared parallels with product diversification, with accompanying products produced and sold 'on the back of' the flagship product. Thus, diversification widens appeal and consumer numbers, bringing in greater revenues whilst enjoying the same brand identification as the central production. Cultural exchange is taking place through the awareness of the varied cultural participants involved with the project and a willingness to incorporate the influences posed. As positive as this may appear to be, in allowing cultural exchanges to help shape the work, other more homogenous factors could be at work. Considering ideas of McDonaldization and Globalisation, the principal driver for these changes to take place lies with the Arts Council having control over investment for the production. Their investment had a significant power to influence the artistic product and was potentially the most dominant (homogenising) influence in contrast to other participants involved (including Kneehigh). Although this is a critique launched at other cultural exchanges, favourable experiences were generally shared and commented on by participants and reviewers within the project's evaluative feedback sheets.

Cultural Exchange

Bill Mitchell stated the aims of the Three Islands Project were to include active incorporation and inclusion of other cultures in the devising process. Pelaez Lyons commented that the start of her creative relationship with Kneehigh evolved out of a project performed in a festival in her home country of Columbia, sharing similar intentions. Pelaez Lyons (was working with the British Council, who were funding *Cymbeline)* gained the opportunity of working with the company as a performer, introducing them to Colombian culture. In my interview with Pelaez Lyons, she described Mike Shepherd and Emma Rice's invitation to work with Kneehigh in the UK, and their commitment to this process by saving money to fly her over (Pelaez Lyons 1). An opportunity for Kneehigh to work with Pelaez Lyons as a practitioner developed another link for international cultural exchange.

Returning to the Three Islands Project, there are many references to cultural exchange illustrated in both reports, particularly in the evaluative report (2005). Cultural exchange was signposted very early with Mitchell outlining the importance of this process within the proposal. Mitchell established that the project should have an international agenda, engaging with other ways of viewing the world. This would be achieved through an international makeup of the team, its music, language and the option to strike up residencies and links:

> We have to be aware of how other cultures express themselves. We have to share cultural forms and ideas and build them into the work. I use everything I can to tell a story. I want to research for narrative ideas anywhere in the world that we make strong connections, develop new work processes and find different company structures to best support the work. [48]

Mitchell continued to outline the ambitions of the project, which explores the 'local meaning of universal stories' [49]The professional core of the team was multi-cultural, with the work being non-text based, using a multi-lingual and invented language, described as 'emotionally transparent.' The report asserted that the work had the power to break down barriers between cultures and nationalities, citing participants from Turkish and Greek Cypriot disparate backgrounds, working together and resolving cultural issues:

> In Nicosia we worked with artists from both sides of the Green Line, Turkish and Greek Cypriots, who had never met people from opposing culture – they had all been born after Partition. Real reconciliation took place, albeit on a personal level. [50]

The evidence of cultural exchange was exhibited in the productions and performances, and also in the community projects and businesses integrated into the overall project. The Three Islands Project displayed evidence of cultural exchange, fulfilling the criteria outlined in Hayle's *Intangible Cultural Heritage* for UNESCO: 'All participants in the Outreach Projects became part of the three islands production community for the duration of the project. A communal sense of ownership of the project is of the essence'[51]. Reflections on the work indicate the use of the community and its environment in the devising process:

> The director, designer and writer were able to weave much of the information gathered from community members into the Hayle production. This is key to the whole project, allowing the story, in the case of *A Very Old Man with Enormous Wings*, to become specific to the host place and community. This includes visual and oral elements as well as community specific practices and rituals being embedded in the action. The specific interaction between place and community becomes all-important for the devising and rehearsal process. [52]

The *Three Islands Project Evaluation Report* illustrated cultural exchange utilising a story that has local references, whilst making connections with broader issues, thereby making this exchange a central factor within the devising process. The totality of community experience is integrated, including the environment, associative rituals and practices. David Micklem, Theatre Officer at the Arts Council, stated the artistic and commercial feasibility of the project, citing it as ideally placed in creating work that caters for the host community.

> On a multitude of levels 'A Very Old Man' is an extraordinary piece of work. In terms of the regenerative effect of a piece of work on a depressed community, the social cohesion that this might inspire, the civic pride in hosting work of this quality and (most importantly in my view) in terms of the artistic quality of the work itself this is an exemplary achievement. [53]

Other comments presented the successful blend of multiculturalism, evidence of cultural exchange and an international focus in their work:

> For me it was one of the most effective Kneehigh productions I have seen. The multiculturalism and the political messages were there and came across superbly, without being heavy-handed. The language worked very well – I took a twelve-year-old with a knowledge of French and a little Spanish who was absolutely fascinated and loved the linguistic mix as well as being transfixed by the story itself. Jennifer Lowe, Cornwall County Council Art Officer. [54]

Western Morning News mirrored this reflection in describing the production's ability to connect and involve 'hundreds of performers across three lands' in addition to 'thousands of people who have witnessed it'[55]. Likewise, *The Cornishman* commented on the global appeal of the work, achieved through use of global elements in its storyline resonating with other communities, blending multiple languages together.[56] Malta Council for The Arts, in their final report, described the possibilities for future development and cultural exchanges/collaborations, building on the successes achieved in *A Very Old Man with Enormous Wings* (2005).

> Future outputs can be expected to result from this project. In addition to the personal achievements of The Maltese Actors, new relationships have been created between The Kneehigh Theatre Company, The Wild Works Company and Malta's Theatre world that are expected to lead to further co-operations in the future. [57]

Not only had new relationships formed between these theatre companies and cultures, but they forged economic networks between two different craft companies in Malta and Cornwall. Those involved in the project hoped to take advantage of the EU's Objective One *Areas of Special Economic Need* status that both areas hold[58]. In the proposals for the Summer School Programme, accompanying the Cornish variant of *A Very Old Man with Enormous Wings* (2005), Kneehigh described the benefits enjoyed by the community and the company:

> This is an invaluable route for Kneehigh to identify talent in the County and to train future company members. It also has the potential to teach a host of life skills, for example communication, confidence and self-esteem. [59]

Feedback for the Outreach projects connected to this production, described the sense of community, growing confidence and cultural diversity emerging from the project:

> The projects helped develop local skills and talent and showcase them in context of a large, high quality theatre project. Participants' confidence increased exponentially as did their sense in their place and community. [60]

Rose Barnecut, from the Penwith District Council, reflected on the positives achieved by the project for the town of Hayle, affecting the local district and underlining the ability of the arts to support community regeneration.

> 'The production proved a great success for the town of Hayle and the district of Penwith. The scale and ambition of the show, its sell out popularity and national reviews have had an impact upon the confidence of the community.

This show emphatically endorsed the role of the art in supporting regeneration in both economic and social terms.' Rose Barnecut, Penwith District Council Arts Officer.[61]

Regeneration is an important focus throughout Cornwall, receiving EU funding pre-Brexit. BBC Cornwall commented on the work and its ability to transform a harbour wasteland into a thriving market and theatre community, displaying the 'potential for the area'.[62] The local newspaper provided further commentary on the barren state of Hayle's environment and economy, questioning the current fortunes of this town.

But Hayle sprawls, around quays and pools and moonscapes of a vanished industry. It is a place with a visible past and a potential future, but still no present. [63]

In reviewing *A Very Old Man With Enormous Wings* connections are made linking the plot of the play with the circumstances of the village hosting this event:

Kneehigh's choice of Hayle as a venue could not have been more apposite, as councillors and worthies are even now locked in negotiations with its latest owners over the very soul of the town and its hopes for the future. [64]

Parallels are clearly drawn between the fictional town in the play, and the real-life factors affecting many of the communities in Cornwall, voicing concerns 'for the future' amongst disparate councillors and community leaders.

In the outreach work in schools led by Anna Maria Murphy, memories and verbal accounts from older and younger generations within the local community generated a project called *Amazing Memories.* Kneehigh described the project as allowing different generations the opportunity to share their histories and experiences, culminating in a performance in collaboration with Penpol School, Hayle. This project, as well as a sense of local pride for the community involved, achieved national acclaim: 'This was one of the highlights of the interval fair and was singled out for praise by the national press. It is easy to imagine the effect that such praise must have had on participants in terms of increasing their pride of place'. [65]

Reflective feedback from the participants of the performance and outreach work of *A Very Old Man with Enormous Wings* portrayed positive outcomes. Admittedly, the feedback selected from the company members in the early sections of the *Three Islands Project Evaluation Report* (2005) is subjective in praise of the work achieved, collated from the three different sites of the performance:

What perceived benefits do you believe you have gained from participating in this event?

'Learning organisation skills for big projects and big groups of people. Planning, resourcing, recognising individual talents and pulling them together. Understood much better English art, Celtic culture, Cornwall.' Melita Couta, Sculptor, Cyprus…

'It is a true privilege to have worked with such a diverse group of people…it is the shared warmth of a common humanity, that always inspires, personally and in work.'Bec Applebee, Actor, Cornwall…

'I believe that this performance 'A Very Old Man with Enormous Wings' had a different impact and significance wherever it was performed, in Malta in September 2003, in Cyprus and this year in Hayle, Cornwall. Kneehigh put emotion and personal connection at the heart of theatre going and do so with such grace and seeming ease that you are left entirely spellbound.' Carmen Callus, St James Cavalier, Malta.[66]

The above quotation displays the varied quality of the work, particularly when performing the piece in three different countries. By acknowledging the performance had a 'different impact and significance wherever it was performed', the report addressed the multi-faceted nature of audience responses based on location and cultural background. Although this is something that created difficulties from devising to performance, they intended to generate a production allowing for cultural diversity. More representative and unedited feedback comes in the form of feedback sheets completed by the participants in the outreach project. The feedback forms are unaltered and placed in the appendix in the report, allowing for unbiased analysis.

Focusing on the benefits of working on the *Three Islands Project* (2005) responses described gaining new skills as a positive experience, with seven respondents stating the chance to learn organisational skills in theatre as a bonus to working on the production. Likewise, participants described the chance to experiment with new art forms, and the opportunity to create their own theatre company as 'a benefit' from working on this production. However, the most overriding response came from those who suggested that a sense of community was a positive experience resulting from the project. Based on these responses, the Three Islands Project was a success in uniting three different countries to create a shared sense of community.

From a more cynical standpoint, including selected evaluation forms strengthen the intended aims and eventual outcomes of the project. Evaluation 3 described the project as 'a wonderful mix internationally and [a] combination of young enthusiastic and older experienced theatre makers'. They commented on the challenging production environment: 'Working with perfectionists can be both rewarding and confidence destroying'[67]. Other respondents described the enriching experience of being part of all three productions and watching it develop and mature, noting the productions were different in the varied locations. Evaluation 12 described the chance to revisit a piece of work through the production's multiple places:

> This project has been a part of you, particularly working with a core group over three years. I have felt part of a real community of Mahale. Relationships have grown and the piece benefited. Playing the Major is now for me one of my most enjoyable Parts. [68]

Interestingly, from an actor's standpoint, the production presented the opportunity to develop roles in each location. What is indicated in the above quotation (although not fully described) is an evolution of characterisation facilitated through cultural exchange and responsive to the environment. Evaluation 27 described the feeling of being looked after by the company, with the 'wonderful food' provided and suggested the carnival interval as a way of involving the community. Evaluation 28 goes further to state that there was a good feeling amongst the entire crew and felt that their own part in the 'greater picture' was valued, despite being tired or wet from the elements. Evaluation 29 commented on the difficulties of the working conditions, viewing them as challenging and excessive of music industry norms, but felt the efforts were 'worth it', listing the themes of the play mirroring the global destruction of communities.

> On a more personal level, the content of the play is something that I can identify with very closely - my concern about the way that so many sustainable (but non-cash based) lifestyles are under threat or undergoing destructive changes as a consequence of a global agenda towards so called economic development. Which all too often equates to explosive and unregulated commercial exploitation. In recent years I have travelled around the Arabian sea from Gujarat down to Sri Lanka and stayed in places that were either in a Mahale-like state of 'transformation'. For me, the play carries a message to humanity that deserves to be conveyed as clearly, loudly, frequently and widely as possible. [69]

This response is pertinent to negative criticism of globalisation, with the respondent expressing the 'humanist' message conveyed whilst working on the project, providing examples of tensions between local and global factors.

Appendix 9 presented Kneehigh's collation of feedback garnered from various cultural agencies. Many of the comments made by representatives from these agencies focused on the successful blending of local, national and global influences. Dot Peryer, writing on behalf of The Works on Truro, reflected on the transformative power of the project to invigorate a once derelict land into a marketplace[70]. The Mayor of Hayle (the site that played host to this event), attended a performance and responded by email to the Kneehigh office. High praise was awarded to this production again with the Mayor stating that she felt honoured that Hayle was chosen to host such a successful and somewhat international event.

Irrespective of the perceived benefits of cultural exchange, criticisms of this ideology are prevalent. Just as homogeny is perceived as a negative aspect of globalisation, culturalisation and de-culturalisation of a performance product (to meet audience demand), can expose cultural exchange to negativity. It is important to consider when discussing cultural exchange, the extent to which creative independence or homogeny were taking place when pursuing cross-cultural projects. Language and dialect presented such a challenge in *A Very Old Man with Enormous Wings* (2005), in adapting the piece for a transnational audience as well as for an international cast. This newly created language included elements of English, Maltese, Latin, Italian, Greek, Turkish and Spanish 'weaving in strands of Cornish dialect and language'.[71] An English bias when combining languages was established, due to the leading company (Kneehigh) hailing from Cornwall. Although the evaluative reports written expose no tensions because of this bias, we can assume the creative process followed the similar global dominance of the English language in business and western culture. Interestingly Fischer-Lichte perceived theatre as a form of globalisation, through cultural exchange, which is the antithesis of homogenisation.

> This concept of a world culture is diametrically opposed to the idea of a unified, one-world culture in which all differences are eliminated – in its ugliest form, a cultural monopoly like Coca-Cola, television, and McDonald's. The somewhat utopian concept of a world culture which theatre seems to be working toward in the productive encounter with elements of foreign theatre cultures is seen more as a communal task of the theatrical avant-garde in the different cultures and is projected in these terms. The intercultural trend in world theatre aims to fulfil this demand, whether implicitly or explicitly. [72]

Within the remit of the Three Islands Project, sharing of artistic and cultural practices fulfilled the 'intercultural' trend described above. However, as debated by Rebellato, amongst others engaging in research within theatre and globalisation, theatre cannot fully escape homogeny, with popularist variants actively seeking and working within the realms of homogenisation.

Reflecting on the evaluations from the participants in the show and the responses from the cultural agencies connecting with the project place, an emphasis is placed on the community enriching aspect of the work. Responses from the cultural agencies supported the claims made by the participant evaluations and offered an external view from those working on the project with Kneehigh. It is difficult to determine how objective and impartial those cultural agencies were in sharing their views. Both the Arts Council England, South West and the Mayor of Hayle offered direct sponsorship and support to Kneehigh, with a vested interest in the work being successful, or perceived to be so. All responses included in the report described the successes of the work. However, as an outside reader, it is unclear how many responses were included, and whether Kneehigh excluded responses that were less favourable about the project. There is a potential bias towards presenting the successes gained by the project, particularly when considering the intended purpose of the report; if used to secure further funding. Therefore, I query the validity of the evaluations and responses from cultural agencies. There may be an untended bias in the selection of responses within the relevant appendices. The documents included in these sections are unedited (or appear to be) and are presented in their original form.

The Marketplace: Precursor to the Asylum

The marketplaces set up alongside the performance area in the production, presented opportunities for local business to sell products and promote their enterprises. It allowed for a diverse range of products to be sold as an 'offshoot' from the main production.

> The role of the arts in supporting regeneration in both economic and social terms was emphatically endorsed by this show. The concept of a total event, incorporating a carnival of local performers, traders and makers provided a new experience for audiences and an innovative platform for local food producers and crafts people. It was an excellent model of how the sectors could work together. It also provided a hub around which a team of creative artists could congregate, and this too has had multiple spin offs with new ideas and collaborations emerging from it. [73]

Rose Barnecut – Penwith District Council Arts Officer regarded the success of the show presented a workable artistic and economic business model, underlining the very important role of the arts in regenerating the economy and society. Erika Fischer-Lichte commented on the theatre's ability for exchange within the arts and other areas of life.

> Theatre, in some respects, resembles a market. For, like a market, where an intense exchange of commodities takes place, an exchange of all kinds of

cultural goods and products goes on between theatre and other spheres of social life – other institutions, cultural performances, art forms, and elements of everyday life. [74]

In the case of the Three Islands Project, a 'literal' market was established, developing an exchange within artistic endeavours and retail. The responses from the evaluation forms in the report presented a positive and optimistic view of this opportunity by the participants as well as a more 'sober' view of the actual economic successes achieved.[75]

Evaluations included in the report were taken from the businesses participating in the carnival/marketplace event accompanying the main production. Many of the businesses commented on the dustiness of the environment, which they felt impeded the promotion and selling of their work. Limiting time constraints was another adverse factor, with demands placed on the audience to make their purchase before the start of the show or the brief amount of time given for the interval. The structure of the business feedback form varied from those supplied to the performers, requesting the businesses specify how much earnings/takings they made from the production (and asked for comments on the suitability of the venue for their business).

Trying to gain a picture of the products on offer at the markets based on the feedback forms, established jewellery and arts and crafts as the predominate businesses represented. Only one organic food and drink establishment was included in Appendix 11. However, this does not mean that only one such business was available. Contrast this with the businesses in trade at The Asylum in the summer seasons of 2010-16 where there was a predominance of local Cornish food and drink establishments.

Most businesses made a profit from the markets and were diverse in their takings: the highest sum earned £1900 for glass pieces and jewellery. However, a business selling gardening tools made none. Whilst appreciating the production and enjoying its experience, this business recognised the unsuitability of their products for sale during a theatre production, but still perceived the benefits of publicity for their company. Most businesses commenting in the feedback forms highlighted the opportunity to publicise their businesses to a local and wider customer base. Evaluation 2 selling 3D weaving products, described the promising opportunity to travel to Malta (due to the new contacts formed through the markets) to develop skills in weaving fishnets. The two evaluation forms by businesses from Malta commented on the opportunity to make contacts in the UK and enjoyed the opportunity to visit the Eden Project. These additional feedback forms engaged with the economic advantages developed by the markets created within and around the production venues: a forerunner of the marketplace environment of The Asylum. Given the range of products on sale at this market, compared to the products on offer at The Asylum, Kneehigh has addressed the suitability or unsuitability of products, presenting a narrower selection of goods. By conducting these evaluations, Kneehigh has a better understanding of what sells in such a performative environment. In progressive seasons held at the Asylum, the company streamlined its products and business associations to contain entertainment products and food and drink. A theatre audience member may be more likely (and prepared) to buy food and drink at a Kneehigh show, rather than a set of garden tools or jewellery.

Adaptation and the sharing of cultural practices evident within the Three Islands Project initiated a process of selection, attempting a balance between local and global factors. *Arts and Business News* offered positive views of Kneehigh's working and collaborative practices, deeming their business model successful: short-listing it for an Arts and Business Award in 2002. They illustrate Kneehigh's creativity and innovation by stating that:

> Working with Kneehigh Theatre has been a revelation. Introducing individuals and teams to concepts, ways of working and feelings not normally associated with the workplace has led to the development of a culture that is as good as putting champagne in the veins. [76]

It is this 'innovative' way of working, which I assert makes Kneehigh a company receptive to cultural exchange. Their identification with the community is at the core of their branded identity, elevating them from being a company governed solely by global forces. Cultural exchange offers varying degrees of creative autonomy, something that Kneehigh worked towards over several years, particularly after their near closure in the 90s. This is in contrast to influences from global business models incorporated to make the company financially viable and globally successful.

Within the narrative for this chapter, what started as an examination into cultural exchange inherent within the Three Islands Project, has also highlighted the focus on Cornish community. This sense of community is at the core of Kneehigh's cultural exchange, using stories containing local references and yet making connections with global issues. It is a core that is 'outward looking' and open to global influences, supported through adaptation. Using an international team is a way of striking local connections, whilst engaging with other ways of viewing the world, encouraging international residencies and links.

A sense of familial community and inspiration from the Cornish landscape is conducive to a successful devising and rehearsal period. Kneehigh concedes their work is conditioned by outside influences, illustrating how embedded cultural exchange is within their practice. My research has revealed that the company can weave these multiple global and local components together, and yet still keep autonomy and artistic integrity. By making an international reputation, the Arts Council England, South West supported Kneehigh, to promote Cornwall and the UK nationally and internationally, presenting the artistic potential of the county. Kneehigh were willing to incorporate 'cultural tourism' within their branding and have continued to attract tourists to Cornwall and the Asylum.

Through de-culturalisation and re-culturalisation within cultural practices, Kneehigh de-construct stimuli for their productions and re-configure them with new local and global material and connotations. Culturalisation may raise questions over community and cultural identity. However, this is an ever-evolving and changing construct. Opportunities to work and collaborate with overseas communities enriches cultural exchange and was supported by responses given by participants in Kneehigh's production work, including performers and businesses.

Evaluative reports for the Three Islands Project highlighted the opportunity to be part of a community and share cultural practices whilst working on *A Very Old Man with Enormous Wings (2005)*. This project mirrored many of the environmental and spatial ambitions held by Kneehigh, realised in the Asylum. Likewise, Pelaez Lyons suggested that a similar process of overseas cultural influences being integrated took place during the Colombian *Festival Americano Teatro*, with Kneehigh enjoying the festival atmosphere with other performance companies: eating, drinking and listening to music after the show.

> The founding directors of the festival create this big tent for all the artists for after their performance, they've got a place to go drink and share with other artists/performers. So they can eat as well and they can find other performers and friends, as it's a place to have fun, like a live performance, a very interesting way to connect...And that was really inspirational for them. [77]

Pelaez Lyons offers reflections on a created post-show environment allowing for further communication and exchanges between the artists and/or the audience. The opportunity to socialise and communicate is central to cultural exchanges and inspirations for future work to take place. Kneehigh bringing these influences back from Colombia, as suggested in the Pelaez Lyons interview, and integrating them into the Asylum, not only ensured that cultural sharing took place but gave Kneehigh control over the environment for these post-show/cross-cultural endeavours.

The next chapter will build on the subject of cultural exchange, exploring national and international collaborations with high profile partners. To examine these collaborations in more detail, I will analyse specific productions in the form of case studies. The productions covered will include; *Cymbeline* (2006), *A Matter of Life and Death* (2007), *Brief Encounter* (2008), *The Umbrellas of Cherbourg* (2011).

Notes

[1] *Three Islands Project Hayle, Penwith, Cornwall,* "A Very Old Man with Enormous Wings – Evaluation Report", 2005, Pg-3.

[2] *Three Islands Project Hayle, Penwith, Cornwall,* "A Very Old Man with Enormous Wings – Evaluation Report", 2005, Pg-4.

[3] *Three Islands Project Hayle, Penwith, Cornwall,* "A Very Old Man with Enormous Wings – Evaluation Report", 2005, Pg-3.

[4] *Three Islands Project Hayle, Penwith, Cornwall,* "A Very Old Man with Enormous Wings – Evaluation Report", 2005, Pg-15.

[5] *Three Islands Project Hayle, Penwith, Cornwall,* "A Very Old Man with Enormous Wings – Evaluation Report", 2005, Pg-16.

[6] Fischer-Lichte, E. *The Show and the Gaze of Theatre – A European Perspective*, University of Iowa Press, 1997. Pg-101.

[7] Smelt, M. *Interview with Sue Hill, Bill Mitchell and Maurice Smelt*, Recorded at 42 Weeth Lane, Camborne, 28th April 2000. Pg-23.

[8] Delanty, G. "Cultural diversity, democracy and the prospects of cosmopolitanism: a theory of cultural encounters", *The British Journal of Sociology,* Vol 62, Issue 4, 2011. Pg-650.

[9] *Three Islands Project* "A Very Old Man with Enormous Wings" Report, 2003, Kneehigh Theatre & Wildworks. Pg-5.

[10] *Three Islands Project* "A Very Old Man with Enormous Wings" Report, 2003, Kneehigh Theatre & Wildworks. Pg-2.

[11] Heddon, D. and Milling, J. *Devising Performance – a critical history*, Palgrave Macmillian, UK, 2006. Pg-120.

[12] Heddon, D. and Milling, J. *Devising Performance – a critical history*, Palgrave Macmillian, UK, 2006. Pg-158.

[13] Saunders, G. *British Theatre Companies 1980-1994*, Bloomsbury Methuen Drama, 2015. Pg-28.

[14] *Three Islands Project* "A Very Old Man with Enormous Wings" Report, 2003, Kneehigh Theatre & Wildworks. Pg 6-7.

[15] *Three Islands Project* "A Very Old Man with Enormous Wings" Report, 2003, Kneehigh Theatre & Wildworks. Pg 8.

[16] *Three Islands Project* "A Very Old Man with Enormous Wings" Report, 2003, Kneehigh Theatre & Wildworks. Pg 4.

[17] *Three Islands Project* "A Very Old Man with Enormous Wings" Report, 2003, Kneehigh Theatre & Wildworks. Pg 6.

[18] *Three Islands Project* "A Very Old Man with Enormous Wings" Report, 2003, Kneehigh Theatre & Wildworks. Pg 7.

[19] Unesco, *Culture,* "Intangible Heritage", 2005.

[20] *Three Islands Project Hayle, Penwith, Cornwall,* "A Very Old Man with Enormous Wings – Evaluation Report", 2005, Appendix 8.

[21] Laera, M. *Theatre and Adaptation: return, rewrite, repeat,* Bloomsbury, 2014. Pg-1.

[22] Laera, M. *Theatre and Adaptation: return, rewrite, repeat,* Bloomsbury, 2014. Pg-1.

[23] Smelt, M. *Interview with Mike Shepherd and Maurice Smelt,* Kneehigh Archive, Recorded at Morrab Library, published 21st March 2000.

[24] Heddon, D. and Milling, J. *Devising Performance – a critical history,* Palgrave Macmillian, UK, 2006. Pg-58).

[25] *Three Islands Project Hayle, Penwith, Cornwall,* "A Very Old Man with Enormous Wings – Evaluation Report", 2005, Appendix 8.

[26] Bettelheim, B. *The Uses of Enchantment - the meaning and importance of fairy tales,* Penguin Books, UK, 1976. Pg-150.

[27] Bettelheim, B. *The Uses of Enchantment - the meaning and importance of fairy tales,* Penguin Books, UK, 1976. Pg-151.

[28] *Three Islands Project Hayle, Penwith, Cornwall,* "A Very Old Man with Enormous Wings – Evaluation Report", 2005, Appendix 8.

[29] Laera, M. *Theatre and Adaptation: return, rewrite, repeat,* Bloomsbury, 2014. Pg-2.

[30] *Three Islands Project Hayle, Penwith, Cornwall,* "A Very Old Man with Enormous Wings – Evaluation Report", 2005, Appendix 8

[31] Govan, E., Nicholson, H. and Normington, K. *Making a Performance – Devising Histories and Contemporary Practices,* Routledge, Abingdon UK. 2007. Pg-138.

[32] Govan, E., Nicholson, H. and Normington, K. *Making a Performance – Devising Histories and Contemporary Practices,* Routledge, Abingdon UK. 2007. Pg-140.

[33] Govan, E., Nicholson, H. and Normington, K. *Making a Performance – Devising Histories and Contemporary Practices,* Routledge, Abingdon UK. 2007.

[34] Govan, E., Nicholson, H. and Normington, K. *Making a Performance – Devising Histories and Contemporary Practices,* Routledge, Abingdon UK. 2007. Pg-144.

[35] Govan, E., Nicholson, H. and Normington, K. *Making a Performance – Devising Histories and Contemporary Practices,* Routledge, Abingdon UK. 2007. Pg-146.

[36] Wang, G. and Yeh, E. "Globalization and Hybridization in Cultural Products: The cases of Mulan and Crouching Tiger, Hidden Dragon", *International Journal of Cultural Studies,* Vol 8, Issue 175, 2005. Pg-187.

[37] Wang, G. and Yeh, E. "Globalization and Hybridization in Cultural Products: The cases of Mulan and Crouching Tiger, Hidden Dragon", *International Journal of Cultural Studies,* Vol 8, Issue 175, 2005. Pg-176.

[38] Wang, G. and Yeh, E. "Globalization and Hybridization in Cultural Products: The cases of Mulan and Crouching Tiger, Hidden Dragon", *International Journal of Cultural Studies,* Vol 8, Issue 175, 2005. Pg-179.

[39] Laera, M. *Theatre and Adaptation: return, rewrite, repeat,* Bloomsbury, 2014. Pg-5.

[40] Butler, J. "Plunge into show's heart", *Three Islands Project Hayle, Penwith, Cornwall,* 2005.

[41] Clayton, Emma "Experienced troupe dress to impress", Telegraph & Argus, published 23rd Jan 2004.
[42] Markwell, R. *Cymbeline Review,* BBC.CO.UK.
[43] Mahoney, E. "A Very Old Man with Enormous Wings", *The Guardian,* published 29/07/2005.
[44] Mahoney, E. "A Very Old Man with Enormous Wings", *The Guardian,* published 29/07/2005.
[45] Bassett, K. "A Very Old Man With Enormous Wings, South Quay, Hayle", *The Independent,* published 2nd Aug 2005.
[46] Skantze, P.A. *Itinerant Spectator*, Punctum Books, New York, 2013. Pg-84.
[47] Skantze, P.A. *Itinerant Spectator*, Punctum Books, New York, 2013. Pg-85.
[48] *Three Islands Project Hayle, Penwith, Cornwall,* "A Very Old Man with Enormous Wings – Evaluation Report", 2005, Appendix 8.
[49] *Three Islands Project Evaluation Report 2005.*
[50] *Three Islands Project Hayle, Penwith, Cornwall,* "A Very Old Man with Enormous Wings – Evaluation Report", 2005, Appendix 8.
[51] *Three Islands Project Hayle, Penwith, Cornwall,* "A Very Old Man with Enormous Wings – Evaluation Report", 2005, Pg-11.
[52] *Three Islands Project Hayle, Penwith, Cornwall,* "A Very Old Man with Enormous Wings – Evaluation Report", 2005, Pg-8.
[53] *Three Islands Project Hayle, Penwith, Cornwall,* "A Very Old Man with Enormous Wings – Evaluation Report", 2005, Pg-14.
[54] *Three Islands Project Hayle, Penwith, Cornwall,* "A Very Old Man with Enormous Wings – Evaluation Report", 2005, Pg-21.
[55] *Three Islands Project Hayle, Penwith, Cornwall,* "A Very Old Man with Enormous Wings – Evaluation Report", 2005, Pg-22.
[56] Ruhrmund, F. The Cornishman, "A very old man earns his wings" *Three Islands Project Hayle, Penwith, Cornwall,* "A Very Old Man with Enormous Wings – Evaluation Report", publishes 4th August 2005.
[57] *Three Islands Project Hayle, Penwith, Cornwall,* "A Very Old Man with Enormous Wings – Evaluation Report", 2005, Appendix 10.
[58] *Three Islands Project Hayle, Penwith, Cornwall,* "A Very Old Man with Enormous Wings – Evaluation Report", 2005, Appendix 10.
[59] *Three Islands Project* "A Very Old Man with Enormous Wings" Report, 2003, Kneehigh Theatre & Wildworks. Pg-5.

[60] *Three Islands Project Hayle, Penwith, Cornwall,* "A Very Old Man with Enormous Wings – Evaluation Report", 2005, Pg-10.
[61] *Three Islands Project Hayle, Penwith, Cornwall,* "A Very Old Man with Enormous Wings – Evaluation Report", 2005, Pg-21.
[62] *Three Islands Project Hayle, Penwith, Cornwall,* "A Very Old Man with Enormous Wings – Evaluation Report", 2005, Pg-22.
[63] *This is Cornwall*, "Hayle Hosts Kneehigh", 4th August 2005. Pg-24.
[64] *This is Cornwall*, "Hayle Hosts Kneehigh", 4th August 2005. Pg-25.
[65] *Three Islands Project Hayle, Penwith, Cornwall,* "A Very Old Man with Enormous Wings – Evaluation Report", 2005, Pg-9.

[66] *Three Islands Project Hayle, Penwith, Cornwall,* "A Very Old Man with Enormous Wings – Evaluation Report", 2005, Pg-18.

[67] *Three Islands Project Hayle, Penwith, Cornwall,* "A Very Old Man with Enormous Wings – Evaluation Report", 2005.

[68] *Three Islands Project Hayle, Penwith, Cornwall,* "A Very Old Man with Enormous Wings – Evaluation Report", 2005, Pg-12.

[69] *Three Islands Project Evaluation Report, 2005,* Evaluation 29.

[70] *Three Islands Project Evaluation Report* 2005 Appendix 9

[71] *Three Islands Project Hayle, Penwith, Cornwall,* "A Very Old Man with Enormous Wings – Evaluation Report", 2005, Pg-15.

[72] Fischer-Lichte, E. *The Show and the Gaze of Theatre – A European Perspective,* University of Iowa Press, 1997. Pg-146.

[73] *Three Islands Project Evaluation Report 2005* Appendix 9.

[74] Fischer-Lichte, E. *The Show and the Gaze of Theatre – A European Perspective,* University of Iowa Press, 1997. Pg-1.

[75] *Three Islands Project Evaluation Report 2005* Appendix 9.

[76] A&B, *Arts and Business News,* "Eden Project and Kneehigh Theatre have been shortlisted for an Arts and Business Award 2002", published 15th Oct 2002.

[77] Pelaez Lyons, Andrea. *Interview by Catherine Trenchfield.* Personal interview recorded at West Thames College, Isleworth. 17th November 2011. Pg-4.

CHAPTER FIVE

'THE GLOBAL' – NATIONAL AND INTERNATIONAL COLLABORATIONS

My exploration into Kneehigh's project work considering local community and cultural identity has so far exposed the company's willingness to engage with global business models to survive and continue to serve their locality of Cornwall. It has also established its ambitions for cultural sharing, forming relationships with different people and countries. This chapter considers Kneehigh's brand ambitions and use of neoliberalist business strategies, considering their national and international collaborations. I use the term 'global' in contrast to the 'local', to discuss Kneehigh's work which displays aspects of globalisation.

This chapter will analyse Kneehigh's 'branded' work in developing classic folk, fairy tales and transforming 'classic' films into theatrical productions (through the examination of specific productions as case studies). Kneehigh has recreated two romantic films from the 1940s, which will be discussed in more detail in this chapter. They two films are *A Matter of Life and Death* (2007) and *Brief Encounter* (2008). It will examine the company's reinvention of these original stories and films, in reference to their national and international partnerships. I will discuss criticisms of globalisation, with arguments suggesting Kneehigh have lost the core elements of the above stimuli, as a result of pursuing their own theatrical style. This has exposed the company to criticism, which will be explored specific to each production (as a case study) within this chapter. It should be stated that the company are not only aware of this critique but are willing to address them and find solutions. The productions discussed are; *Cymbeline* (2006), *A Matter of Life and Death* (2007), *Brief Encounter* (2008), and *The Umbrellas of Cherbourg* (2011). These productions established national and international collaborations with the National Theatre, the British Council (with sponsorship to tour South America), the Royal Shakespeare Company and French musical composer, Michel Legrand.

Kneehigh, as well as other contemporary British theatre companies, have developed ambitions of gaining an international audience and fanbase. This ambition was encouraged within the political climate of the UK in the 90s and 00s, as a way to increase funding to support artistic expansion. The political age of 'New Labour' in 1997, saw arts funding being doubled to support the cultural industries, recognising them as being central to the country's prosperity. The Labour party embraced neoliberalism, free market and privatisation as a way of encouraging cultural and economic growth. According to theatre scholar, Liz Tomlin, by taking on board globalism, Labour reinforced capitalist business strategies advocated by Thatcher, as a response to 'the failure of socialism in Eastern Europe'.[1] In 1993, the Arts Council dissolved into national constituencies, and despite funding cuts during the 90s, the National Lottery was used as a 'saviour of the arts'.[2] Kneehigh was affected during this time, despite support from Arts Council England, South West, and as discussed in Chapter 3, faced near closure in 1991, but have since received some of their funding from the National Lottery.

From 2000 onwards, theatre was allocated additional funding as part of an initiative to highlight theatre as one of the strategic priority areas to receive an increase in funding; from £40 million in 2000/1 to £70 million in 2003/4[3]. This expansion offered the opportunity for the theatre sector to rebrand and reinvent itself; an influence also felt by Kneehigh and discussed in the company's own evaluation reports. The impact of globalisation within British politics, expansion of the EU, and support of the British Council, encouraged many theatre companies to embark on overseas touring:

> The dissolution of many of the national boundaries that had previously existed on the continent did have an impact on British artists and cultural organisations over this period, who found partnerships and movement across and within the continental European countries significantly easier than had previously been the case. [4]

This is the case with the productions examined within this chapter, extending the work for global appeal. As mirrored by Tomlin's research above, Kneehigh productions became more national and international in scope. This was encouraged by government policy for the 'strategic priority' of theatre to receive arts funding and present work on national and international platforms.

As part for the artistic vision for 'Brand Kneehigh', the company had aspirations for many years to build the strength of their brand, affording them greater financial independence and creative autonomy over performances they wished to generate. Part of Kneehigh's 'strategic

priority' incorporated branding connections with Cornwall, attracting
national and international attention for the company and the county. Within
the *Penlee Project Outline* (2001), by developing a bid to gain support for
the production, Kneehigh discussed their willingness to be part of the
cultural brand of Cornwall and encourage tourism.

> Promoting Cornwall as a tourist destination with a rich cultural identity,
> offering a diverse range of evening events for tourists and thereby ensuring
> that Cornwall retains a significant share of the high spending cultural
> tourism market. [5]

The appeal of being recognised as a quality cultural product of Cornwall
was discussed later in this outline, as was the suggestion that Kneehigh was
working within a sector perceived as one of the fastest-growing industries
in Britain. With an increase in cultural products created by the company
being exported outside the UK and promoting the Kneehigh brand, it also
capitalised on the demand for Cornish cultural products. In this capacity,
this growing opportunity could 'promote Cornwall and its economy on the
back of cultural products worldwide'.[6] Kneehigh also cited the project as
contributing to 'a lifelong learning culture' that had the potential to impact
all areas of the community[7]. Further explorations into the strategies used by
Kneehigh to develop work between local, national and international
collaborators will be examined in this chapter. It will also reflect on their
potential to generate creative autonomy, whilst generating a global pull
away from producing work in Cornwall.

Global 'Mindset' and the Business Model

The analysis of the Global ideologies outlined in Chapter 1 unveiled a
movement towards 'going global', or as described by Michael A. Hitt,
developing a 'global mindset'. Hitt outlined a 'global mindset' as being
beneficial to running a profitable and thriving business. Many of the
qualities of a 'global mindset' described by Hitt shared aspects found within
cultural exchange; including diversity, knowledge of sociocultural/
institutional systems, and the ability to work with people from different
cultural backgrounds:

> Global mindset is a set of individual attributes that, combined, enable the
> global executive to succeed in influencing those from different parts of the
> world to work together to achieve corporate objectives. [8]

According to research conducted by Hitt, the increase of globalisation in business provoked the necessity for global 'mindsets' within business management.

Hitt provides a pragmatic view of the importance of this business model within a perceived globally driven free market. However, Hitt appreciates the difficulty in achieving a balance between the varied components to make this strategy work:

> As globalisation increases, MNCs [Managers in Multi-National Companies] are exposed to concurrent and often contradictory pressures for global integration and local responsiveness. [9]

As outlined by Tomlin earlier, globalism was a key influence in government funding for theatre, despite the 'contradictory pressures' affecting companies locally. A 'global mindset' was the preferred strategy for Arts Council policy, encouraged by political engagement with neoliberalism and the arts. Kneehigh has actively sought a multi-cultural working environment, particularly in the Three Islands Project, which displayed elements of a 'global mindset' through cultural exchange. An evaluative process, through participant questionnaires, was employed to access the 'degrees of exchange' taking place. Despite the overall narrative of 'success' perceived within the project, there were still difficulties in cultural sharing. The development of a language specific to the production, and ill-judged product placement within the marketplace being examples of the difficulties encountered.

The term 'business model' is used in response to reflections made about Kneehigh in the commentary of this chapter. However, it requires a brief discussion to clarify its meaning, to allow for the formalisation of the term within this research. Professor Bernd W. Wirtz has conducted investigations into the origins of the term business model, underlining its connection with globalisation and associations with gaining a competitive advantage. This term has been in use for over fifty years, and during that time it has developed in meaning and emphasis. A business 'model' can refer to conceptualisation and strategic planning, and due to its evolving state and frequent use as a term, lacks a definitive structure. Because of its shifting state, the notion of the business 'model' has encountered criticisms from a range of theorists concerning its meaning, according to (referenced by Wirtz) Michael E. Porter in 2001:

> The definition of a business model is murky at best. Most often, it seems to refer to a loose conception of how a company does business and generates revenue. Yet simply having a business model is an exceedingly low bar set

for a company...The business model approach to management becomes an
invitation for faulty thinking and self-delusion. [10]

These are critical words to describe a term still in use and one referred to in
this research, communicating the complexity of defining what it means and
using it in practice. Kneehigh resolved to refine its business plan to become
more financially stable, preventing closure. They often cite business models
in evaluative appraisals of a company's economic viability and evolution to
develop and diversify their products. Although appealing as a solution for
change and development, the criticisms above suggest confusion over its
definition, leading to a misinterpretation in its construction and
implementation.

More recent concepts of the business model link the phrase 'model' and
'strategy' together, acknowledging their differences, but embracing the
areas where they intersect: 'Strategy and business model, though related,
are different concepts; a business model is the direct result of strategy but is
not, itself, strategy'[11]. Exploring a further breakdown of this concept,
presents 'strategy' as involving a vision, an idea of future direction. The
business model provides a 'coherent implementation of a strategy'.[12]
Kneehigh was keen to embrace an alternative business model to save the
company from financial collapse by encouraging greater participation in
international and globally based productions. Relating to the of this term in
this text, Wirtz's ideology underpins a cohesive implementation of a
strategy, incorporating a vision for future direction incorporating work with
national and international collaborators.

The strategies utilised by Kneehigh in the productions explored in this
chapter show the 'global mindset' and the growth of the company. These
are ambitions shared by Kneehigh, but also by their collaborators. The RSC
and the British Council approached Kneehigh to develop *Cymbeline* and
tour the production in South America. Michel Legrand, creator of
Umbrellas of Cherbourg, contacted Rice to apply 'Brand Kneehigh' and
generate a theatrical version of the film. The National Theatre and producer,
David Pugh worked with Kneehigh in developing *A Matter of Life and
Death* and *Brief Encounter* respectively. By following the encouragement
of the Arts Council and their own ambitions to expand the theatrical brand,
Kneehigh formed the above collaborations, bringing with them a range of
factors attributed to globalisation, localisation and cultural exchange.

Cymbeline (2006)

Shakespeare's play *Cymbeline* was based on the Celtic stories about
British King Cunobeline. The production featured a play adapted by

Kneehigh; written by Carl Grose and directed by Emma Rice. In speaking to *The Telegraph,* Rice describes *Cymbeline* as a modern tale, involving broken families, step-parents and lost children.[13] Rice has indicated her interest in cultural memory and personal experience, often reinforcing these areas within her forewords to production programmes. Lilley, in an appraisal of *Cymbeline,* observed this same engagement with cultural memory and personal interest. The focus on dysfunctional families within the production exposes their 'damaged, multi-faceted nature', whilst Grose (scriptwriter) was attracted to the 'pulp fiction violence' inherent in the story.[14] Describing how the production came to life, Robin Markwell stated the RSC's desire for Kneehigh to give *Cymbeline,* a little known and somewhat forgotten Shakespearean play, 'the once-over' as part of its Complete Works Festival. In rising to this challenge, the company placed their 'trademark stamp' on the product, displaying their theatrical style, receiving awards and acclaim for breathing life into an archaic text.

Kneehigh's 'trademark' theatrical style was seen in several performances and production elements (becoming familiar to me as spectator having formerly seen *The Wooden Frock* and *Tristan and Yseult*). Kneehigh modernised this Shakespearean production, introducing elements found commonly within other productions. The performance featured comedy and a direct address to the audience, balanced with moments of pathos. Cornish references were explicitly established by the character Joan Futtock (a Cornish housewife), played by Shepherd in drag, acting as narrator. Contemporary music combining punk, rap and east European folk music generated an urban yet ephemeral quality of fairy tales. Metal bins were set on fire, with the chorus dressed as members of a homeless community: communicating abandonment and poverty. Other familiar elements utilised props such as a remote-controlled car used to deliver important news and a set incorporating different stage levels allowing for multi-configuration. The steel cage staging provided a platform for the actors to climb and jump from different areas, facilitating physical theatre, supporting the urban aesthetic alongside the metal bins.

The above elements within Kneehigh's theatrical style displayed an eclectic yet specific combination of performance components characteristic of their production. Considered individually, these elements can be found within other contemporary theatre companies and holistically, they form the company theatrical 'brand'. In addition to communicating and debating Cornish cultural identity, this style incorporates the talents and skills of the cast and crew influencing many elements on stage. Rice and Shepherd's ambition to discover the best way to tell a story in production, whilst also being receptive to influences from their devising company, comes across as a core component to their work and was established within *Cymbeline*. The patchwork quilt displayed at the end of the production was a visual representation of this, triggering several associations; it was supportive of Kneehigh's theatrical brand, it reinforced their role as storytellers, and provided commentary on the potential impact these stories generated within their audience.

The patchwork quilt evoked connotations of the rustic charm of the Kneehigh brand. Through the interpretation of the imagery and symbolism of the quilt in this performance, associations are formed with 'homeliness'; family and comfort within a traditional and old-fashioned construct. The patch-work style of the quilt drew attention to the 'rough' and 'patchwork' nature of Kneehigh's devising style, fitting in with their drive to create work for Cornish village halls and community centres. As storytellers, the image of storytelling created by the quilt generated familiar childhood images of bedtime stories - showing that *Cymbeline* contained themes and narratives that have a 'universal' and global resonance. In terms of audience impact (and in keeping with the function of fairy tales), the story is told from the safe confines of the home: specifically, under the comforting covers of a quilt. From the safe (and local) environs of the bedroom, challenging narratives were explored within a broader, more global arena. Through this approach: broken families, abandonment, political uprising and violence could be examined, and then safely put aside, just as a parent closes a book as their child settles down to sleep. In this 'world' anything too difficult or disturbing can be placed out of sight, no longer immediately dealt with, reducing the powerful immediacy of the narrative. Interestingly, what was evoked in my spectatorial experience was the sense of childhood innocence, overshadowed by 'adult' concerns not fully pacified by the quilt.

The presence of the quilt on stage also signposted Kneehigh's role as storytellers, displayed explicitly on stage at the end of the performance. Storytelling is integral to their brand, which can be achieved through theatrical productions; site-specific performances (including narrated coast walks), educational workshops, and other entertainment experiences. Although storytelling is part of their theatrical style, it is also part of their brand. It is a quality that can be found and attributed to their work, but also as an aspiration for brand development as storytellers on a range of platforms and entertainment experiences.

As I have discussed earlier, an 'experiential archive', encompassing a range of materials, in addition to performance and traditional documentation, is valid as research. It also contributed to my spectatorship. During my exploration of the Kneehigh Archive, I discovered an artefact used to promote the production *Cymbeline* (2006). This material was unlike other promotional products I had encountered within the archive, which included posters, CD's, programmes, leaflets, reviews and production reports. Within this box, amongst colourful tissue paper and shiny metallic material, was a small plastic toy motorbike with a label attached to the handlebars. One side read *Kneehigh Theatre Cymbeline*, while the other stated: 'Please join us on one of our friend's nights for music, fun and fireworks on Friday 18th and Friday 24th August 2006 xx'[15]

Fig. 5-2. *Cymbeline* Memento, Kneehigh Archive, Falmouth University, C. Trenchfield (July 2012)

Looking at what was inside the box caused me to consider several questions: how could I record this item usefully? What would its use be within my research? Unlike the paper documentation used throughout my research, this material was in part non-literary and therefore required a unique approach. While looking at the materials contained within the box, my experience of exploring the item differed from those who had received them as an invitation to the performance. My experience also evoked memories of seeing *Cymbeline*. The small motorbike was a direct link to a prop used in the show, where a remote-controlled toy car delivered a letter carrying important news. The company used similar props to convey news in other performances with effective comic effect.

The discovery of the toy motorbike memento generated experiences triggered after the event, in contrast to the intended experience of promoting the show. For those who experienced it as an invitation, there would be no recollections or connotations to remind the 'experiencer' of the performance: only impressions of what the production might include. However, an experience post-show has the potential to provoke any number of associations with what has been seen in performance. In fact, there would be a pre and post-show experience, triggered by this memento for the original receiver of this item to enjoy. Exploring the archive and encountering this object several years after the event, established two experiences, one post-show as outlined above and another as a researcher. Both experiences are different, but interconnect - and with further consideration of the 'experiential' archive, this interconnectedness becomes much more grounded. Embracing the artefacts and mementoes connected to the show, noting their experiences as research, allowed for varied experiences of spectating this production. My encounter with this resource is in keeping with the theories of Pine and Gilmore, as an 'approach to extending the experience'.[16]

The physical embodiment and experiential encounter with this artefact, presented evidence of Kneehigh's globalised business model and brand ambition. Economic and business theorists Pine and Gilmore described the power these mementoes have to reinforce brand loyalty and promote repeat custom. Kneehigh incorporated this strategy for this performance (as displayed through this artefact) and other productions. This 'gift' helped define brand associations for the company, acting as a physical and tangible way to prompt the show and the company. As a memento given to those in the 'Friends of Kneehigh' scheme, brand loyalty through paid membership was rewarded. In this capacity, privilege is established, setting apart 'friends' of Kneehigh in contrast to other audience members. Other brands follow similar reward schemes to ensure continued engagement with their products. During my spectatorship of *Cymbeline* at the Lyric Hammersmith, the toy motorbike gift was not in evidence.

As part of a national and international collaboration, *Cymbeline* toured nationally with support from the RSC, before being selected as a production to perform in South America by the British Council. In the British Council's *General Report*, Kneehigh's work on the production of *Cymbeline* is regarded as challenging 'traditional' views of UK society and Shakespeare performances:

> ... because Latin American interest in Shakespeare remains as powerful as ever we decided to bring this production of *Cymbeline* to reinforce an image of contemporary and innovative Britain...[We wished to] show broader

target audiences the work of one of the best UK's contemporary theatre companies and combat a persistent image of the UK as a traditional society.[17]

As commented in the British Council's report, Kneehigh, through their production, challenged 'preconceptions' of the UK in Latin America by showcasing contemporary, innovative British Theatre. Within this version, the performance featured urban, contemporary music, costumes, a set with cages, graffiti, metal bins on fire, and modern colloquial dialogue. The image of contemporary Britain was also portrayed; just as Rice had focused on the familial issues of the play, the aesthetic of the 'mise en scene' was powerfully evocative of a dystopian society.

My own spectatorial connections (at Lyric Hammersmith in January 2007) reminded me of the political phrase 'Broken Britain' (a phrase used within tabloid journalism during 2007 onwards to describe social decay in the UK[1]). The world of *Cymbeline* was very reminiscent of this view of British society, through the presentation of homelessness and social unrest on stage and in the music of the production. From a more localised view, the economic degeneration of Cornwall was a pertinent issue, with EU funding allocated to the county since 1999. The stage was evocative of this narrative, reminiscent of the many derelict buildings; a reminder of Cornwall being one of the poorest areas in the UK. However, the narrative of *Cymbeline* offers positive resolutions to these political and social factors, with social and moral justice being restored.

The production also introduced an international audience to 'Brand Kneehigh', showcasing the company themselves and their theatrical style. It is important to state that the Arts Council and the British Council are separate organisations, with different artistic remits, with the British Council concerned with global ventures, whilst the Arts Council works on national projects. The research of Gillespie and Hennessey argues that successful strategies for local business are the same tactics used by global companies: 'Often the global firm's strongest local competitors are those who watch global firms carefully and learn from their moves in other countries'[18]. In doing so, Kneehigh work globally, ensuring the company's artistic associations are also displayed. Kneehigh's global endeavours are not overtly ambitious; but have the ability to develop and grow: 'Global expansion is not just a decision to venture abroad. It is a commitment to learn from experience'.[19]

---

[1] From 2007, *The Sun* ran many stories under the 'Broken Britain' theme, documenting violent crime, child neglect, teenage pregnancy and benefits cheats.

Several favourable production reviews cited Kneehigh's ability to 'inject life' into an often-overlooked Shakespearean text. Kneehigh's development of the play led to a script with a modern voice, allowing non-native English speakers the opportunity to understand the material. Rice discussed her own difficulties in working with the text in its original form:

> Then I read it. Or should I say, tried to read it. The language is tough, dense and archaic. My modern, sluggish brain struggled with the complexity of the plot and the long descriptions of emotion. No one talks about how hard Shakespeare can be, what an alien form his work has become. I plough on. Slowly, the fog lifts, the stories emerged and blow me! There is nothing archaic or alien about it. [20]

Despite the difficulty in comprehending the language, the narratives embedded in *Cymbeline* interest and excite Rice; something she was keen to share in the Kneehigh adaptation with Grose as writer. Rice has experienced a backlash in her comments about Shakespeare within reviews for this production, and particularly during her role as artistic director at The Globe theatre.

The production was both acclaimed and criticised for its adapted script, with many feeling it had become too homogenised and diluted from the original version. Theatre reviewer Peta David stated that although the show was entertaining, it is unrecognisable in its Kneehigh form due to a 'script grittily dumbed down for the masses'. Michael Billington's review concurred that the production made no pretence in offering Shakespeare's original play, but instead offered one written by Carl Grose and adapted by Emma Rice.[21] In this capacity Kneehigh's theatrical style, as a part of 'Brand Kneehigh', was in place and visible within the production, overshadowing the original 'Shakespearean' core. Billington described his disappointment with the performance and Kneehigh's dominant presentation of their theatrical style, pushing Shakespeare's own work to the background. 'What disappointed me, however, was that I felt we were being asked to celebrate Kneehigh's cleverness rather than explore Shakespeare's own mysterious, experimental genius'.[22] Billington goes further to suggest that integral qualities from the original source were lost in the Kneehigh translation and reinvention for modern and global audiences.

As a criticism levelled against them, Kneehigh used their theatrical style to adapt the play, in preference to keeping a greater proportion of the original Shakespearean text. However, the company were approached by the RSC, with the intention that Kneehigh would place their theatrical 'stamp' on the production and generate a 'Kneehigh' version of *Cymbeline*.

In the case of Kneehigh, *Cymbeline* was commissioned by the RSC because its fairy-tale origins were seen to fit Kneehigh's style. Cymbeline's convoluted plot meant it was a play that was rarely staged and a bit inaccessible so maybe it was felt it would benefit from Kneehigh's intervention. Additionally, Kneehigh hadn't done any Shakespeare before, so this was a good opportunity. [23]

Critique within the above-cited reviews exposed negative associations with globalisation and brand identity. To make *Cymbeline* more globally viable, local differences (in this case Shakespearean language), have not only been 'watered down', but virtually removed. In doing so, the performance is unrecognisable from the original script, generating a negative response from audience members and theatre reviewers. However, the production offered the British Council a global performance suitable for promotion in Latin America, to satisfy a demand for Shakespearean material for a wider audience (particularly for audience members in which English was a second or third language). What is revealed is a critique of the treatment of Shakespeare's work in order to engage in global encounters, making it more appealing to a wider cohort.

The World Shakespeare Festival in 2012 was another project that sought to produce a global platform to experience and enjoy Shakespeare around the world. The festival featured 50 companies, performing in 50 different languages, led by the RSC, but also developed with The Globe. This project encountered similar difficulties in its globalised approach. Amongst the logistical challenges experienced by the companies performing on an Elizabethan style stage: 'diplomatic relationships have sometimes been strained' according to *The Guardian* journalist, Andrew Dickson.[24] Further descriptions reveal power struggles between the main organisers:

> The Globe doesn't deign to link to anyone else's Shakespeare projects on its website: more seriously, a bitter dispute about whether an Israeli company should be allowed to perform erupted on the letter pages of this newspaper, because it has performed in the Occupied Territories[2]. [25]

Dickson concluded his article proposing that the work of Shakespeare is no longer the sole province of the UK, opening it up for a global reinvention.

> But even these disputes prove that Shakespeare reflects the world around us, its conflicts as well as its shared values – and the World Shakespeare

---

[2] The Israeli-occupied territories are described by Amnesty International as being in breach of human rights because of violence and abuse issues through the long standing military occupation between Israel and Palestine.

festival, this 'great feast of languages' to borrow from *Love's Labour Lost,* reminds us that Shakespeare is no longer ours alone. Everyone knows the line from *As You Like It*, 'all the world's a stage'. This summer, if all goes to plan, the metaphor will be vividly recast: The Globe's stage will itself become the world. [26]

Dickson raises an interesting issue concerning the 'global' ownership of Shakespeare's work. The scripts (because of their age) can be performed anywhere, without infringement of copyright laws. However, Dickson's global ownership of Shakespeare overlooks the powerful national branding of Shakespeare and companies like The Globe, the Royal Shakespeare Company, and the town of Stratford-upon-Avon. All capitalise on their location and connections with Shakespeare and are fundamental components of British tourism. Although Shakespeare has been performed around the world, part of British cultural identity is entwined with Shakespeare and his work. However, just as Cornish cultural identity is ever-evolving, British cultural identity (and its connection with Shakespeare) are also subject to change.

The Globe experienced criticism against its resistance to the modernisation of Shakespeare while Emma Rice was Artistic Director (just as Rice has also experienced critique relating to her creative ideas). However, Dickson's article illustrated the difficulties and criticisms levelled at theatrical experimentation of performing Shakespeare. It highlighted a power struggle between traditionalists, resistant to change and collaboration, and those in pursuit of global translation and adaptation. But also calls into question the ownership of Shakespeare's work, with the argument that the work no longer belongs to the UK but has a global resonance that everyone can engage with, despite associations with Shakespeare and British cultural identity.

A Matter of Life and Death (May-June 2007)

The company's first production based on a film, *A Matter of Life and Death* (2007) directed by Emma Rice, received mixed responses from theatre critics, provoking then National Theatre's Artistic Director Nicholas Hytner to make the infamous 'dead white men' comment regarding theatre criticism. Hytner made this comment, in defence of Rice, suggesting the majority of theatre reviewers were white, ageing and male, with views bordering on misogyny. His commentary instigated a number of journalistic articles considering and arguing against his claims, with some pointing out his bias towards Rice and his role as Artistic Director.

The play closely follows the plot of the film it is adapted from which was written, produced and directed by British film makers, Powell and Pressburger in 1946. The plot features a fantastical love story between Peter a fighter pilot and June, a radio operator. Peter survives a fall from his plane and is then pursued by celestial figures meant to intercept his fall and conduct him to heaven. His romance with June poses a difficult question relating to fate and moral justice, questioning whether love can redeem the karmic balance destabilised by Peter's survival.

Kneehigh's adaptation (in collaboration with the National Theatre) of this classic film also exposed them to criticisms directed towards many projects; specifically, when transforming from one art form to another. Most film or television adaptations have experienced unfavourable comparison with the original source material, particularly when adapting literature into performance. In a review for *The Guardian,* Claire Armistead describes receiving a 'scornful' letter from a relative of one of the original filmmakers, Pressburger. The letter presented a very pertinent point, forming the basis for many of the criticisms directed at the company: 'It was nonsense to try to adapt the film – or any other for the theatre - because the medium of any great work of art is part of its very essence'.[27]

Armitstead, in defence of working theatrically on this film, suggested the production (unlike the film), was able to offer two different endings. Either ending was selected by a flipping coin, deciding on the fate of the lead male protagonist Peter. Dependant on whether it landed heads or tails, Peter would either live or die. Rather cleverly, as observed by Armistead, it generated the opportunity for audience members to see it again in order to witness a different outcome, increasing Kneehigh's income two-fold:

> By the time I got home, I had decided I would have to go and see it again. But how many times would I have to go before I witnessed the survival of Peter Carter? Might the coin even, like Rosencrantz and Guildenstern's, come down the same side up 85 times in a row? [28]

As a spectator, this premise drew me to return, in the hope of experiencing an alternative ending. Luckily, this was achieved on my second visit. Would I have returned if I did not expect to experience this alternative ending? Several factors would affect this decision; the financial ability to pay for another ticket, seat availability, and the desire to see the show again. The potential to see multiple endings is evident within a number of immersive theatre productions, offering unique experiences in each spectatorship. A number of productions have capitalised on dual casting, allowing audiences to see actors swap roles. A notable example is *Frankenstein (2011)* also performed at the National Theatre, with Benedict Cumberbatch and Jonny

Lee Miller alternating between playing the doctor and monster. It is a trend not uncommon within contemporary theatre, used effectively and with powerful connections to the narrative dealing with fate in opposition to free will.

The argument for working on stories, films, legends etc. can, as Kneehigh has suggested, be a way of connecting with timeless themes and emotions. It can also provide tried and tested stimuli with a proven track record in terms of successful plot/storyline exposition. Working on pre-created stimuli may attract with it an audience with interest in the project already because of the subject/content. This can be a way of securing audience figures and revenue, ensuring other venues book these productions due to the popular and well-known choice of subject matter. Kate Bassett in her review for this production stated that Kneehigh had created their own form of originality in working on this project which 'slavishly borrow[s] from the movie', devising its own original dialogue combined with physical theatre and film projections.[29]

However, working with this form of stimuli can attract criticisms from audience members and critics alike. Re-imaginings of classic folktales and stories can go against the pre-conceived ideas of audience members, provoking feelings of anger felt towards the production. This anger is generated by the re-interpretation of film or TV into a completely different medium or art form. Reviews for this production varied, some suggesting that the theatre production breathed new life into the film and was full of energy, whilst other commentary stated that it was a case of style over substance (with further critique relating to the dominance of the Kneehigh theatrical style).

Considering my own visits to see this production at the National Theatre during its run from 3rd May to 21st June 2007, I witnessed three different endings to the show: providing a Brechtian turning point. Firstly, the preview show ending was dictated by a voting audience, raising hands to decide the fate of the lead characters. In my second and third viewings, the ending of the performance was decided by the flip of a coin. These multiple endings underlined a bittersweet moral dilemma. The cultural and social contexts displayed in the production provoked ethical questions relating to the lead character. Should Peter, the main protagonist, be granted a happy ending with the love of his life after killing hundreds of civilians through his work as a fighter pilot during WW2? Or should he die as fate had initially intended as 'just' punishment for his war crimes? The first of the three shows I witnessed encouraged the audience to vote whether this character should live or die, forcing the audience to respond to this challenging ethical question. Audience members were reluctant to vote, appearing to be reticent to actively participate in the decision. Out of the three shows, this appeared to be the most Brechtian version. However, the audience voting system was later abandoned after the preview shows for the random flipping of a coin; proving to be more acceptable for the audience. For whatever reason, Kneehigh felt that this method did not work, and in my viewing of the show, I felt that it detracted from the overall quality the production was striving to achieve. It created an unnecessary drop in pace, with the audience seeming to find this level of participation awkward and embarrassing.

In my final two viewings of the production, I was lucky enough to witness the outcomes of both sides of the coin, one in which Peter lives and the other where he dies. During my second viewing, I was struck by the mixed feelings and thoughts experienced when seeing the lead character survive. By introducing the deceased families at the celestial trial illustrating their losses accompanied by a wall of faces of all those killed through bombings in Germany, I was made very aware of the cost incurred by others for one person's happiness. A moral question now replaced the usual joyous feeling of a fully resolved happy ending over this character's punishment for the pain and suffering he has caused. Rather than basking in the glow of happiness and the sentiment that 'love conquers all' as the main characters embraced, I was left to consider the unfortunate fates of those who had lost their lives during the bombings in Dresden, whose pictures adorned the cyclorama of the Olivier theatre. In fact, the pictures of those who had lost their lives in World War Two was the final image displayed at the end of the show, overshadowing the happy embrace between Peter and June. Arguably, this was the effect Kneehigh intended to generate, through the projections of the real-life victims of the war; an indication of the moral complexity inherent in the story.

On first examination, introducing factual scenarios presented a move away from symbolic fairy tales, offering material more social and political in nature. However, a secondary reflection revealed Kneehigh's adaptation of this film, presented all facets of the fairy tale, exposing both light and the dark elements within their retellings of classic stories. Looking at the story from a social and political perspective: 'locally' the audience witnessed the happiness of a couple in love 'enduring against the odds'; 'globally' the destruction caused by one person is exposed affecting many with dire consequences. By acknowledging the social implications presented by Kneehigh in this adaptation, the 'happy ending' became bittersweet through its global impact, making it potentially 'immoral' for Peter to cheat death twice: with him being 'rewarded' whilst having killed hundreds of innocent people.

The darker and more complex implications associated with the lead protagonist and war were evidently an image Kneehigh intended the audience to engage with, reinforced by the inclusion of the *Charter of the United Nations (1945)* in the production programme. The charter discusses the 'scourge of war', with the hope that successive generations could be spared its impact. The charter seeks to affirm fundamental human rights, with an emphasis on 'international peace and security'. These 'implications' of war are stressed in both the performance and accompanying literature, exposing the 'cultural baggage' Rice alluded to in her conversation with Welton: 'I think I always want to retell stories, and on some level that's what I consider myself to be, a storyteller'.[30]

Rice's 'cultural baggage' was described in the production foreword in the programme, discussing memories of her Grandad and his experiences during WW2. In particular, Rice discussed her Grandad's set of handbells, which he carried with him throughout the war: 'He and his fellow soldiers would play them over the graves of the friends that had fallen' (*A Matter of Life and Death* 21). Handbells, based on Rice's own familial memories or 'cultural baggage' were included in this adaptation, with injured soldiers in hospital ringing the bells to announce another life lost to war. Acknowledging the personal relevance of the story for Rice provoked similar associations within the spectator. This was certainly the case for me, also having a Grandfather share his own wartime stories of WW2. Likewise, in Rice's descriptions of using these very same handbells during rehearsals, feelings and memories connected to her Grandad are shared, illustrating the personal toil experienced.

> None of us will ever know what he was like before the war - I'm sure he was always kind and placid, but I suspect that a piece of him died in those years, or perhaps it was buried so deep that it was lost forever. [31]

Rice also included a brief timeline of her Grandad, with historical events affecting him during his life, with her own commentary. Rice's anger at war and the sacrifices made by her grandparents are shared emphatically:

> But I do swear and I do scream. I scream that my Gran was left with a young family, no running water, no electricity, no husband to help, I scream that this gentle man was forced to be part of horrors unimaginable and I scream that we are still at war now. [32]

This anger was evident within the production, through the creation of the character, the Dresden Woman, in Rice and Morris' adaptation. This character formed a spectral presence on stage, only seen by Peter until the celestial trial, during which she reveals Peter as the cause of her and her children's death. The Dresden Woman did not exist in the film version, but her inclusion provided Rice with a platform to reveal the horrors of war and her anger towards them. Within my own spectatorial experiences, I found her presence and eventual revelations haunting, reminiscent of the ghostly apparitions in Dicken's *A Christmas Carol.* Illustrated by Rice's foreword is the adaptive process, exploring stories as research, finding commonality and connection:

> At the heart of Kneehigh's approach to adaptation is a desire to explore the mutability of stories, revealing and invigorating their relevance within contemporary culture, through exploration of their personal resonance. [33]

Rice used her own familial experience within her adaption of this production, and by doing so developed her own knowledge and connection with her Grandfather: dedicating the production to him, to those who fought with him and 'for the dead of all wars'.[34] Likewise, within the audience's own 'cultural baggage', a varied range of connections could be made, triggering memories and associations.

During my third visit to see *A Matter of Life and Death* (2007), I was able to watch the darker version of this tale, with the main character Peter dying in the arms of June. As with the second viewing, the fate of these characters resulted from a spinning coin turning the outcome into a random act of destiny as opposed to a conscious choice (experienced in my first viewing). As the coin finally came to a standstill and Peter's fate was sealed, a much more sombre and depressing ending ensued through his demise. This ending, with Peter framed as a killer of hundreds of civilians, getting 'justice' however 'morally just', resonated as an anti-climax. Locally as a spectator, I had invested time and emotional energy in these characters, with Peter and June coming across as highly likeable. I felt that in order to achieve a happy ending, I would need to ignore the global impact these characters had on the world. Having watched this third show, I questioned whether I could overlook these implications, in order to gain an ending that was much more uplifting and potentially satisfying. On leaving the theatre after this version, I felt glad that I had witnessed both endings, satiating my curiosity for either result: leading to my conclusion that the production warranted both endings. Through Kneehigh's development of the wider social and political factors influenced by these characters, the 'happy ending' becomes somewhat morally unpalatable. However, the sad ending offered, from a dramatic viewpoint, also becomes unedifying; feeling cheated out of a resolution or denouement that warranted my emotional investment in the lead protagonists. Providing both endings allowed for a moral and dramatic resolution to co-exist. Economically it allowed the company to capitalise on audience members wishing to see both versions of the production. As written by Armitstead for *The Guardian,* she herself had experienced a 'dull disappointment' at viewing the sad ending and realised that she would need to go again to experience the happier version.

Brief Encounter (2008)

Brief Encounter (2008), directed by Emma Rice, was the company's second re-imagining of a classic film from the 1940s. Despite receiving critical reviews for *A Matter of Life and Death*, this production established Kneehigh's creativity to experiment with cinematic imagery and immersive environments. Staging the premiere of *Brief Encounter* (2008) at the Cinema Haymarket, instead of a West End theatre (through the influence of Theatre producer David Pugh), allowed for an immersive cinematic experience to take place before the theatrical performance. Pugh was confident that such a marketing technique would be successful in promoting the show and encouraging further sales. Pugh also indicated that Cineworld was interested in returning to 'the old days for good'; transforming the Cinema Haymarket into its original form as the Carlton Theatre[3]. This has not been developed further by Cineworld. However, experiences like Secret Cinema have grown in popularity since this production, evidencing a demand for immersive cinema entertainment. Likewise, the use of immersive environments has been incorporated into business strategies, visible within other brands to increase the economy and popularity of the product: evident in this production and the Asylum.

Brief Encounter premiered at a cinema in the West End, a venue very much in reference to its source material. The foyer area and auditorium were restored to their 1930-40s furnishing and decorations. Actors from the company dressed in period clothing as cinema ushers bearing torches and old-fashioned ice-cream boxes. Although the cinema screen for this production was transformed into a proscenium arch stage, a cinematic environment and etiquette were observed. In keeping with the 1940s cinema experience, an intermission was announced instead of an interval, during which old-style adverts promoting fictional washing powder, grooming products and soap were played. These components, during my own visits to this production in the West End as well as the Birmingham Rep, added to

---

[3] Cinema Haymarket was formerly the Carlton Theatre, opening on 27th April 1927 and was last used as a theatre in March 1960, before becoming the Carlton Cinema until 1977 before closing down.

the enjoyment of the production and strongly contributed to the feeling of an 'immersive branded experience'.

Through the decorated foyer area and costumed ushers and usherettes, Kneehigh were effective in developing the world of the play beyond the confines of the auditorium. Arguably this strategy provided layers of experience within the performance whilst increasing the likelihood of additional purchasing. For example, the novelty of themed products such as cream teas and old-fashioned ice creams sold within this themed environment were extremely inviting to a consumer whilst 'cocooned' within this specifically created world. Although this particular variant of the production was pre-Brexit, the image of war-time Britain, with tea served with a 'stiff-upper' lip is a highly evocative image of British cultural identity. This same identity has been cited as an alluring, yet 'fairytale-esque' representation of the UK before joining the EU, providing an ideal for some to vote to leave. In this production, Kneehigh were indirectly addressing British culture (as opposed to Cornish heritage), particularly in light of the international scope of the tours this production had embarked on. This image of Britain contrasted with the dystopic cultural identity portrayed in *Cymbeline*, an identity at odds with a return to the romanticised version offered in *Brief Encounter*. This environment, with added products, allowed the audience to actively participate within the experience, but regarding Susan Bennett's ideas of 'interpretative communities' engaged with 'meaning-making' on a broader platform. It gave the spectator an opportunity to 'consume' this form of British identity, through the cream teas available pre-show and at the interval.

The consumerism established with the novelty factor of this environment (unlike other theatre and cinema productions), encouraged spectators to purchase the above items: extending the experience beyond the realms of the actual production. As suggested by Pine and Gilmore in *Authenticity: What consumers really want (2007)*, a transformative process can occur when a consumer is provided with an experience, increasing the amount of money they spend: 'With experiences, customers pay for the time they spend with a company, rather than for the activities the company delivers'[35]. During my own visits to see this production in March 2008, I found that I purchased extra items at the Haymarket production, including the cream tea offer. I was admittedly taken in by the surroundings, wishing to fully participate in the experience which added to the overall enjoyment of the evening. The production at the Birmingham Rep, although very similarly decorated, could not recreate the same period cinema feel, and did not contribute to the total experience effect as successfully as the West End show.

The production of *Brief Encounter* (2008) received plaudits and criticisms in Kneehigh's re-imaginings of a classic film, again returning to 'universal' themes of love and loss at the core of their theatrical style. Within the director's note for the production, Rice stated: 'I love romance. I also love folk tales. *Brief Encounter* has surprisingly embraced both these passions'.[36] One reviewer commented on the production's ability to make the characters more likeable and human through adjustments to make them more modern.[37] Haydon commented that he preferred the stage version of *Brief Encounter* compared with the film version, although critiqued Kneehigh's 'overuse' of symbolism through physical theatre.

In questioning Kneehigh's reasons for using a predominance of physical theatre, Haydon likened the artistic promotion of their brand to Shared Experience, acknowledging another branded theatrical style: 'It's like Kneehigh doing Shared Experience doing *Brief Encounter*'.[38] Shared Experience is another contemporary British Theatre Company, known for their performance work which combines a union of physical and 'text-based' theatre. The physical theatre elements are described as being expressionistic, displaying the inner emotions of a character. This was seen in Laura's physical motif of being caught in a wave, submerged under water. Whenever Laura left overwhelmed by her emotions, this physical motif would be performed accompanied by a filmed projection of waves and an underwater swimmer. Haydon's comment on the branded influence of Shared Experience on the work of Kneehigh has a critical slant, implying negative connotations with Kneehigh's utilisation of this style. Both Shepherd and Rice have been transparent in their theatrical influences. Theatre as a product and art form is global in nature and subject to cultural exchange. Rice's use of her training with Polish theatre company Gardzienice, introduced physical theatre elements to the devising process and performance work. However, I cannot affirmatively state whether Kneehigh had intentionally 'copied' Shared Experience's physical theatre style in this production.

Brands offering similar products can share common strands in their work and can be influenced positively by each other. Within the contemporary theatre genre, there are a number of theatre companies who are grouped together through style and shared influences. Many companies have been compared unfavourably with Punchdrunk, perceived as the forerunners of immersive theatre. While there are companies who have copied Punchdrunk's performance, there are others who have adopted elements whilst also generating new qualities within the genre. Branded products outside the realm of theatre also mirror the same process of influence, innovation and replication. Some companies will copy a brand using substandard materials, generating an inferior performance experience. Others will develop work comparatively and progress further through innovation. It is my interpretation of Haydon's commentary, which alludes to this process of replication. However, such replication does not have to be regarded in negative terms, as it can display an act of influence and cultural sharing. It can also instigate development and innovation within a theatrical genre, performance style and product.

Returning to the emotional components of *Brief Encounter,* Emma Rice in an interview with *The Telegraph* suggested that the emotions involved in this story provided a timeless quality that allows a re-imagining and re-branding of the work:

> 'I would argue that there's not much difference from today,' says Rice. 'The pain involved in meeting someone you shouldn't, in wanting to be with someone you can't be with – I don't believe there's any difference. There's a more liberal attitude towards what the options are, but the basic emotions are the same.' [39]

This adaptation allowed for new contemporary perceptions on this love affair, considering the infidelity in a more sympathetic light, but also embracing the notion of self-discovery or as suggested by Rice, 'personal awakening'. As observed by Kara Reilly: 'Each generation remakes the classics in their own image for their own contemporary moment, engaging with texts of the past in the present' (Reilly xxiii). This notion of self-discovery and identification for the female lead Laura (separate from housewife and mother), is arguably a more recent philosophy and not openly acknowledged in the 1930-40s. Rice reinforced this theme by stating: 'There can be no happily ever after until this true self, or nature has been accepted and embraced' (Rice 2007 7). By including this theme, Rice provided an uplifting tonality to the end of the play. Rather than being completely immersed in the grief of a love affair ending between Laura and Alec, the spectator can 'celebrate' Laura's reconnection with 'self'.

Despite this more positive ending, Billington concluded his review of *Brief Encounter (2008)* with the above suggestion, that despite Kneehigh's inventiveness, valuable qualities that made the original so powerful are no longer evident in this production:

> In the end, however, the show friskily demonstrates Kneehigh's skill but at the cost of the quiet integrity that makes the original Brief Encounter so peerlessly moving. [40]

The review written by David Benedict for *Variety*, voiced similar concerns as Billington and argued that although the film is suitable for a theatrical transformation, Kneehigh have not lived up to the challenge, despite the resources afforded to them by the National Theatre:

> Working via the audience's imagination more than film does, theatre would appear to be well suited to this particular story. And director Emma Rice (and co-adaptor Tom Morris) have certainly utilised the National's plentiful resources. What they haven't done is marshal them into an effective whole.[41]

Irrespective of these reservations, since the opening of the production in 2008, *Brief Encounter* toured internationally in Australia in 2013 and the USA in 2014 (with further performances in 2017 and 2018 in the UK). My spectatorship has not extended to viewing these international productions due to location and expense. However, what can be observed is the company's success in transferring this production in two very different global locations, for an extended period of time.

Through Kneehigh's recreation of an old-fashioned cinema, the company paid homage to the source material, incorporating a way to make it work theatrically through the use of multi-media, period costumes and set. Unlike other devised performances, *Brief Encounter* took on a more fixed structure, according to Lilley. This is owing to Coward's screenplay, and earlier play *Still Lives*; responding to this material through adaptation, rather than taking the form of a devised play. In this capacity, according to Lilley, Kneehigh has developed into a 'devising company' who utilise their theatrical devising skills for adaptation.[42] Arguably this is integrated within the company's theatrical brand, which has been sought after in recent years to adapt pre-existing scripted work. As discussed earlier, adaptation from one art form to another invariably attracts critique. The same was encountered by Kneehigh when adapting *A Matter of Life and Death,* with resistance found by the loyal fanbase of the original film, theatre reviewers, and from the Powell and Pressburger estate.

Building on the critique of *A Matter of Life and Death*, this production utilised the format of the 'original' film within the adaptation, rather than completely transforming it as a solely traditional theatrical production. The play itself was presented in the auditorium as a film within a cinema. Filmed sections were projected, with live actors interacting with digital performers and vice versa. The infamous romantic train scene was inventively brought to life through a moving curtain and filmed projection of a train. Again, live performers communicated with digital counterparts, in which illusion allowed a smooth transformation with a live actor appearing through the cinema screen. Arguably the more positive reception to this production was due in part to the clear link between the original film and this adaptation.

Rather than creating something different and 'new', this production appeared to celebrate its filmic heritage.

The Umbrellas of Cherbourg (2011)

The company's third foray into classic films presented a departure from the 1940s, turning to a cult French musical film from the 1960s. The plot features a romance between a young Frenchwoman (working at a boutique selling umbrellas) and a mechanic. However, their love affair is cut short by war, and the lovers are separated despite a pregnancy. This adaptation was scripted by Carl Grose and directed by Emma Rice. However, in contrast to Grose's work on Cymbeline, this version does not deviate too far from the original film script and is a musical sung throughout the performance. Shepherd is not listed within the cast and crew for the production; however, as artistic director, it can be assumed that he assisted in some form of consultation.

Reflecting on the production *The Umbrellas of Cherbourg (2011),* Rice described being approached by the writer of the original musical, Michel Legrand, who had been impressed by the Kneehigh adaptation of *Brief Encounter*, and wanted the same 'magic' to be recreated for his own proposed revisiting of *The Umbrellas of Cherbourg*. Likewise, David Farr from the Bristol Old Vic is quoted as providing an overview of their appeal:

> They are just very, very good at telling stories. And when you get innovative visual theatre allied with classical storytelling, you get something that audiences respond to immediately. [43]

Rice commented on the global themes of love and 'endurance' that have primarily encouraged her to work on this production during an interview with *The Times* in 2010, conducted just under six months before its premiere. Rice expressed to Tom Gatti, her intention of finding a way to 'inject the anarchic Kneehigh theatre style into the work'.[44] In retrospect, these ambitions did not pay off: the production was deemed unsuccessful and closed after two weeks of opening in London. Shepherd in the same interview, is quoted as stating that he had no interest in producing a slick, perfect show, suspecting that it might be a bit boring and would 'rather present humanity on stage'.[45]

Perhaps the 'failure' of this production resided in the presumption that the material would automatically generate an audience, because of the association with 'Brand Kneehigh'. At this juncture, the perceived strength of the brand was tested and proved unreliable for this particular project. The Kneehigh brand and Rice as director were used for their creative merits and 'star' name to attract potential audience members. This had been done previously at the Lyric where members of the Kneehigh team were used in collaboration, working on *Nights at the Circus (2006)* and *The Odyssey (2006)* to greater success. Unfortunately, the tactic did not work for this production, and despite Kneehigh's loyal audience fan base, *The Umbrellas of Cherbourg* closed within weeks of its premiere.

This may have been an enlightening time for Kneehigh; reflecting on the reasons why the production did not 'work'. The closure of the production reveals the difficulties and potential limitations of marketing the arts but may have also acted as a provocation for the company to gauge their 'successes' in local and global theatrical arenas. Arguably, the supposed failure of *The Umbrellas of Cherbourg* reinforced the need to maintain a local, loyal fan base, when global and more adventurous projects do not achieve the expected or planned 'successes' predicted. In this capacity, there is a need to maintain their local work, as a way to survive and generate enough funding to venture forth into more national and international venues. In regard to *The Umbrellas of Cherbourg (2011),* were Kneehigh influenced by high profile collaborators to move away from their artistic stance to create a 'perfect' show? Were they encouraged to move away from the creativity that has developed their brand and reputation in the first place? A musical with all the dialogue sung was an ambitious and adventurous project to undertake. The closing of this production, along with criticisms launched at the company for their interpretations of *Brief Encounter* and *A Matter of Life and Death*, would affect their brand and creative sensibilities.

The notion of 'value' and the perception of 'success', given the perceived financial failure of this production, is an important factor to discuss. If we are to follow neoliberal economic definitions of 'success' and 'value', *The Umbrellas of Cherbourg* lacked both. Using a neoliberal gaze to regard this production, reduces its merits to financial terms, ignoring other achievements. Although theories of globalisation and branding have been used to consider the work of Kneehigh, it should be specified that whilst common factors exist between global theories and theatre practice, there are marked differences. Artistically, 'valuable' or 'successful' cannot always be linked to financial gains. In this arena, more personal or individualistic notions of success and what is of 'value' are formed. Kneehigh Theatre Company began with such a premise, with Shepherd developing a company to perform in Cornwall as a way of expressing themselves, irrespective of whether they were paid. Referring to Shepherd's journal found within the Kneehigh Archive, many of the earlier productions in the first few years of the company were unpaid.

A performance can still be of artistic value, despite low audience numbers. Again, the process of artistic creation and the eventual production are still valid entities and regarded as successful and of 'worth'. However, the reviews for this production were extremely mixed. Costa, for *The Guardian*, described her initial reservation about reviewing *The Umbrellas of Cherbourg*, replaced by feeling the production had 'genuinely changed my life, by encouraging me to start a blog, to tell people how much I'd loved it – and so reigniting my passion for writing about theatre'[46]. Costa shared her feelings on the 'value' of the production, inspiring a response to her own creativity. In direct contrast, Charles Spencer for *The Telegraph* was much less complimentary, describing it as a 'damp squib'. The review starts with a somewhat patronising and sexist analogy, regarding the 'type' of female audience member who would find this production appealing:

> I'll get stick for saying so, but this strikes me as the kind of evening that will appeal to susceptible women in the audience, who will wallow in the bittersweet romance of it all, while most of the chaps will be bored stiff, though they will just have to grin and bear it if they want to keep their partners happy. [47]

Spencer acknowledged that some would take offence in his negative commentary of the production, signposting his own positionality (and sexism). This was established by a stereotypical (and somewhat chauvinistic) viewpoint, stating that the only audience members to find 'value' in the production would be those identifying with his 'sentimental' female description.

Revealing less artistically driven objectives for working on *The Umbrellas of Cherbourg,* Rice described the business 'value' Kneehigh could provide and also benefit from, by embarking on the collaboration in an interview with *theartsdesk.com*, stating:

> There's the fact that I was there and that so much of my experience comes from Kneehigh, the creative team was nearly all Kneehigh but then there's also the business side of things. To be completely frank, it wasn't going to be a Kneehigh show, but the producers asked us if it could be because our name was going to help sell tickets and we're no fools.[48]

Whitney conducted this interview after the closure of the production on the West End, with Rice displaying an element of defensiveness about the project and the creative restrictions imposed. Although through these comments, Rice expressed her freedom to share her thoughts (despite these views being perceived in a negative light) after the production had closed. This indicated another layer of complexity to the working relations of this venture differing from the positive inspirations Rice shared in an interview placed in the education resource pack:

> I didn't find The Umbrellas of Cherbourg, Umbrellas found me. Michel Legrand had been to see Brief Encounter and decided that I should direct the first version of The Umbrellas of Cherbourg in 30 years. The courtship started with a series of very passionate, charming and persuasive calls until I agreed to watch the film. And then, and then... The courtship was no more – the love affair had begun. I adored this piece from the moment I saw its colours, felt its heartbeat and recognised its characters. I said 'yes' with no questions or doubts, and the love affair continues. [49]

The above quotation reveals Rice's own assertions on how she was drawn to material to work on. During her conversation with Martin Welton, Rice responded to a question posed about adaptation. Welton questioned whether there was a 'formula' to the Kneehigh adaptation process. Rice confirmed that there is no 'formula', rather there was a commonality that holds an attraction: 'The simple thing that binds all these projects together is that I wanted to tell "that" story. I call it the itch!'.[50] The later quotation above presents Kneehigh recognising the financial benefits from this collaboration appeared at odds with 'the itch'. It is, however, possible that Rice and Kneehigh experienced both standpoints. Positionalities can change; and as evidenced in earlier work, Kneehigh has worked artistically whilst also responding to financial challenges and external demands.

My spectatorship of the production offered an enjoyable show, presenting elements of Kneehigh's signature theatrical style and the original film. I found validity and value inherent in the production but felt the source material was too obscure to attract audience members in the same way that other productions had when using more popular material. In this capacity 'Brand Kneehigh' was not 'strong' enough to attract a greater audience, resulting in its West End closure.

In an interview for *Clifton Life*, Rice is sanguine about the external factors that impact their creativity and dictate their work. On reflecting on the potential dangers, the company may face by becoming a popular and potential mainstream product, Rice asserted that the company must stay true to their principles. She is realistic that changes due to outside factors will occur: 'Change is inevitable and wonderful; you can't stay the same. But neither are we about to move to London and join the rat race...'.[51] In an interview with *The Times*, Rice responded honestly, and in an unguarded fashion when asked about the influences of big budgets, high profile collaborators and international tours posed for the company. Gatti, conducting this interview, questioned whether Kneehigh could keep their 'rawness'.[52] Rice provided her answer by stating that the company had the best of intentions, maintaining the qualities they developed during their formative years, qualities at the core of their own artistic identity. However, there was no guarantee in maintaining this amongst powerful influences, with Rice questioning whether these influences have not already affected the company in this manner.

> 'I look at *Brief Encounter* and I think 'I've really learnt my craft',' she says. 'But then I look back at *The Red Shoes* and think, 'Have I lost something along the way?' I don't want us to be a manicured, middlescale theatre company.' [53]

This is an ongoing challenge for the company, and as discussed in Chapter 3, smaller scale productions within Cornwall (whilst also producing national and international work) offered solutions to address this question. Arguably the recruitment of Carl Grose, a longstanding member of the company, as Joint Artistic Director appeared to be a logical decision, following Rice's departure. Grose has worked with the company for two decades and has been present during the different phases of Kneehigh's 'theatrical' career and the evolution of 'Brand Kneehigh'. Grose's Cornish roots additionally reinforced 'local' elements of the Kneehigh brand, having a stabilising effect on the company. The recruitment choice for this post was extremely important, not only in terms of artistic direction but for its social and cultural associations. A different choice could have introduced the company to more international and national associations. Instead, the choice of Grose, a known artistic component, was a supportive selection of Cornish talent. It was also a drive towards maintaining 'core', 'local' elements, in light of the company's expansion in national and international arenas.

Former company member, Mary Woodbine, an actor with Kneehigh during 2008, suggested that Kneehigh's policy of members bonding and becoming part of a responsible community gave actors 'a really strong sense of ownership in the company'.[54] This outlook instils a sense of loyalty to the company through shared responsibility, creating an opportunity for the actors to feel like shareholders in the company (with a vested interest in its success encouraging higher productivity). This community bond encouraged trust between all participants through mutual care about the production and the company, with an intense bonding process being forged during rehearsals. Kneehigh Theatre Company members working on a project can expect to get up early in the morning for a jog before breakfast, rehearse throughout the day, take meals and breaks together and rehearse well into the late evening. This is followed by drinking and socialising, playing music and games well past midnight into the early morning, with the onus on actors and crew participating throughout the rehearsal period.

Kneehigh company members have consequently found their own career opportunities develop either through positive associations of working with Kneehigh leading to other outside work; or like Emma Rice and Carl Grose who have found their role within the company become greater and more important. An experience working on a Kneehigh production is another component to their brand identity, embracing the opportunity to work with long term company members, local and international artists. The experience of working in the barns at Gorran Haven, participating in morning runs and yoga, eating and drinking together are elements specific to the company's pre-production process. Creativity and playfulness are qualities fostered by Rice and Shepherd, and collectively form the artistic ethos for making work. High profile performers such as Douglas Hodge (*A Matter of Life and Death*) and cabaret star Meow Meow (*The Umbrellas of Cherbourg*) have performed in these respective productions, participating in the Kneehigh rehearsal and devising process. Performance experience is central to the brand and rehearsal as a function serving performance is a form of experience containing its own qualities. Actors working on a production can experience 'Brand Kneehigh' as a rehearsal experience, and as part of a performance. This is, of course, a different branded experience to the spectator.

This chapter has examined national and international collaborations within four noted productions as case studies. Inherent within each production are qualities associated with Kneehigh's branded theatricality, in contrast to criticisms relating to their theatrical style. One of the principal arguments posed has suggested a dominance of Kneehigh's theatrical style over the original source material. *Cymbeline* was criticised over the virtual elimination of the Shakespearean text. However, Kneehigh received positive commentary on updating the play for a contemporary, international audience: receiving sponsorship from the RSC and the British Council. *A Matter of Life and Death* established another high-profile partnership with the National Theatre and displayed ambitious new creative directions in working with classic films; receiving mixed reviews in their adaptation from the original medium. *Brief Encounter* received more favourable responses, embracing media components in a celebration of the original film. Likewise, the production experimented with immersive environments through the themed transformation of venues, developing the world of the production. In the case of *The Umbrella of Cherbourg,* Rice and Kneehigh were approached by Legrand (attracted by their associative brand name and 'star' power) to work on a theatrical adaptation of the original film. The narrative had an unintended outcome through mixed reviews and the closure of the production due to poor sales and the failure of the Kneehigh's brand to secure longevity for this project. Rather than focus on the perceived critique of these respective productions, an examination of these case studies exposed challenges inherent within local, national, and global collaborations.

In terms of Kneehigh's branded theatricality, familiar aspects of their work in performance were evident; actors made a direct address to the audience with comedy and pathos, with music and song included to underpin key themes. Physical theatre was also used, as were props on either a miniature or grand scale (as seen by the tiny bike in *Cymbeline* or the large-scale ping pong game in *A Matter of Life and Death)*. Projection and multimedia elements were included (specifically in *A Matter of Life and Death* and *Brief Encounter),* and despite not being included in all productions, are still associative elements within their work.

The next chapter examines the physical manifestation of the Kneehigh brand: the Asylum. I will also discuss case studies of productions in reference to this unique space, with references to the Asylum's multiple locations and configurations. The chapter will explore the development of the venue, considering Kneehigh's own ambitions for this branded performance space.

Notes

[1] Tomlin, L. *British Theatre Companies 1995-2014*, Bloomsbury, 2015. Pg-3.
[2] Tomlin, L. *British Theatre Companies 1995-2014*, Bloomsbury, 2015. Pg-27.
[3] Tomlin, L. *British Theatre Companies 1995-2014*, Bloomsbury, 2015. Pg-32.
[4] Tomlin, L. *British Theatre Companies 1995-2014*, Bloomsbury, 2015. Pg-1.
[5] *Penlee Project ERDF BID Project Outline*, Perfect Moment, Kneehigh Theatre, Feb 2001. Pg-2.
[6] *Penlee Project ERDF BID Project Outline*, Perfect Moment, Kneehigh Theatre, Feb 2001. Pg-3.
[7] Penlee Project 200, Pathways Synopsis
[8] Hitt, M. et al. *The Global Mindset - Putting it All Together: So What is a Global Mindset and Why is it Important?* Emerald Insight, 2015. Pg-2.
[9] Hitt, M. et al. *The Global Mindset - Putting it All Together: So What is a Global Mindset and Why is it Important?* Emerald Insight, 2015. Pg-12.
[10] Wirtz et al. "Business Models: Origin, Development and Future Research Perspectives", *Long Range Planning,* Vol 49, 2016, Pg-37.
[11] Wirtz et al. "Business Models: Origin, Development and Future Research Perspectives", *Long Range Planning,* Vol 49, 2016, Pg-38.
[12] Wirtz et al. "Business Models: Origin, Development and Future Research Perspectives", *Long Range Planning,* Vol 49, 2016, Pg-38.

[13] Sierz, "Cymbeline", *The Telegraph,*2008. Pg-2.
[14] Lilley, H. "Kneehigh's Retellings", Reilly, K (ed). *Contemporary Approaches to Adaptation in Theatre,* Palgrave Macmillan, 2018. Pg-10.
[15] Kneehigh Theatre Cymbeline, Archive Box 15.
[16] Pine, Joseph. & Gilmore, James. *The Experience Economy: Work is Theatre & Every Business a Stage*, Harvard Business School Press, Boston, 1998. Pg-57.
[17] British Council, *General Report Cymbeline*, Kneehigh Archive, Falmouth University. 2008.
[18] Gillespie, K. & Hennessey H.D. *Global Marketing*, South-Western, Cengage Learning, Third Edition, UK, 2011. Pg-158.
[19] Gillespie, K. & Hennessey H.D. *Global Marketing*, South-Western, Cengage Learning, Third Edition, UK, 2011. Pg-6.
[20] Rice, E. *Cymbeline Programme,* Lyric Hammersmith, 2006. Pg-4.
[21] Kneehigh Archive Press Cuttings 2012. Kneehigh Archive Falmouth University, 2012.
[22] Kneehigh Archive Press Cuttings 2012. Kneehigh Archive Falmouth University, 2012.
[23] Radosavljevic, Duska. "Chapter 4 Kneehigh Theatre", ed. Tomlin, Liz. *British Theatre Companies 1995 - 2014*, Bloomsbury, 2015.
[24] Dickson, A. "World Shakespeare festival: around the Globe in 37 plays", *The Guardian,* published 20th April 2012.
[25] Dickson, A. "World Shakespeare festival: around the Globe in 37 plays", *The Guardian,* published 20th April 2012.
[26] Dickson, A. "World Shakespeare festival: around the Globe in 37 plays", *The Guardian,* published 20th April 2012.
[27] Armitstead, C. "A matter of life, death and two different endings", *Guardian Unlimited: Arts blog – theatre, 2007.*
[28] Armitstead, C. "A matter of life, death and two different endings", *Guardian Unlimited: Arts blog – theatre, 2007.*
[29] Bassett, K. "A Matter of Life and Death", *The Independent*, Published 13th May 2007.
[30] Laera, M. *Theatre and Adaptation: return, rewrite, repeat,* Bloomsbury, 2014. Pg-230.
[31] Rice, E. *A Matter of Life and Death Programme,* National Theatre. 2007. Pg-21.
[32] Rice, E. *A Matter of Life and Death Programme,* National Theatre. 2007. Pg-23.
[33] Lilley, H. "Kneehigh's Retellings", Reilly, K (ed). *Contemporary Approaches to Adaptation in Theatre,* Palgrave Macmillan, 2018. Pg-6.
[34] Rice, E. *A Matter of Life and Death Programme,* National Theatre. 2007. Pg-23.
[35] Pine, Joseph. & Gilmore, James. *The Experience Economy: Work is Theatre & Every Business a Stage*, Harvard Business School Press, Boston, 1998. Pg-47.
[36] Rice, E. *Brief Encounter Programme,* Birmingham Repertory Theatre. September 2007. Pg-4.
[37] Haydon, A. "Brief Encounter – Kneehigh at the Haymarket Cinema", *Postcardsgods.blogsot.com*, 20th February 2008. Pg-2.
[38] Haydon, A. "Brief Encounter – Kneehigh at the Haymarket Cinema", *Postcardsgods.blogsot.com*, 20th February 2008. Pg-1.

[39] Cheal, D. *The Telegraph,* "Brief Encounter", 09/02/2008. Pg-2.

[40] Billington, M. *The Guardian,* "Brief Encounter", 18/02/2008.

[41] Benedict, D. "A Matter of Life and Death", *Variety*, Published 18/03/2008. Pg-1.

[42] Lilley, H. "Kneehigh's Retellings", Reilly, K (ed). *Contemporary Approaches to Adaptation in Theatre,* Palgrave Macmillan, 2018. Pg-11.

[43] Gardner, L. "We like our plays to be foolish", *The Guardian,* published 2005.

[44] Gatti, T. "Where theatres wild things are", *The Times*, published 24th July 2010.

[45] Gatti, T. "Where theatres wild things are", *The Times*, published 24th July 2010.

[46] Costa, M. *The Guardian,* "Musicals we love: The Umbrellas of Cherbourg, Published 31st March 2014.

[47] Spencer, C. *The Telegraph,* "The Umbrellas of Cherbourg, Gielgud Theatre, review", published 23rd March 2011.

[48] Whitney, Hilary. *theartsdesk.com,* "Q&A: Director Emma Rice", 16th July 2011.

[49] *Notes for Students – The Umbrellas of Cherbourg,* Kneehigh Theatre, 2011. Pg-10.

[50] Laera, M. *Theatre and Adaptation: return, rewrite, repeat,* Bloomsbury, 2014. Pg-229.

[51] Robins, D. "Flights of Fancy", *The Clifton Life,* 2010. Pg-39.

[52] Gatti, T. "Where theatres wild things are", *The Times*, published 24th July 2010.

[53] Gatti, T. "Where theatres wild things are", *The Times*, published 24th July 2010.

[54] Costa, M. *The Guardian G2,* "Arts: Theatre: Troupe therapy: Kneehigh", Published 2008. Pg-2.

CHAPTER SIX

ASYLUM – BRANDED WORLDS

This chapter discusses the company's own venue, the Asylum. It will consider whether this venue makes the Kneehigh brand stronger and more successful, harnessing a greater autonomy over the company's creativity. Importantly this has been suggested by Kneehigh themselves as their own solution to the difficulties of producing work that appeals to a global audience but serves their local community. Connections with the Asylum will be made in contrast to global theories discussed earlier, establishing the Asylum as an experiential 'world' in which consumers spectate and take part. The chapter will establish the Asylum as an environment to reinforce 'Brand Kneehigh'. Likewise, it supports my form of spectatorship and research: the experiential archive. Finally, it will reflect on the tensions encountered by the company, tensions provoked by a local and global dichotomy, exploring ways in which the Asylum provided solution and sanctuary.

Fig. 6-3. Asylum, The Dome Company, Cornwall (2010)

Background and Inspiration for Asylum

An earlier emergence of 'Brand Kneehigh' and their concept of a total entertainment experience was evident in the Three Islands Project. In this production, Kneehigh created a 'festival' environment including; food and drink vendors, arts and craft stalls with the cast and the Kneehigh band providing extra entertainment[1]. Descriptions of this venue appear as a precursor to the Asylum entertainment 'ethos' with a variety of products to buy and enjoy.

> Huge crowds pour into Kneehigh's little world every night, wandering through the Glastonbury-type settlement of tents, sideshows, fast food and crafts to the main arena where the angelic parable takes place, with the mixture of humour, pathos, marvellous live music, superb design and effects, and dashes of breathtaking adventure for which this company is so famous. [2]

As discussed in Chapter 1, the Kneehigh brand has ambitiously forged associations with 'lifestyle' and entertainment to develop their theatrical product. The descriptors within the above journalistic review signpost this potential, drawing highly evocative comparisons with Glastonbury. The term 'Glastonbury-type' is extremely descriptive of a 'festival' style configuration. This is a term used by other reviewers of Kneehigh's work, with 'festival-like' comparisons utilised within this study. During this project Kneehigh forged links with other local brands: 'We've teamed up with Cornwall Taste of the West, and suppliers like Cornish King and Cornwall Organic Partnership to offer a choice of drinks and hot pre-show meals. We think it will add to the atmosphere at these three venues'[3]. In doing so, Kneehigh reinforced their branded experience, making their marketplace stronger through a combined brand synergy – with the common denominator being their Cornish locality.

The 2005 evaluation report commented positively on Kneehigh's perceived understanding of the communities involved in this project, through their development of an entertainment product involving pre-show entertainment and the facilities to sell and share local merchandise.

> The final event was a great testament to the ability and confidence Kneehigh (and particularly Bill) have in understanding the communities and overall context in which they are working: from the selection of the artists and caterers who provided the stalls for the market to the partnership with Creative Partnerships in developing the shop. [4]

As outlined in this chapter, this 'festival' environment provided opportunities within the communities of each island (with people of all ages) to work in the marketplace and side-shows accompanying the main production. In the third and final incarnation of the Three Islands Project in Cornwall, Kneehigh collaborated with Cornwall Arts to gain their support and verification to attract and work with local businesses to sell their products at the performance venue.

> Kneehigh worked with Cornwall Arts Marketing who seconded a project manager to co-ordinate this element of the event. This person in turn worked with Creative Kernow to identify crafts people producing high quality work in Cornwall which would match with the themes of the performance: and Taste of the West to identify food suppliers who could offer high quality Cornish food on site [5]

This description of business collaborations between Kneehigh and local high-quality food suppliers displayed the initial developments of a total entertainment product and associations with Cornish tourism. The project developed at each island with different partnerships being formed locally to develop the marketplace and side-shows. Peter Boyden, in the foreword to the *Three Islands Project Evaluation 2005*, advocated that powerful cultural endeavours, such as theatre or sport, hold to unify a community. He reflected on its humanising abilities through cultural exchange, consolidating identity, culminating within this performative environment.

> When we gather together in celebration (in a theatre, a football ground or in a public space at the heart of a city), the world functions at a more human scale than when we experience it alone. One way or another, all cultures have used 'performance' to nurture and celebrate the 'stories' which form and hold our identity. [6]

This was a space allowing for 'celebration' and exchange, but also for the development of a branded environment facilitating performance, entertainment and consumerism. *The West Briton Redruth* argued that the production was 'more of a festival than a traditional theatre show', likening it to the Eden Project and used the terminology of 'brand' to compare both companies: 'In many ways it is a setting every bit as wondrous as that other Cornish brand – Eden' (Dyer 1). The dome shape of the Asylum bears more than a passing resemblance to the Eden Project constructions, with positive comparisons made as a tourist attraction. Both Kneehigh and the Eden Project developed partnerships outside Cornwall, as a way of developing their work further afield, gaining popularity and financial rewards outside the local environment. They also used their popularity to draw attention back to Cornwall and to the county's plight/struggles.

Tim Smit, co-founder of the Eden Project, has commented favourably on Kneehigh's ability to generate local and global appeal, highlighting Kneehigh as a Cornish attraction:

> Kneehigh is the champagne in the veins – heartbeat of Cornwall although rooted in the community which spawned them, their timeless imagination has an international language that brings pleasure to 'Everyman' wherever they are. [7]

Smit uses highly complementary language to describe how fundamental the company is to Cornwall. The analogy of 'champagne in the veins' in place of blood, and the 'heartbeat of Cornwall' establishes Kneehigh at the 'heart' of the county, as its cultural lifeforce. Smit is also diplomatic in his comments, with relationships between both companies previously established by workshops and training facilitated by Kneehigh.

As a 'template' for a site-specific, movable venue, the Three Islands Project offered a successful development for the Asylum. The structure of Three Islands Project performance venue was built and disassembled in three locations. As described above, this structure fostered creative and cultural relationships, 'festival' entertainment experiences Kneehigh wished to continue with further.

Plans discussing a multi-purpose performance and entertainment venue were recorded in production reports (found in the Kneehigh Archive) as early as 1998 – twelve years before the first summer season. The proposal displayed its intentions for cultural sharing, including training and experiences offered by landscape theatre, reaching new audiences who would not attend a more traditional theatre setting.[8] Gil Gillingham of the Dome Company built the Asylum, which was one of their largest projects.

> It consists of two geodesic half domes bridged by a cathedral-like fabric atrium, with a soaring, vaulted roof supported by a geometry of leaning arches. The twin half domes are built of curved, laminated timber beams (using timber from sustainable sources) and galvanised steel anchors and connectors, the arched auditorium is supported by aluminium trusses, and the entire structure is tented with acrylic-coated polyester. [9]

The *Design Project for Kneehigh Theatre* by The Dome Company emphasised the necessity for creating a flexible and adaptive space. This space would allow for Kneehigh's 'signature' performance style, generating a more intimate relationship with the audience.

> The structure must enable this style to continue. It would be a mistake to produce a structure which dictates a rigid relationship between the audience and the performance, or between the performance and the architecture. Instead, the space should be adaptable, enabling the theatre to be staged in many ways and enabling a direct relationship with outside space. [10]

This book has commented on the performance style synonymous with the Kneehigh theatrical brand, listing the elements that are commonly found within a Kneehigh show. Arguably, part of their devising/adaptation strategy, highlighted by The Dome Company, is flexibility. Kneehigh have been receptive to a range of influences; incorporating environments, stimuli, people, cultures, etc. This has been highly influential to their performance style, which is flexible, adaptive and continually changing. Skantze has also observed the fluidity and flexibility of the performance space, which can act as an invitation to explore in non-conventional ways.

> The architecture announced itself as a space apart with an area blocked off by benches for reflecting, a small garden, a conscious change in the mode of inviting bodies into a space not given, or not solely given, to commerce. [11]

The configurations of the Asylum, allowed for exploration in varied displays, art installations and stalls. The configuration of the stage space has been adapted each season, allowing for a greater freedom in set design and audience proximity. As indicated by Skantze above, the redesign and configuration of the performance space was not 'solely given to commerce' but contributed to the entertainment experience.

The Dome Company in the accompanying letter dated 4th February 2005 expressed their interest in assisting Kneehigh in 'providing a long-term mobile arts facility for Cornwall'.[12] Incidentally, Springboard Design Partnership developed an earlier proposal for the Asylum, showing the difficulties in getting the project off the ground based on the scale and cost of the project. Applications to gain Arts Council funding were rejected as the council felt that Kneehigh, as a small-scale theatre company, were not appropriate owners of the venue 'and could not show adequately how they could maintain, run, and finance the venture on an ongoing basis'[13]. This news would have been difficult for Kneehigh to receive, as it was a project with ambitions spanning many years. Inadvertently, the initial response from ACE mirrors the external barriers Kneehigh are attempting to navigate around by building the Asylum. There was no documentation within the archive that noted Kneehigh's response to this news. However, contemporary theatre companies are experienced in making applications for funding and receiving rejections.

Further justifications for the previous abandonment of this project tied in with high levels of unemployment in Cornwall. Unemployment is something Kneehigh have reflected on as a barrier to creating theatre in Cornwall. Springboard stated that the project should be given to a local builder and thus generate employment opportunities. Springboard Design Partnership is based in Bristol while The Dome Company who gained the contract for the project are locally based and have previously created structures for the Eden Project. The Cornish link with The Dome Company is obviously stronger than Springboard Design Partnership, enjoying links with the Eden Project. These shared connections would also reinforce the Cornish Tourism branding of the Asylum. Within Kneehigh's own promotional materials for the Asylum, the company presented an overview of their venue, explaining both its structure and creative ambitions.

A discussion of these plans for the Asylum is displayed on their company website in March 2009, describing their need to raise £3/4 million to build it, with funding and partnership from Cornwall County Council and the Arts Council. This provides an interesting turn of events with the Arts Council now in support and funding the project. Kneehigh acknowledge that they are close to achieving this financial target but need financial support to build the construction. This is of course met through revenue from the *Friends* scheme, business investment, and patron donations.

The first brochure for the Asylum, printed a year later in 2010, advertises for financial support for the project, with affiliations to become a supporter of Kneehigh included. The company also describe the historical inspirations behind this venture:

> The Kneehigh Asylum is truly modern in its conception and yet it is inspired by ancient building methods and rooted in circus, troubadour and folk traditions. [14]

The links between the past and present are demonstrated in the circus-style canvas structure, but as indicated above, connect with other modern Cornish attractions. Through this statement, Kneehigh is transparent in presenting and acknowledging the importance of heritage, displaying their own theatrical evolution within a theatre-style encompassing 'circus, troubadour and folk traditions'.

In an interview with *The Spectator,* Emma Rice and Mike Shepherd discussed the inspiration behind the Asylum. Rice described the tension the company felt with their success, reaching a point where they could have gone anywhere and left Cornwall, and in response, created Asylum.[15] Rice explains how Kneehigh came up with the title for their new venue:

On paper, the Asylum is a glorified and glorious purpose-designed tent. The name, Rice confesses, was 'nicked': The Asylum was a Nottingham nightclub she once frequented, where the rejects hung out, the Goths, the punks. In Kneehigh's hands, it is a space that 'feels like home and is home', where 'we can do whatever we want, with whoever we want, eat whatever we want'. It is a place of sanctuary, of refuge, with 'a little bit of madness in there, too'. [16]

Within this identification with Rice's formative years in Nottingham is a connection between the 'other' and a rebellious, subversive freedom. These are qualities Rice and Shepherd have used to describe being Cornish. They acknowledged their aspiration to be viewed as unique, to be 'other', and to pursue the freedom to express this stance. Notions of 'other' have been explored in *Tristan and Yseult* with the 'Club of the Unloved', and through *Blast*, with the 'other' represented by everyone not from Cornwall. The work of Bettelheim, exploring the search for 'self' in fairy tales, mirrors the search that Kneehigh has embarked on in their productions, in their cultural identity, but also in the conceptualisation and eventual construction of the Asylum. A place they can call home, but also a space for Kneehigh (as 'other') to belong, explore their identity, and artistic pursuits.

Mike Shepherd goes into greater detail regarding the concept of the Asylum establishing an environment conducive to creativity, presenting an observation that this is a luxury not always afforded to drama classrooms or rehearsal spaces. The paper, *The Kneehigh Creative Asylum* (Shepherd 2012*)* presents the necessity for the company's own performance space which should include air, light and colour, besides food and drink[17]. In 'Background', Shepherd illustrated the desirability for a room to create an atmosphere, describing examples of creative spaces lacking this capacity as a justification for developing their own venue. Shepherd illustrated the difficulty in being creative when the space provided is uninspiring.

The drama studio was a peripheral hut, all black, no windows, airless, the odd ripped theatre poster on its wall and a proliferation of used Blu-tac. It was quite literally rank, and we were ghettoised there. [18]

Shepherd's critique established a contemporary move away from rehearsal spaces and drama studios painted black, with many spaces providing a bright, light environment: facilitating the appearance of a 'blank canvas'. The *Kneehigh Theatre Application to the ACE National Lottery Funding Capital Programme for Equipment October 1998 Reference 98-642,* charted the construction of the Asylum as embedding the company's aims for autonomy.

The brief for the feasibility study, set out three requirements which the Company had set itself to achieve artistic autonomy;
-       to commission and operate an adaptable touring performance structure giving the Company much greater control over artistic and audience development.' [19]

Interestingly, Kneehigh lists the construction of a touring structure as a primary 'requirement' in achieving creative autonomy. Kneehigh has found inspiration from other European touring companies who have also developed touring venues (particularly Footsbarn, another Cornish theatre company who formed ten years before Kneehigh).

When touring in mainland Europe with our outdoor work we sit within a well-established popular tradition of companies creating visually spectacular work. The companies that Kneehigh take particular inspiration from are Dogtroep, Footsbarn, Archaos, and Companie Jo Bithume. [20]

Although landscape theatre has contributed to their touring work in Cornwall and the Three Islands Project in Europe, the construction of the Asylum has been a long-term goal, reinforced by similar practice by their contemporary theatrical peers.

Further justification for Kneehigh developing their own space arose from the difficulties experienced by the company when hired to lead workshops around the country in uninspiring spaces. Shepherd commented it is 'nigh on impossible to conjure innovation or inspiration in such circumstances'.[21] Likewise, Shepherd is aware that legislation and other responsibilities can impede other environments, conditioning Kneehigh's opportunities to display individuality and freedom of expression. Of course, health and safety legislation would still be observed within the Asylum. The ability to configure and reconfigure their own performance environment, as they do within the barns at Gorran Haven offers additional layers of autonomy.

Shepherd has formerly discussed an earlier factor concerning Kneehigh's desire for artistic freedom, negatively experienced from the varied perceptions of local and global audiences when performing *Tregeagle* (1989). In contrast, their local Cornish audiences were unhappy over Kneehigh's evolution from children's theatre into performance material suitable for adults, dealing with darker themes, whilst global audiences embraced this style of work. Commenting on Kneehigh's experiences of *Tregeagle*, Shepherd stated: 'It went to Edinburgh where it went down an absolute storm: we got into trouble in Cornwall because it was the first show that we've done that was obviously not particularly family-orientated'[22]. The fact that *Tregeagle* (1989) was the first show in a decade of work that was non-family orientated provides an understanding for their local audience's surprise and dislike of the work. Kneehigh's local community has experienced the company's TIE work over several years, developing artistic expectations on their work. A national and global audience (who have not experienced their earlier work in children's theatre), have no expectations, allowing for a non-biased view and response to the production. By travelling nationally and globally to perform their shows, Kneehigh used the opportunity to reinvent their artistic identity and communicate their cultural identity. The creation of Asylum allowed for similar forms of experimentation: providing a base from which to showcase new work.

Returning to the paper, *The Kneehigh Creative Asylum,* Shepherd cites Asylum as a way for the company to offer flexibility, creating a practical touring space enabling the company to work in Cornwall, 'one of the "longest" counties in the UK'[23]. The Asylum, according to Shepherd, would allow the company to travel to these communities with their own environment.

> Cornwall needs practical infrastructure to support the arts and education into the future. The Asylum run by Kneehigh, in possible partnership with Gil Gillingham and Creative Partnerships, is a tangible asset for Cornwall. In addition to the exciting educational possibilities of a specially commissioned creative space The Asylum would help address a major issue facing Kneehigh. [24]

Shepherd expressed the tensions experienced in wishing to create work for Cornwall but needing to work away from their home due to artistic demand and financial necessity. He regarded the Asylum as the solution to this dichotomy facing the company, providing them with an opportunity to produce more work in Cornwall on their own terms without other external influences. Additional benefits included working in an environment Kneehigh have shaped with full control and ownership. The flexibility of the construction allowed for transportation and matched the adaptable style of their theatrical brand. While Kneehigh were still running, The Asylum had been moved to three different locations within Cornwall, with each location providing new semiotics.

In recent years, the location at The Lost Gardens of Heligan has reinforced Kneehigh and Asylum as a tourist attraction, with options to purchase combined entry to both venues. Within my own spectatorship, the 'cultural materialism' associated with the Asylum was entwined with its physical locality. Buying the combined ticket to see a show at the Asylum and visit the gardens, I was very aware I was visiting Cornish tourist attractions, with a strong emphasis on heritage. The Lost Gardens of Heligan are themselves described as amongst the 'finest gardens in England', obscured by brambles and the outbreak of WW1.[25] In my first attendance to the Asylum, based in Heligan, I visited the gardens, and the 'market-style' restaurant area, before moving on to the Kneehigh performance area. Unlike the two seasons at the Asylum, which featured food and drink stalls within the auditorium area of the tent, the residency at The Lost Gardens of Heligan allowed food to be consumed in their restaurant, ultimately encouraging a shared leisure/hospitality experience.

The most recent Asylum venue: Carlyon Beach (St Austell), offered new associations. Part of Cornwall's tourism is connected to the coastline, with this location establishing cultural heritage associations with another facet of Cornish tourism and identity. In fact, support from the Coastal Communities Fund provided support to Kneehigh and other Cornish performers, encouraging tourism locally and 'further afield'[26]. By relocating to the beach, Kneehigh is aligning themselves with other entertainment on offer such as live music, food and drink, again evoking a 'festival-like' event, encouraging a wider audience demographic. Carlyon Beach is still close to The Lost Gardens of Heligan and the Eden Project, with Kneehigh contributing to these notable tourist attractions within the area.

The placement of Asylum, on top of the foundations of the Coliseum at Carlyon Beach (an iconic music venue opened in the 1930s and closed in 2000, before being demolished in 2015), provoked links between Cornish history, at the same time as revisiting political debate. The Coliseum was a noted music venue, attracting international artists before 'falling into disrepair' in the 1990s[27]. For many years, the venue remained derelict, causing dismay and critique amongst the local community, with the abandoned building gaining unfavourable comparisons with 'war-torn Beirut'. It created much debate within the local community, even leading to a satirised postcard featuring the Coliseum (and other dilapidated parts of St Austell) stating: 'Wish we were not here', to be sent to the then-Deputy Prime Minister, John Prescott[28]. Subsequently, long-standing plans to redevelop the site by Commercial Estates Group (CEG) had been 'put on hold' in 2016, due to Brexit.

> The result of the EU referendum introduced significant political and economic uncertainty, which makes it impossible for us to continue with the planned investment programme across our portfolio, so we have had to make some difficult decisions. [29]

Losing this development was met with mixed responses, some feeling that the plans for redevelopment were 'too excessive', dominating the local community, with others conceding the benefits the proposed development could have made to the economy[30]. This history and political context were embedded within the foundations of the Coliseum but reconfigured through the Asylum.

Diana Taylor has formerly discussed the re-categorisation and re-validation of a place, once used as a dump and abandoned by culture, now re-branded as a magical, significant place through performance. Referring to a performance of *Yo también de la rosa,* a one-act play by Emilio Carballido, in a Mexican rubbish dump, Taylor comments on the transformative powers of repertoire to invigorate a space:

> This space that has been dumped on, devalued, that transforms our most intimate objects into abject, dead things is also the space of magical transformation. Things grow in the dump; there is evidence of new life and endless possibilities for reconfiguration. [31]

Kneehigh achieved this transformation of space and place in not too dissimilar ways. They achieved this through the Asylum, and through their capacity to inhabit abandoned sites and reinvigorate them into their own world and performance environment. Performances at the Asylum were welcomed at Carlyon Beach, reinvigorating the cultural scene. Likewise, recreational areas outside the main performance environment have been incorporated, including bars, live bands and sit-down areas allowing audience members the opportunity to continue with the experience. Oddey has commented on the ability of the spectator to explore and 'read' the space, free from the artist's intended narratives.[32] Arguably, these 'free' spaces are constructed with a narrative in mind but can offer opportunities to make choices, allowing for areas of focus and consideration and re-contextualisation.

An earlier example of Kneehigh's ability to transform, yet also be inspired by a derelict location, can be seen in the production *Hells Mouth* (2000). In this production Kneehigh displayed a willingness to celebrate and support the Cornish community, working with the 'moon-crater' like holes left by the mining industry. The play written by Nick Darke, was an adaption of Sophocles *The Thebans*, developed site-specifically for the clay pits in St Austell. In addition to the local community, the local Hell's Angels bikers were also recruited to perform stunts in the clay pits; influencing the name of the play and forming relationships between disparate communities. On describing the project, *The Western Morning News* commented on the initiative set up by Kneehigh and the Clay Area Leader Project, allowing the local community the opportunity to work on the production in an area once viewed as the 'epicentre' of Cornish economy but now a derelict landscape. The general manager of Kneehigh, Julie Seyer, reflected on the potential for the creative industries to use these abandoned clay pits.

> The clay pit has got endless potential in terms of the landscape. It's a kind of ready-made theatrical experience, and we just want to say to people locally that they have a great resource here and we can help.[33]

The clay pit 'resource' was used creatively by Kneehigh. It was embedded within the play and realised within the production, utilising the skills of the local community, whilst strengthening their branded association for creating landscape theatre. The production provided opportunities for work as a way to 'help' the community, irrespective of its temporality. Interest in the area from the press (through interviews with company members and theatre reviews), drew focus on the area and its specific needs. Again, this was short-lived, and despite the intentions of Kneehigh, the issues attributed to a derelict location with social and economic deprivation were too big to resolve by this production.

The creation of the Asylum, building on Kneehigh's reputation for site-specific performance, was the realisation of the tourist 'epicentre' formerly described by Govan, Nicholson and Normington, attracting audiences to Cornwall to see Kneehigh productions and offer opportunities to buy local products. Sue Hill (former company member) reflected on Kneehigh's commitment to playing in Cornwall despite the difficulties the company faced to survive; acknowledging a lack of funding, and an inability to afford the cost of tickets.

> I think I'd like to talk about Cornwall, about Kneehigh's relationship with Cornwall? And the tension in it because it's quite hard for us to survive, financially, in Cornwall. Historically, there's been a pull on the company to perform everywhere else *but* Cornwall, because the economy is so fragile…In Cornwall it's hard because lots of people can't afford the ticket prices, and the promoters find it increasingly hard to pay the fees that we need to make work. But there's a really strong commitment from the company to keep making work in Cornwall, and I think – if anything – that's getting stronger and stronger. And it's to do with recognising that it's because we come from somewhere, and it's one of the things that makes us special. [34]

In creating the Asylum, Kneehigh was re-addressing this balance by creating affordable theatre for the county. During the summer season in 2012, ticket prices were reduced from the full price of £20 for those living in the Cornish locality and for those who booked before the summer season; with greater discounts for bookings made in April/May in contrast to those booking in June/July[35]. In doing so, Kneehigh is mindful of the economic circumstances of the county and committed to making the work accessible through affordability. 'Brand Kneehigh' and Asylum provide a space to perform, achieving their ambitions of performing locally and affordably. The construction of the Asylum has embraced the 'cultural baggage' of Cornwall, a heritage that has suffered economic loss, but sought to develop ways to improve this situation through a commitment to community. Rice in conversation with Welton elaborated on further complexities in building the Asylum.

> Kneehigh's been going for long and there was certainly a moment 5 or 6 years ago, when the work was really taking off and the opportunities for the work were threatening to shatter the company. So that was when we decided to build a tent so that it was nomadic, but also because tents are magic, aren't they? [36]

This was a very revealing comment, exposing the difficulties experienced that were effectively pulling the company in different directions. So far, the narrative of 'Brand Kneehigh', has portrayed a company following global, branded ambitions to survive financial difficulties. Cultural exchange through national and international collaborations had been successfully incorporated into Kneehigh's adaptation and devising processes, contributing positive associations to their theatrical brand. Within the reports written by the company, Kneehigh have commented on their 'global' pursuits (encouraged by ACE), providing them with financial backing to create work in Cornwall. The above statement by Rice indicated a shift, with national and international successes creating a divide within the company. Globalisation has had a negative impact on Kneehigh, with the Asylum offering unification, a centralised place for performance and their theatrical identity (in addition and separate from the Gorran Haven rehearsal barns).

Rice, in the above statement about the Asylum, underlined the 'magical' nature of performance tents. It shares similar semiotics with circus big tops, with cultural perceptions of the space and the ability to configure and re-configure. Joss Marsh described the magic inherent within a circus tent, observing the impressive 360-degree panoramic view lending itself to 3D illusions: 'The experience was no trick of mesmerism or magic carpet, but the effect of the first "panorama"...[a] 360-degree view'.[37] Marsh highlighted the qualities of a circus tent, arguably one of the first immersive performance spaces 'the spectator did not merely look at but stood within the illusion'[38]. The circus tent big top has often been described as a space that looks smaller on the outside but transforms into a vast performance arena once inside. The symbolism of circus tents, which Rice is aligning the Asylum with, has other connotations with a 'nomadic' lifestyle and travel. In this capacity, this local space can travel nationally and internationally. Even within the localism embedded within the place, a space primarily constructed to serve the county, there is a global 'mindset' allowing for temporality from the local to the global.

Spectatorship and 'Experience Economy'

Performance can trigger a spectator's own memories and reflections, in addition to shared social and cultural memories, leading them to find meaning based on experiences intrinsic to their personal history.

> Will you create narratives having to do with identity and categories of exploration by looking, listening, receiving in tandem with me, categories I seek not to define for the very reason that the contours or shapes of the land mass may create different coordinates dependent up on your own spectatorial coordinates? [39]

My 'spectatorial coordinates' shifted in the second summer season at the Asylum. By inviting friends to join me on a 'Cornish road trip', the emphasis of my spectatorship grew, inadvertently engaging in the Asylum as a broader 'product' than simply a theatre performance, into 'a Kneehigh branded short-break' or 'package holiday'. This is where my use of Skantze's 'itinerant' model developed into an experiential archive (influenced by Pine and Gilmore's definitions of an 'experience economy'), illustrating a turning point in my own branded spectatorship. This shift allowed me to engage in 'Brand Kneehigh' in an immersive, undiluted way, an unanticipated yet highly beneficial outcome. We consumed food and drink within the Asylum (and later in the Gardens of Heligan), purchased programmes and original prints by the artist and illustrator Daryl Waller, attended gigs and dances both pre and post-show.

Over the years, as the Asylum and its configurations changed, so did mine and my friends' ambitions for our 'road trip'. We sought additional activities specific to the location and consumed local Cornish cuisine. Skantze considered memories provoked through eating a dinner pre-show before attending *Mahabharata* in a theatre in New York, discussing racial stereotypes, tensions and associations experienced when eating fried chicken (Skantze 111). I found that dinner at the Asylum (later outsourced to the Gardens of Heligan) triggered similar connections: the food, provided by local companies, appeared to wrestle with its own stereotypes, through providing pasties and cider but also organic and vegan options. However, I would argue that the consumption of vegan and organic foods is stereotypical of those employed and interested in the arts (of which I qualify to some of these descriptors), in contrast to traditional Cornish foods.

> I cannot deny a form of identity or identification persists in what can so quickly become a cliched symbol of national affiliation: so is food, the enduring sense that how we eat and what we eat does make for a sturdy kinship. [40]

As observed by Skantze, the act of eating becomes a part of spectatorship, which can create a sense of 'kinship' within this shared experience, as well as being part of a branded entertainment package. I felt a sense of connection and authenticity in the experience, especially when consuming traditional Cornish food and drink. This is not unlike tourists wishing to enjoy local cuisine on holiday to gain a genuine, specific, local experience. The pursuit of authenticity grew between me and my companions in setting the challenge of consuming a Cornish cream tea, Cornish Pasty, Cornish Cider and/or Cornish Ice-cream, 'branding' this 'The Three C's'. Kneehigh's relocation to the Gardens of Heligan made it easier to achieve all three or four of the challenges in one sitting - if you had the constitution for it! Just as Skantze has observed food and associated stereotypes experienced pre-performance, their connections can also be problematic in the 'reading' of a performance. My 'reading' of *Blast,* discussed in Chapter 3, generated 'tension' when considering the traditional Cornish food served pre-show, satirically discussed as problematic for the County. My observations, through experiences at the Asylum, illustrates how evocative food can be in association with cultural identity and place. This became something that my 'road trip' friends and I actively engaged with each season of the Asylum.

Skantze established that many triggers, unique to both the performance and the spectator, can generate these connections.

> Not an individual agency but one that can be provoked by an atmosphere the theatre creates temporarily through producing associations in the spectator, a potential coordinate of endowing agency according to what individual makes of her or his reception. [41]

Spectatorial connections can occur through a dialogue between audience members, but also from an internal monologue within the spectator. Skantze described this as a spectator 'vertigo', provoking the spectator to question what they feel during the performance (both immediately and retrospectively). This 'vertigo' can incorporate considerations from a materialistic viewpoint (Gilmore and Pine) and appraise theatre in economic terms. As stated by Skantze:

> Exchanging the theatre space can at times replicate a gift economy, the close of the transaction comes to hyper marketing consumer exchange, the more the spectator becomes the assessor of his or her stocks. [42]

This critique by Skantze is symptomatic of other products and brands and validates the global lens through which I have experienced and examined Kneehigh's performances. Notions of value and 'worth' are tensions that occur when considering performance in neoliberalist terms. Skantze also raised this as an important question: 'Is the spectacle performing well enough, that my investment in the share of a ticket is worth it?'[43]. Pine and Gilmore's 'experience economy' would ensure this tension was appeased. Through the act of engaging in a memorable experience; the investment would be worth it, encouraging audiences to come back and see the show again or continue to follow work by the company. I experienced a form of spectatorial 'vertigo' as a result of attending every Asylum summer season from 2010. Immersing myself in 'Brand Kneehigh', attending performances, discussing their work at conferences, and using the archive, questioned my ability to enjoy the work on its own merits. This 'brand fatigue' experienced is a potential consequence for many companies who follow the philosophy of repeat custom by inadvertently triggering the opposite to their intended outcome. Likewise, 'brand fatigue' can be triggered when a brand fails to introduce new components to invigorate and reinvent the product. In terms of the Asylum, part of the variable components featured its location and auditorium structure. It was important for Kneehigh to adapt the Asylum for each summer season, providing a new experience with different productions. Arguably, it was not enough for the productions to be changed as the Asylum (following the ideologies of leisure brands) encompasses a broader notion of entertainment. In fact, it is testament to Kneehigh's ambitions in branding and the Asylum as an integral part of 'Brand Kneehigh', that their venue is regarded in these terms. As a critique within my spectatorship, I found the Asylum experience at The Lost Gardens of Heligan post-2016, too familiar. It was during this time I considered it necessary to take a break from experiencing the brand at the Asylum in order to 'recalibrate' as a spectator.

Pine and Gilmore's ideas on branding and experience outlined the potential for specifically designed environments to strengthen the possibility of a client making a purchase, encouraging consumer loyalty and 'repeat custom'[44]. Following this argument, the 'experiences' offered by

Kneehigh within their specifically created environment. The Asylum, could also encourage brand loyalty. Areas of the auditorium decorated in the style of the set allowed audience members to freely explore, with a range of merchandise available. According to Pine and Gilmore (1998), the purchasing of such goods or memorabilia from these shows can act as an immersion and brand reinforcement by continuing the experience for the audience member long after the live production has ended. These mementoes can act as a tangible artefact, as 'selling memorabilia associated with an experience is one approach to extending an experience'[45]. These products may not be any different from mementoes offered by other theatres or producing houses. However, Kneehigh created an experience with a strong link between the performance environment, the production itself and the products people can buy.

Kneehigh's use of 'universal' themes exploring love and loss, coupled with their exploration of classic myths and legends were transparent in these experiences, forming connections between past and present shows, displaying their brand associations. Just as the Disney Corporation established its own signature style for its treatment of fairy tales, reinforced by their self-contained environment and accompanying products, Kneehigh presented its own darker re-imaginings in the Asylum. The 'Brand Kneehigh' experience is strengthened by selling commodities unified to represent these core values and themes.

The experiences in the Asylum provided the opportunity to explore this created or imagined world devised by Kneehigh. This world did not end with the productions seen at the Asylum but continued beyond the world of the play. In relation to specific productions, art installations, separate themed areas, locally sourced food and drink, merchandise, gigs and dances as well as a bar area, these were invented and reinvented in each yearly reincarnation of the Asylum. Peggy Phelan indicated that after the act of performance, nothing else remains, with the onus on the audience to use up its resources before it goes to waste.

> The idea that performance art, when it happens is non-reproductive and is wholly consumed: '... in performance art spectatorship there is an element of consumption: there are no leftovers, the gazing spectator must try to take everything'. [46]

The theories of Pine and Gilmore contrast with this view, implying that experiences are consumed beyond the world of the main production. This can heighten the experience further and allow it to live on. I disagree with Phelan, situating myself alongside Pine and Gilmore, sharing commonalities with Pearson with his 'imperfect archaeology', re-establishing the notion of the experiential archive. The 'leftovers' Phelan stated as non-existent are contained within several performance artefacts, some are traditional paraphernalia associated with attending a performance, whilst others included official and unofficial recordings.

Regarding my experience of the 'present' given out as an invitation to *Cymbeline*, Kneehigh like other theatre companies, create material given to audience members as a memento of the theatrical experience. This will be separate from merchandise purchased before or after the show, often free, and the presentation may be embedded within the performance itself. Examples of this 'memento material' can be seen in Kneehigh's, *Quicksilver* (2002) with bags featuring miniature mining equipment; Punchdrunk's, *A Drowned Man* (2013) with masks worn during the performance given out to audience members at selected shows, and Les Enfants, *Alice in Wonderland* (2015) and *Alice Through the Looking Glass* (2017) provided a printed playing card associated with material from the show as a souvenir. What is illustrated in offering this memento to the audience is an awareness of the strong association between object/artefact and memory of an experience. This association has been exploited by theatre companies to strengthen the memory of the show, incorporating a positive connotation through a free gift, with the incentive of repeat custom. By developing this 'gift' and presenting it during the performance, the appeal of the authenticity of a 'unique' experience is strengthened. As an audience member, you feel you have taken part in something 'original' and specific to the company and the time of performance. This feeling is in contrast to a globally mass-produced and repeated product – irrespective of whether this is the case.

The Red Shoes (2001 and 2010)

My viewing of *The Red Shoes* at Asylum in 2010, was the first production I had experienced in the venue and instigated my combined 'experiential' spectatorship via the Asylum and the Kneehigh archive. *The Red Shoes* was an extremely important production within the company's history, charting a shifting point in Kneehigh's national and international success and establishing Rice's success as a director, prefiguring Rice's role as artistic director. Appropriately, this was one of the shows revised for the opening of Asylum, realised in the 'circus-like' space with simplicity in its staging and costumes.

In terms of Kneehigh's theatrical style, *The Red Shoes* provided examples of the company's ability to use simple production elements to create a timeless, broad global appeal within the production. This production toured China, in the municipality of Shanghai and the capital city, Beijing. According to the accompanying British Council's report written by Rice, the production was positively received. Rice would have a vested interest in highlighting the benefits of this tour in this evaluative document. Rice also confirmed the important educational exchange work produced as a product of the tour: 'We have made links and friendships with like-minded Chinese artists and have enjoyed meeting and teaching exceptional students in both cities [Shanghai and Beijing]'[47]. Rice indicated that further work and connections between both parties were needed to achieve a greater understanding of the Chinese culture, particularly regarding censorship of live performance and Chinese Theatre's preoccupation with Stanislavskian theatre.

> We were approached by Nick Yu from Shanghai about a possible co-production in the future, using half Chinese, half English actors and a Kneehigh creative team. We will be following up this possibility with email contact and a continued friendship. [48]

Although Rice has not developed this cultural exchange further during her time with Kneehigh, Rice indicated the opportunity to shift international perceptions of theatre, presenting a theatrical style which included Brechtian influences (amongst other elements).

In the reprised version of *The Red Shoes* in 2010, Brechtian theatrical elements were used in performance, including; direct address to the audience, placards (indicating objects and places), a minimal set, and a semiotic use of props. The combined effect of these elements generated a non-time and location specificity, providing a contemporary relevance for the story; further supported by the selection of modern props and costumes (including clogs and y-front underpants). The selection of props and use of placards provoked comedic responses and associations from me as a spectator. Despite my initial surprise over the eponymous red shoes portrayed in this incarnation as red clogs, the shift in my own perceptions allowed for this congruence to be replaced with new connections. In other representations I have encountered, the red shoes presented have included; ballet shoes, stilettos, and in the case of *The Wizard of Oz,* sequinned heels. Implicit within these examples is an aesthetic of desirability embedded with the social and cultural context of the original tale. In my spectatorship of this tale, I have associated; desire, power, freedom, skill, beauty, temptation and domination as attributive themes. Initially, the cultural symbolism of a pair of red clogs did not offer the same agency or desirability. However, through Rice's direction, I formed new connotations. The red clogs in this production, through their functionality in folk dancing, were well placed to portray the power of 'the dance'. Unlike the graceful representation offered by ballet shoes, the choice of clogs effectively portrayed the danger of the 'cursed' footwear: the 'stomp' sounds made by the clogs matched the jerky, uncontrolled movements of The Girl. Likewise, Patrycja Kujawska's physicality as The Girl, wearing these shoes for the first time, convincingly established their desirability and sexual appeal. A scene featuring a flirtation between The Girl and The Soldier transformed my associations of these shoes from unflattering 'clomping' footwear to an 'earthy', yet exciting sensuality.

Reviews contained in *The Red Shoes Press Report Edinburgh Festival (2001)*, indicated Kneehigh's notoriety as a company who focus on the universal and fundamental themes within classic folk and fairy tales. Several reviews for this production argued that the company had returned to the 'original' and darker version of the story. Whilst other reviewers reflected on the bloody and violent retelling of this tale, far removed from Victorian or even more recent Disney reinvention. One press cutting underlined Kneehigh's ability (and theatrical brand) to fuse physical theatre, entertainment and the grotesque nature of these tales into a highly successful production.

> The fusion of folk fable and physical theatre is not an easy one, but Kneehigh Theatre pull it off with style, proving glorious, grotesque entertainment for anyone who likes their fables to be dark, extravagant and filled with funky moves. [49]

The production was described as suiting all age ranges: not too frightening for children, but also 'thought-provoking enough for sophisticated adults', retaining the darkness of the source material whilst appealing to a range of audience members and age groups[50]. This view is shared by press cuttings compiled by Thom Dibdin in *The Stage Edinburgh Preview 2001* (listed as one of the top ten shows in Fringe 2001). The production is again described as the 'dark version of Hans Christian Anderson story', and despite its darker undertones, still appeals to a broad demographic[51]. Considering my own viewing of *The Red Shoes*, the production did not shy away from exploring darker issues on stage, doing so imaginatively. Red ribbon was used in staging the scene in which The Girl has her feet cut off by The Butcher. Although not as visceral as fake blood or paint, Kneehigh were able to fully present the gorier aspects of the scene, provoking both humour and repulsion from the audience.

Fig. 6-4. *Global Cornwall,* C. Trenchfield (2012)

Global Cornwall

Kneehigh has been willing to engage in political and social discussion about Cornwall, using a number of productions to share their ideas and arguments. However, an opportunity to directly communicate with an audience occurred during *Global Cornwall* (2012). This was a one-off event, chaired by Chris Hines MBE[1], featuring performances by Linton Kwesi Johnson (a noted Jamaican born artist and poet), Kurt Jackson (environmental artist from Dorset), Holly Holden (a Cornish based musician), and Seth Hampshire (a poet from Truro). In addition to performances and presentations of their artwork, participants in the event were encouraged to highlight their Cornish identity in contrast to their global experiences and discuss Cornish and global issues. The resulting analysis formed another layer of meaning, used as part of the discursive process, contributing to the contextual and associative 'reading' of the Asylum. However, the event was unsuccessful in addressing local and global concerns coherently. Kneehigh's performance work, particularly the production *Blast* (2010), was much more thought-provoking and sophisticated in its response. Use of humour and emotion presented the very real difficulties and dilemmas the main protagonists were caught in, relating

---

[1] Chris Hines MBE was the co-founder and director of Surfer against Sewage from 1990 till 2000. He has worked as the Sustainability Director at the Eden Project for 5 years and was awarded an MBE in 2006 for 'services to the environment'.

them to the individual and allowing for a personal and multi-layered reflection.

Kneehigh has previously defended their right to take part in political discussions within *Kneehigh Report on the Debates on Cornwall and its Future November 1998*. Opening sections of the report illustrated justifications for engaging in a political and cultural debate.

> Why should a theatre company host a series of public fora? Kneehigh is of and from Cornwall, we care about where its future lies, and we hope to be part of that future. The people who live here are our inspiration and primary audience - it is vital that we hear their fears and aspirations to inform our work. [52]

This statement presented a passion for the place and its people, irrespective of how 'successful' Kneehigh deemed these events to be by participants and outsiders alike. Introducing a political symposium established Kneehigh's desire to offer direct commentary whilst also changing the functionality of the Asylum. Skantze has observed the capacity for a performance space to allow for political and social analysis, placing the spectator on 'a metaphorical map where the coordinates do actually combine into interpretation'[53]. Knowles highlighted the broader impact a performance event can have, commenting on the influence this can have within a range of areas:

> Meaning is ultimately produced in the theatre through audiences' lived experience of the entire theatrical event, and the social, cultural, political impact of the theatrical event lives in the ways in which that experience is knitted into the social fabric of the day. [54]

Kneehigh's statement in the *Debates on Cornwall* report, and eventual *Global Cornwall* event, acknowledges theatre's ability to be integrated into the 'social fabric of the day', as illustrated by Knowles' observation. Recent discussions have been varied, relating to those within the public eye and their ability to speak about global, moral and ethical issues. Such argumentation has been raised against performers and speeches made at awards events (such an example can be seen in a critique on Joaquin Phoenix's *Oscars* speech in 2020 discussing the global meat industry). Although Kneehigh may not be immediately associated within the same artistic 'circles', the company and respective Artistic Directors are still public figures, 'enjoying' publicity and a platform to discuss a range of topics. Within their statement, Kneehigh displayed a duty to expose the difficulties Cornwall faces, raising questions pertaining to its future.

It is important to stress that Cornwall as a 'place' is varied and multifaceted, reduced in its diversity for the *Debates on Cornwall* report. The report generalised Cornwall and its cultural identity on a macro-level, simplifying the notion of Cornwall to strengthen and simplify its meaning. What can be appreciated is a desire to start a political/cultural dialogue. Dorney suggested that performance studies and archival research are similar: 'Both are concerned with acts of creation; with witnessing and the effects of witnessing; with memory and the preservation and memory and with appraisal' (Dorney 8). Such an appraisal of *Global Cornwall* and the above statements made by Kneehigh in sharing their political voice displayed multifaceted layers; because of their commitment to Cornwall and localisation, intensified by their willingness to engage with a political debate. Likewise, 'creation, witnessing, memory, preservation and appraisal' are present in the 'experiential archive' described in this chapter.

By hosting *Global Cornwall,* Kneehigh were openly working with international artists to be more globally inclusive, establishing the event as an act of provocation for political and social developments. Taken from the Hall for Cornwall website (a place advertising cultural events in the county), the following was displayed to promote *Global Cornwall* (2012):

> Politics and debate: In a space dedicated to freedom of thought, innovation, irreverence and challenge, we consider tension and change, and how it can help progress. With music, comedy, poetry, food and drink; we also welcome debate and questioning as we explore why we should care and how we can make a difference to the world around us. Do the people in positions of power remember they are working for us all? Do they realise that we are watching? Does accountability and responsibility resonate in the inner conscience when making decisions, on our behalf? Come into the belly of the beast, light or reignite your fire, take to the soapbox, join in the debate. Theatre is all about provocation and passion, let us take this moment to look outwards… with optimism. [55]

The event was Kneehigh's direct engagement with their own global debate, defining Asylum as a 'safe space' offering freedom and creativity. It is a space that provided the company with the platform to discuss the complexities of globalism and their place within it.

The questions posed in the above statement comment on power, indicating an imbalance created by those in positions of authority. These provocations underpinned negative connotations of globalisation, highlighting a domineering power deciding on behalf of a subjugated group. These are views expressed within localisation, providing a counterpoint to global forces. The terms within the statement 'they' and 'we' generated the tensions described, asserting a difference in stance between the two parties.

It can be assumed that 'they' are authority figures with 'power' to make decisions affecting Kneehigh (and Cornwall), outside the Cornish locality and with national or international scope. 'We' identified Kneehigh Theatre; those invited to the event, and audience members in attendance. Likewise, the 'we' also included the locality of Cornwall and those who may not be Cornish but shared similar artistic and political visions.

Kneehigh encouraged further provocation by stating: 'Do the people in positions of power remember they are working for us all? Do they realise that we are watching?'.[56] The statements had a political activist tone, mirroring the arguments of anti-globalists and the fears expressed by those in defence of localisation. It was an active response to readdressing power and focus from the global to the local. The assertion that 'we' are watching implied that 'they' are being scrutinised, while this power imbalance still occurs. The company tried to instigate provocation by questioning: 'Does accountability and responsibility resonate in the inner conscience when making decisions, on our behalf?'.[57] This comment addressed opinions on Cornwall and its frustrations at being governed nationally. It attacked the 'they' identified in this statement, declaring a response from their 'conscience' over decisions affecting the localised, and powerless 'we'. Concluding with an invitation to 'take the soapbox' and join the debate, they are aware that doing so evokes both 'passion and provocation', with optimism and an ambition to look 'outwards'. Considering the theories of globalisation in Chapter 1, global advocates would perceive this statement as 'outward-looking' affirming a global pull or 'global mindset'. Arguably, despite localised ideals, a global framework is the only strategy to communicate and negotiate within society.

Although the debate could not unpack the intricacies of Cornwall's (or Kneehigh's) place within the world, they engaged with this discussion with an earnest ambition to share ideas and opinions. As part of the research exploring both the Kneehigh Archive and the Asylum (as part of my spectatorship and experiential archive), I attended *Global Cornwall*, finding it to be mixed and somewhat confused in its purpose. Its advertised function was to showcase Cornish talent (intermixed with international artists), inviting them to perform and reflect on their experiences of Cornwall. The audience was engaged with an open debate, posing and attempting to answer questions on globalisation and Cornwall's relationship with this dichotomy. As an audience member, I found the responses tokenistic and superficial. I concede my research into globalisation exacerbated this at the time of attending the event. The event failed to ignite the political debate outlined in the promotional material; but provided the opportunity for it to take place.

Globalisation has many implications: one concerns the criticism of capitalism as a system no longer fit for purpose. Leslie Sklair underpinned key areas in which capitalist globalisation negatively impacts society: 'Capitalist globalisation cannot provide the conditions for most people on the planet to have satisfying lives and alternatives to capitalist globalisation are urgently required'[58]. This statement displayed the difficulty the event encountered in generating a debate that offered solutions and ambitions for the future. Many people in attendance at *Global Cornwall* could identity with Sklair's statement, but despite the necessity for an alternative to globalisation, one has so far failed to materialise. The immensity of the global question proved too complex to be resolved at this event. These are difficult ideologies to unpack and are at the core of how we live today. Returning to my opinions of the *Global Cornwall*, it is commendable that Kneehigh, feeling affected by these factors, wished to discuss them in a discursive and exploratory endeavour; however, the resulting discussion was superficial and ill-equipped to deal with globalism.

The Asylum and the 'experiential world'

During an extensive career, Kneehigh have contended with homogenising influences of developing a global theatrical product. With these influences, Kneehigh have afforded themselves the opportunity to have full control of the environment and lifestyle entertainment product through the Asylum. Brands such as Nike, McDonalds, Disney etc., according to Naomi Klein in *No Logo* (2010) become so successful, they have the funds and ambitions to create product diversity, but also expansive environments or 'towns' built to reinforce their identity. Examples such as Disney's development into Disneyland and Disneyworld are mirrored by companies like Nike, with Niketown on Oxford Street, London, and M&M world in Times Square New York and London. Anti-globalists (addressing negative traits of globalisation), including Klein's research, underlined the possible insidious motives and power behind a brand overtaking large spaces with their own 'towns' and 'worlds'. Global sceptics observed branded companies overpowering consumers with their products and company ethos.

Klein described the creation of a branded environment and experience as synergy, which reinforced the brand and product experience in an 'integrated branded loop'.[59] She continued by stating that 'Disney and Mattel have always known this - now everyone else is learning too.'[60] This business strategy has facilitated the rise of the 'one stop shop' philosophy; simplifying purchasing decisions by housing everything under one roof. It should be stated that Kneehigh and Asylum does not follow this strategy completely. The entertainment with associated products were Kneehigh's, the environment was themed from shows past and present; however, the food and drink were provided by other suppliers and brands. However, parallels can be seen between McDonalds supplying their own food while forming associations with Coca-Cola to provide beverages. In most, if not all branded 'worlds', partnerships are formed to enable an offering of a range of products and services.

Anti-globalists are cynical about 'brand's' unregulated control to create these environments, also commenting on aggressive marketing campaigns dominating public spaces, making the experience of these branded campaigns unavoidable. However, Kneehigh's reasons behind wishing to create such an environment appeared to be artistic rather than purely economic. Companies like Nike, M&M's and Disney are driven towards creating these 'worlds' and 'towns' out of a desire to engage a consumer's attention and sensory experience whilst obliterating any other competition; extending the range and power of their brand. Pine and Gilmore theorised in *The Experience Economy (1998)* that businesses which generate experiences, elevate their products from commodities to services that consumers are happy paying more money to enjoy as 'consumers value experiences more highly'[61]. The above 'valued' experience is described in *The Asylum* brochure where Kneehigh give an example on how this venue will facilitate 'Brand Kneehigh' as a complete entertainment product.

> Imagine what a night in the Kneehigh Asylum might include: top international companies; film showings; fantastic exhibitions; ear tickling gigs; excellent food and drink, as well as Kneehigh shows both old and new. After The Red Shoes we could dance the night away. If the show were Tristan and Yseult we'd all take part in the karaoke of the unloved! We could have a tea dance like you've never known it with Brief Encounter – ballroom, banburys and balloons! Or bring the whole family and eat homemade pizza before Rapunzel! [62]

Just as Kneehigh had created a village for *The Very Old Man with Enormous Wings* containing both the performances and markets selling a range of products, the Asylum offered a more fully formed creation of this lifestyle entertainment project. As perceived in the above quotation, a few of those activities have already been achieved, whilst others, such as the film showings and tea dances yet to be realised. They may still prove to be aspirational for the future, with Kneehigh growing their product and the environment of Asylum to allow for multiple activities to take place.

Brands such as Disney also have an environment or 'world' that allows for participants or consumers to experience unique products simultaneously. Pine and Gilmore argued that environments or 'experiences' should be engaging to keep consumer interest. They predicted that consumers will demand more unique experiences and will look 'in new and different directions for more unusual experiences'[63]. Although written in the late nineties, Pine and Gilmore indicated the current theatrical environment allowing for theatre companies like Kneehigh (Punchdrunk, DotDotDot and Les Enfant Terrible) to create an entertainment space that audience members can explore and submerge themselves in, contrasting with a more traditional performance atmosphere.

In *The Guardian: G2*, Kneehigh discussed the touring ambitions of the Asylum that can present Kneehigh productions in 'urban car parks, wastelands, cliff tops and fields'.[64] These plans would not only reprise past productions but re-inject life into derelict and overlooked spaces. Kneehigh have an established experience of doing this, through their use of landscape theatre, transforming specific locations, regenerating them for their productions. In *Pandora's Box* (2002), the company created 'site sympathetic staging' individualistic to the venue.

> The installation for the piece has been designed individually for each venue and comprises 16 tonnes of specially created rubble, which covers the entire stage. Two eight-foot chandeliers hang from the roof, as does a massive sheet which forms the backdrop for pre-recorded video projection. [65]

Specificity to the site was addressed in *Hell's Mouth*. Kneehigh extend this notion of individuality beyond a location's physicality to embrace its history, as seen in the production *Quicksilver* in reference to the Carnglaze Caverns and mining.

Pine and Gilmore cite creating an environment to immerse your clients as being the most desirable format in shaping a successful experience. The environment can eliminate any negative cues that may be evident in a pre-existing environment, inventing a purer form of immersion. Everything contained in the confines of the environment is shaped by the company, making a much more unique and less mundane experience. My experiences of the summer seasons at Asylum in 2010 to 2016 have been multi-dimensional and sensory events. Theatre shows, gigs and debating events contained artwork/photography displays, dances, food and drink within the Asylum under the Kneehigh brand umbrella. One such example featured Kneehigh holding a bar and disco after the production *Midnight's Pumpkin* (2012). This post show entertainment continued until midnight with Cornish and Somerset ales and ciders sold for refreshment. As described by Pine and

Gilmore, this provided an opportunity for the experience to 'live on', generating associative memories.

One of the fundamental elements of Pine and Gilmore's theories of the 'experience economy', is the success of the experience to repeat custom for a brand. 'Brand Kneehigh' has effectively established this through their theatrical/performance style. However, the Asylum offered an additional experience for the brand, based on their own created 'world'. All brands use imagery and associations to make their product more appealing, however the notion of lifestyle brands, as discussed by Legrain, are much more immersive with the need to dominate the consumers' experiences and be transformative of the consumer's purchasing habits and way of life. Pine and Gilmore (1998) described the benefits a business can enjoy if they create an environment or experience that creates brand loyalty. Through this created immersive environment, repeat custom is generated that grabs their attention: 'Occurring over a period of time, staged experiences required a sense of place to entice guests to spend more time engaged in the offering.[66]

Pine and Gilmore advocated that businesses, in order to generate sales for their goods and commodities, must go beyond providing services for consumers and create an experience. The above description of Asylum concurs with Pine and Gilmore's statement by providing a multi-sensory experience. Kneehigh manifest this affirmation of brand through their own environment: emphasis is placed on positive cues reinforcing their brand, eliminating negative cues detracting from the intended experience. A successful experience that is staged correctly should generate repeat custom as 'it's very design invites you to enter and to return again and again' (Pine and Gilmore 43).

Kneehigh offered a unique opportunity, like other companies with a stationary home, to 'return to again and again' (mirroring the ideas of repeat custom by Pine and Gilmore), enjoying novel experiences in a location that is their own.

> We start this journey in Cornwall and our planning for the next three years will see us return here. Cornwall is our HOME. [67]

There is a relevance that this journey into a branded environment started in Cornwall, a place they assert as their home. The statement is a message to this community, underlining in capitals the importance of this 'HOME'. It provided a strong stance against criticism on their national and international creative endeavours, reinforcing their commitment to Cornwall. The subtext for Kneehigh's need to outline Cornwall as their home illustrated the tensions explored in this book of being caught between local and global interests. This was the dichotomy that provoked their 'message' that

Cornwall is home and they were returning to this place despite their national and global projects.

The Asylum as a 'solution'

Kneehigh demonstrated a desire to create work for Cornwall and have been transparent about the difficulties encountered financially in doing this. The emergence of the Asylum fulfilled their creative ambitions, taking into consideration the global and financial influences drawing their production work away from the county. The Asylum has been a way of developing a space conducive to creativity and experimentation which has been missing in other theatrical environments. Likewise, it was a space allowing them the opportunity to share political concerns and engage in debate. Within this chapter they have been likened them to other brands, paralleling their development of 'worlds' in a similar capacity to Disneyworld or Nike Town, ensuring control over the consumer's surroundings and purchasing options. The Kneehigh brand and Asylum are linked, producing a popular brand displaying product diversity and allowing for creative autonomy in their own environment. My own experiences of 'Brand Kneehigh' were intensified during my visits to the Asylum. Surrounded by their own performance and entertainment environment I was fully immersed. However, variations of the brand have still been encountered at other venues (such as BAC, the Lyric Hammersmith and the National Theatre). I found the brand experience to be much stronger within the Asylum and intensified further through its Cornish locality. Just as Klein has reflected on brand synergy in *No Logo*, the environment allowed for interconnection between the products and performances available. This generated a unique, individual 'experience', strengthening the brand through its product diversity and availability. Through well-chosen locally sourced businesses and products, a greater connection with Cornish culture and identity contributed to this experience within the Asylum. Arguably, the uniqueness of the Asylum, in comparison with other venues housing Kneehigh productions, allowed the support and integration of Cornish products in their production and venue facilities.

Although this chapter has made comparisons with other branded environments to create an environment to strengthen 'Brand Kneehigh' and encourage repeat custom, Kneehigh were not driven by the same economic ambitions or philosophies. As stated within company reports and interviews with Shepherd and Rice, the Asylum allowed for a greater control over their creativity and an opportunity to work for their local community. Because of the flexibility of the venue, the Asylum could be moved and set up in different locations (utilising the potential for different configurations). This is born out of a creative ambition, allowing for a collaborative partnership more in keeping with cultural exchange than homogenous globalisation. In relation to the production *The Umbrellas of Cherbourg*, consideration of financial 'success' in contrast with the perceived 'value' of a creative pursuit/endeavour is pertinent to the debate on globality. What is abandoned and what is kept, based on perceived 'importance' describes globalisation, but presents Kneehigh's own value system through the creation of the Asylum. The company's focus in serving their own 'local' ambitions has not been homogenised in favour of solely making money and appealing to a global market. The Asylum provided Kneehigh with a local platform to fulfil their creative objectives, whilst refining their brand identity and attracting a global audience to their Cornish locality. This philosophy builds on Littlewood's and Price's 'Fun Palace', providing culture and entertainment for the community. Just as national and international successes were threatening to 'shatter' the company, the Asylum offered stability within their local environment.

Has the Asylum provided the 'solution' to the tensions Kneehigh cited and defined as the narrative found within the Kneehigh Archive? In response to this question, the Asylum provided the company with a chance to be both epic (global) and down to earth (local) and offered the chance to return to their roots of outdoor theatre. Although I indicated that the company can be both local and global through the Asylum, is debatable whether the incarnation of the Asylum 'resolved' these issues. In fact, these factors proved too immense to be settled, and as my discussions in the conclusion to this book presenting Kneehigh's response to the Brexit referendum in 2016, and closure induced by the Covid pandemic reveal, this is a debate that will continue. The Asylum allowed the company the opportunity to escape these complexities through the creation of their own world for nearly a decade. In this space the needs of their local community, ambitions of global collaboration and redefining their cultural identity were able to co-exist harmoniously. In addition, Asylum was used as a venue to look 'outwardly' into a global arena; provided a safe environment with their own financial income, and a platform from which they discussed both Cornwall's and Kneehigh's place in the world.

Notes

---

[1] *Three Islands Project Evaluation Report 2005.*
[2] *This is Cornwall*, "Hayle Hosts Kneehigh", 4th August 2005. Pg-25.

[3] Parker, S. "Tales of fish and fire, wolves and water", *Western Morning News*, published 18/6/02.

[4] *Three Islands Project Hayle, Penwith, Cornwall,* "A Very Old Man with Enormous Wings – Evaluation Report", 2005, Kneehigh Theatre. Pg-21.

[5] *Three Islands Project Hayle, Penwith, Cornwall,* "A Very Old Man with Enormous Wings – Evaluation Report", 2005, Kneehigh Theatre. Pg-12.

[6] *Three Islands Project Hayle, Penwith, Cornwall,* "A Very Old Man with Enormous Wings – Evaluation Report", 2005, Kneehigh Theatre. Appendix 8.

[7] *Three Islands Project* "A Very Old Man with Enormous Wings" Report, 2003, Kneehigh Theatre & Wildworks. Pg-6.

[8] *Three Islands Project Evaluation Report 2005.*

[9] Shepherd, M. and Rice, E. *Kneehigh Theatre, The Asylum Summer Season 2010,* Kneehigh Archive Falmouth University. 2010.

[10] The Dome Company, *Design Project,* 2005.

[11] Skantze, P.A. *Itinerant Spectator*, Punctum Books, New York, 2013. Pg-219.

[12] The Dome Company, *Design Project,* 2005. *Letter to Kneehigh.*

[13] Springboard Design Partnership, *The Mobile Theatre* 2.

[14] Shepherd, M. and Rice, E. *Kneehigh Theatre, The Asylum Summer Season 2010,* Kneehigh Archive Falmouth University. 2010.

[15] Feaver, J. *The Spectator*, "Magical mystery tour: Jane Feaver goes behind the scenes with Kneehigh, a theatre company with an international reach that remains resolutely close to its Cornish roots", published July 23rd 2011. Pg-1.

[16] Feaver, J. *The Spectator*, "Magical mystery tour: Jane Feaver goes behind the scenes with Kneehigh, a theatre company with an international reach that remains resolutely close to its Cornish roots", published July 23rd 2011. Pg-2.

[17] Shepherd, M. *The Kneehigh Creative Asylum*, Kneehigh Archive Falmouth University. 2012. Pg-1.

[18] Shepherd, M. *The Kneehigh Creative Asylum*, Kneehigh Archive Falmouth University. 2012. Pg-1.

[19] Kneehigh Theatre. *Kneehigh Theatre Application to the Arts Council of England National Lottery Funding Capital Programme for Equipment October 1998 Reference 98-642*, Kneehigh Theatre. Section 4.

[20] *The Kneehigh Plan 1997-2000*, Kneehigh Theatre. Pg-20.

[21] Shepherd, M. *The Kneehigh Creative Asylum*, Kneehigh Archive Falmouth University. 2012. Pg-3.

[22] Smelt, M. *Interview with Mike Shepherd and Maurice Smelt*, Kneehigh Archive, Recorded at Morrab Library, published 21st March 2000. Pg-5.

[23] Shepherd, *The Kneehigh Creative Asylum.* Pg-3.

[24] Shepherd, *The Kneehigh Creative Asylum.* Pg-6.

[25] *The Lost Gardens of Heligan,* <https://www.heligan.com>

[26] Hards, S. "Kneehigh's Asylum at Carlyon Bay praised for boosting economy", *Cornwall Live*, 13th September 2019.

[27] Hards, S. "The inside story of iconic music venue Cornwall Coliseum three years after it was demolished", *Cornwall Live*, 8th April 2018.

[28] Hards, S. "The inside story of iconic music venue Cornwall Coliseum three years after it was demolished", *Cornwall Live*, 8th April 2018.

[29] Hards, S. "The inside story of iconic music venue Cornwall Coliseum three years after it was demolished", *Cornwall Live*, 8th April 2018. Pg-4.

[30] Hards, S. "The inside story of iconic music venue Cornwall Coliseum three years after it was demolished", *Cornwall Live*, 8th April 2018. Pg-4.

[31] Taylor, Diana. *The Archive and the Repertoire: Performing cultural memory in The* Americas, Duke University, 2003. Pg-97.

[32] Oddey, A. *Re-framing the Theatrical – interdisciplinary landscapes for performance*, Palgrave MacMillan, 2007. Pg-64.

[33] Parker, S. *The Western Morning News 1st August 2000*, "Moulding a different view of the Clay", Published 1st August 2000. Pg-2.

[34] Smelt, M. *Interview with Sue Hill, Bill Mitchell and Maurice Smelt*, Recorded at 42 Weeth Lane, Camborne, 28th April 2000. Pg-22.

[35] Hall for Cornwall 2012.

[36] Laera, M. *Theatre and Adaptation: return, rewrite, repeat,* Bloomsbury, 2014.

[37] Tucker, Herbert F. "Spectacle." *A New Companion to Victorian Literature and Culture.* Oxford, UK: John Wiley & Sons, 2014. Pg-302.

[38] Tucker, Herbert F. "Spectacle." *A New Companion to Victorian Literature and Culture.* Oxford, UK: John Wiley & Sons, 2014. Pg-303.

[39] Skantze, P.A. *Itinerant Spectator*, Punctum Books, New York, 2013. Pg-7.

[40] Skantze, P.A. *Itinerant Spectator*, Punctum Books, New York, 2013. Pg-111

[41] Skantze, P.A. *Itinerant Spectator*, Punctum Books, New York, 2013. Pg-19.

[42] Skantze, P.A. *Itinerant Spectator*, Punctum Books, New York, 2013. Pg-136.

[43] Skantze, P.A. *Itinerant Spectator*, Punctum Books, New York, 2013. Pg-136.

[44] Gilmore, J.H. & Pine, B.J. *Authenticity what consumers really want*, Havard Business Press, USA. 1-191. 2007. Pg-42.

[45] Gilmore, J.H. & Pine, B.J. *Authenticity what consumers really want*, Havard Business Press, USA. 1-191. 2007. Pg-57.

[46] Phelan, Peggy. *Unmarked the Politics of Performance,* E Library, Routledge, 2005. Pg-161.

[47] Rice, E. *British Council Report on Kneehigh Theatre's Tour of China – The Red Shoes*, care of Falmouth University Kneehigh Archive, Falmouth University, 2001. Pg-1.

[48] Rice, *Tour Report – The Red Shoes*, 2001. Pg- 4.

[49] Kneehigh Archive Press Cuttings 2012. Kneehigh Archive Falmouth University, 2012.

[50] Blackmore Vale Magazine 2001.

[51] Dibdin, T. "Critics' hit parade", *The Stage Edinburgh Preview 2001 ,*2001. Pg-VIII.

[52] *Kneehigh Report on the Debates on Cornwall and its Future November 1998*. Pg-2.

[53] Skantze, P.A. *Itinerant Spectator*, Punctum Books, New York, 2013. Pg-132.

[54] Knowles, R. *Reading the Material Theatre*, Cambridge University Press, 2004. Pg-101.

[55] "Global Cornwall", *The Asylum*: Truro, Cornwall, Kneehigh Theatre, 12th Aug. 2012.

[56] "Global Cornwall", *The Asylum*: Truro, Cornwall, Kneehigh Theatre, 12th Aug. 2012.

[57] "Global Cornwall", *The Asylum*: Truro, Cornwall, Kneehigh Theatre, 12th Aug. 2012.

[58] Sklair, L. "Capitalist Globalisation: Fatal Flaws and Necessity for Alternatives", *Brown Journal of World Affairs,* Fall/Winter 2006, Vol XIII, Issue 1, Pg-1.

[59] Klein, Naomi. *No Logo*, Fourth Estate, 2010.

[60] Klein, Naomi. *No Logo*, Fourth Estate, 2010. Pg-146.

[61] Gilmore, J.H. & Pine, B.J. *Authenticity what consumers really want*, Havard Business Press, USA. 1-191. 2007.

[62] Shepherd, M. and Rice, E. *Kneehigh Theatre, The Asylum Summer Season 2010*, Kneehigh Archive Falmouth University. 2010.

[63] Gilmore, J.H. & Pine, B.J. *Authenticity what consumers really want*, Havard Business Press, USA. 1-191. 2007. Pg- 31.

[64] Costa, M. *The Guardian G2,* "Arts: Theatre: Troupe therapy: Kneehigh", Published 2008, Pg-2.

[65] Cornish Guardian, "Kneehigh takes the lid off a brand new production", published 11/04/02.

[66] Gilmore, J.H. & Pine, B.J. *Authenticity what consumers really want*, Havard Business Press, USA. 1-191. 2007. Pg-42.

[67] Shepherd, M. and Rice, E. *Kneehigh Theatre, The Asylum Summer Season 2010*, Kneehigh Archive Falmouth University. 2010.

CHAPTER SEVEN

CONCLUSION – WISE CHILDREN AND KNEEHIGH CLOSURE

This book has considered the effects and impact of globalisation on Kneehigh's creative ambition, their economic reality, and ultimately their local/global survival. Kneehigh, like the many other contemporary theatre companies, contend with profound tensions influencing their artistry, sense of identity and financial stability. Despite these 'tensions' Kneehigh have realised their ambition to create performances and communicate their local cultural identity. This is part of their brand ethos and is something they consider to be their creative 'responsibility'. Kneehigh has experienced significant influences from external funding bodies to create work that will appeal on local and global platforms, whilst also promoting the positive aspects of Cornish cultural identity. My research within the archive and Asylum has revealed Kneehigh as a company that has skillfully incorporated these influences, while also meeting Arts Council and UNESCO objectives. My use of an 'experiential archive' (including performance mementoes/ artefacts), offered layers of meaning and opportunities for analysis, if not a full sensory experience of the performances discussed as case studies. I have argued that connecting these mementoes/artefacts with the original performance allows the original encounter to live on, encouraging repeat custom, spectatorship and consumption.

During a career which has spanned decades, Kneehigh has been able to continue to work on their chosen creative areas of interest, producing work for and within Cornwall. Community as a core theme, allowed and encouraged an interaction between Kneehigh, the Cornish county, and the devising process; blending collective creativity and influences from all participants involved. This working environment generated a familial safe space conducive to creativity that was inspired and shaped by the Cornish landscape. The company wished to develop themselves into a recognisable brand synonymous with their unique theatrical style and quality. Like other brands, Kneehigh has achieved the art of reinvention. This has been accomplished by updating their brand, promoting their creativity and capacity to reinvent and reinvigorate products. In some instances, they have transformed material previously deemed outdated and obscure. Offering merchandise at performance venues immersed audience members within the production whilst reinforcing the brand, and allowed the experience to continue, long after the live production had ended.

Kneehigh's theatrical style has a range of mediums performed with an emotional commitment to tell stories by the actors, including; use of song, dance, movement, puppetry, music, props (on a tiny and epic scale) and direct address to the audience. Each production has a robust performance energy in portraying the narrative that is characteristically underpinned by Cornish references. The desire or 'the itch' to tell a story is central to all their work, embraced by their ensemble and embedded within the production. Although these elements in isolation are not uncommon in other theatre companies, collectively they form the specific quality of the Kneehigh theatrical brand. This is strengthened by their cultural identification with Cornwall and reinforced by the creative freedoms established in the rehearsal rooms at Gorran Haven and Asylum.

The company has a reputation for theatre that presents darker re-imaginings of fairytales, myths, and legends. This is a stimulus they feel is important to human development, dealing with issues they perceive as global and timeless. The work of *Cymbeline* and *Brief Encounter* found Kneehigh confronting critique against their theatrical 'brand', drawing arguments regarding their theatrical homogenisation of the original work. Notions of 'value' questioning what is 'successful' posed a conflict between global business and artistic paradigms, particularly when considering the production, *The Umbrellas of Cherbourg*. Success, from a globalist stance, is defined in economic terms. However, other perspectives considered the artistic 'successes' achieved by Kneehigh, acknowledging these despite the closure of the production.

Kneehigh appeared forward thinking in reconfiguring and redrawing lines around their own theatre community and cultural identity. Much like other brands who monitor their product/s through questionnaires, Kneehigh analysed performance audience data and demography to develop their performance/experience. Questionnaires, in reference to the Three Islands Project, was a vital way to access the perceived level of cultural exchange achieved. The analysis of the questionnaires for this project indicated that a range of cultural sharing occurred. Sharing of theatrical practice was achieved through collaborations between performers and artists from all three countries. Comments made by participants including those recruited for stalls in the marketplace, brought to light areas that did not work as well.

However, emphasis on the positive aspects of the project illustrated that cultural exchange had successfully taken place.

Further analysis of this data has acknowledged the potential bias by Kneehigh and other parties involved in constructing a definitive argument for exchange. Inclusions of favourable theatrical reviews from all three production sites are in advocacy of the project, supporting its validity in evaluations for Kneehigh, WildWorks Theatre, St. James Cavalier Centre for Creativity, Malta, and the Cyprus Theatre. Positive outcomes would be beneficial for future funding and collaborations for all involved, influencing the tonality of evaluative documentation. Unedited questionnaire responses were included in the appendix. However, the removal of critical responses was impossible to establish.

The Asylum provided the company greater control in response to potentially unwanted outside influences. It offered creative autonomy, conceived when Kneehigh's success generated pressures to leave Cornwall, and operated as a centralised force to keep the company from dividing into separate factions. The Asylum was Kneehigh's answer to these tensions, with 'Brand Kneehigh' and the Asylum linked in producing a recognisable brand with product diversity within their own environment. In response to globalisation and its effects of squeezing out local influences, the company has tried to readdress the balance with Cornish culture and stories presented at the forefront. In considering the ambitions for 'Brand Kneehigh', it is my assertion that the company is not motivated by homogenous globalised ideology, but displayed a balancing act using cultural exchange. Likewise, it is their sense of Cornish identity and responsibility to the county that grounds them within localism. However, their openness to the evolutionary nature of cultural identity facilitated an engagement with other global cultures and collaborators. 'Brand Kneehigh' is a product of cultural exchange but is indelibly linked to the Cornish community. It embraces globalised notions of branding and product diversification, evident through a range of products developed under the Kneehigh 'umbrella' and their own branded environment, Asylum.

This concluding chapter will discuss recent Kneehigh productions, and will also consider the evolution of the company since Rice's departure as artistic director. Considering the perceived developments of the Kneehigh brand, I will direct focus to an emerging future for the company and artistic directorship. Rice left Kneehigh for The Globe in 2016, working only two seasons there as artistic director, resigning in 2017 to form her own theatre company, Wise Children. Kneehigh appointed Carl Grose as joint artistic director in 2018 (he had worked with the company for over twenty-four years). Rice's departure posed a critical juncture for Kneehigh, which this chapter will now explore. As mentioned earlier, Rice's appointment as director was fundamental in achieving success and critical acclaim for the company in the early 2000s. This success assisted in the national and international development of the brand, with increasing finances contributing to the development of Asylum. Losing Rice would have been felt by Kneehigh, however, Rice attempted to allay any fears of change during a post-show talk for *Rebecca* (2016) at the Birmingham Rep. Theatre, stating that once you become a member of Kneehigh 'you never really leave'.[1] Core members of Kneehigh have joined Rice in new posts in her new company Wise Children, with a fluidity achieved for performers working for both companies. Mike Shepherd took on a key performance role in the production *Wise Children*: his appearance strongly communicating support for Rice in this new venture.

The appointment of Grose as joint Artistic Director (sharing this with Mike Shepherd) represents a new theatrical era for Kneehigh. I will discuss this in light of productions since his recruitment to this role. Likewise, the productions of Wise Children will also be reflected on. The methodology of this chapter is slightly different, as I do not use the Kneehigh archive, as the productions analysed do not currently have material placed there. However, drawing in my experiential archive I will examine these productions embracing Skantze's 'itinerant spectatorship', Knowles' 'materialist semiotics' and 'cultural materialism', and Pearson's 'imperfect archaeology'. Through looking at both companies, links between them can be revealed and discussed in branded terms: how this has affected Kneehigh, whether this has weakened or reinforced 'Brand Kneehigh', and what this could mean for the future for both companies.

Emma Rice, The Globe and Wise Children

Rice's appointment as Artistic Director at The Globe in April 2016, fitted the job description requiring 'visionary and charismatic leadership'. Given Rice's years as Joint Artistic Director with Kneehigh, and the success achieved in transforming *Cymbeline* for the RSC, this appeared to be a 'bold' yet assured recruitment decision. When asked for commentary, Dominic Dromgoole, Rice's predecessor stated:

> [Rice's appointment is] in keeping with the Globe's traditions of boldness and adventure. Over many years, Emma has created at Kneehigh a body of work that shares the same principles of imagination, populism, wit and passion that have always been central to the Globe. Kneehigh have also pulled off the same happy trick of a fierce local attachment in Cornwall and

a broad international reach, which is so important to the Globe, in Southwark and everywhere.' [2]

Interestingly, Dromgoole highlighted Kneehigh's local yet global appeal, citing Rice as instrumental in this 'populism', advocating this influence at the Globe, which he observed was an important component to the theatre. Other commentators observed the surprise in Rice's employment; with Michael Billington stating that although he disliked Kneehigh's *Cymbeline*, he appreciated Rice's ability to reinvigorate other classics. Lyn Gardner underpinned the company's 'joyful anarchy', suggesting that Rice would be a 'breath of fresh air' and have the audience 'swinging from the chandelier'.[3]

During her time at the Globe, productions featured a mix of Shakespearean texts such as; *Romeo and Juliet*, *Twelfth Night* and *Much Ado About Nothing*, balanced with Kneehigh classics *Tristan & Yseult* and *The Flying Lovers Of Vitebsk*. Links between Rice (at the Globe) and Kneehigh were clearly established, both parties receiving 'benefits' through association. Kneehigh were able to perform several shows at the highly prestigious venue, while Rice could continue her work with Kneehigh, acting as a transitionary period for both Rice and Kneehigh. However, Rice's tenure and artistic direction received mixed responses and reviews, contributing towards her resignation in 2017.

Rice received criticism at the start of her artistic directorship for admitting she had not read many Shakespeare plays, and that she sometimes found his work hard to understand. With hindsight, Rice acknowledged that this honesty was ill-conceived because of her role. Other factors were at play: initially defined as Rice's introduction of artificial light and sound as the reason for Rice's departure, the Globe sought a new Artistic Director. Controversy arose from Rice's artistic decisions, encouraging experimentation with the technical aspects of productions.

Arguments against this provoked a debate between traditional representations of how Shakespearean drama should be performed using natural lighting effects and live sound. Those in opposition to Rice's plans felt it was going against the artistic mission of the Globe, to recreate performances authentically as would be seen in the Elizabethan era. In contrast, many supporters of Rice's plans felt that theatre should not become a 'museum' exhibit, and artistically the Globe should be willing to experiment theatrically. Rice opined that the Globe did not wish to be a heritage site, but due to conflict within the organisation, was 'unsure what it wants to be'.[4] However, the issue over lighting and sound was symptomatic of wider issues relating to decision making and artistic direction, with Rice stating in an open letter posted on the Globe's website at the time of her resignation: '[that it] was about personal trust and artistic freedom'.[5]

Rice continued to outline her 'fight' in standing up for her rights within the organisation and alluded to her exclusion from meetings where key decisions were made[6]. As reported by BBC News: 'She decided to quit, she said, because "the theatre's board did not love and respect me back and began to talk of a new set of rules that I did not sign up to and could not stand by"'.[7] Dromgoole, Rice's predecessor in the role, supported Rice in his own open letter, describing the inner conflicts within the company: 'There are structural problems, there are personality problems, there is too much fighting for territory, and there are too many who feel free to comment on work without ever taking the risk of making it'[8]. He conceded, within the report, that he did not agree with Rice over her move away from 'shared light' (in which actors and the audience are under the same lighting effect).

> For me, shared light was the unique Globe tool, which subverted the orthodoxies of director's and critic's theatre, and which handed back to the actors and the audiences the capacity to collaborate together freely on making an imaginative experienced occur. Taking away that uniqueness doesn't strike me as radical, it strikes me as conformist. Every theatre has light and sound, the Globe didn't. [9]

Despite Dromgoole's opinion that the dispute over lighting and sound was 'at the heart of her disagreements with colleagues and the board', he argued that he could not agree with the 'block' made by the board against her choices (Young 1). Rice, also acknowledged her mistakes in this process, citing an excitement in working for the Globe as instigation for these changes. In an interview with *The Telegraph*, Rice stated:

> But clearly I hadn't understood something profound about the organisation,' she said. She behaved 'like a kid in a playbox' by installing lights and radio microphones. 'The Globe is the most exciting venue on the planet… I was electrified by the experience and absolutely I turned up the volume. Now I can look back and go, of course that was inflammatory. And I don't think I had explained that to them, so I completely take responsibility for that'. [10]

Mark Brown for *The Guardian* observed that this was 'a battle between the traditional and the experimental, with Rice – and the latter – coming out the loser'[11]. Brown elaborated further on Dromgoole's open letter, which commented on the 'bile' directed towards the Globe and all previous artistic directors, which he considered targeted 'newness' and innovation. Dromgoole argued that Rice was in fact continuing a tradition towards 'originality and invention' instigated by all artistic directors since its reopening. In an interview with *The Observer* in 2018, Rice formed the analogy of her experience at the Globe with *Hamlet,* casting herself as Polonius in reference to his stabbing behind the curtain. She elaborated that:

> They were surprised when I didn't get up. That's my guess. When I started working at the Globe, I came on too strong. I met the space with artistic frenzy, it was so exciting – the lights, the sounds. I don't think they imagined I'd leave. They thought I'd accept new guidelines, that I'd want the job more than my practice. My guess is they were shocked when I said: 'Absolutely not'. [12]

Further debate questioned the Globe's recruitment of Rice, indicating that the company was potentially naive and ill-equipped to fully engage with their choice. In retrospect, Rice was surprised by the outcome: 'It was very shocking because, from my perspective, it had all gone so well. I didn't see it coming because audience figures were astronomical, reviews great, and a fizz was happening around the building'.[13]

As stated earlier, reviews (in addition to opinions on Rice's tenure) were mixed, establishing debates over traditionalism, sexism, class and theatrical experimentation. When questioned if Rice would have achieved the same treatment if she were a man: 'Do you know what? Actually, I think that it's possibly down to my education - possibly more down to class than gender. I've got 2 A-levels, and I went to a comprehensive in Nottingham'[14]. There are a number of complexities relating to Rice's appointment and resulting departure from the Globe. Commentary written immediately and sometime after Rice's departure offered a myriad of theories, allowing Rice more freedom to express her thoughts, uncensored during her tenure, but also causing tension for the Globe.

In juxtaposition to Rice's shared artistic directorship with Shepherd at Kneehigh and her role at The Globe, the same sense of creative rebellion and pursuit of cultural, artistic identity can be perceived. Within interviews contained in previous chapters, Rice has expressed her desires, in alignment with Shepherd's and Kneehigh's, to develop a place they can express themselves with theatrical agency. They have also discussed their feelings of being an 'outsider', and, in reference to their Cornish identity, different from the rest of the UK. Essentially these observations were confirmed by her experiences at The Globe. However, it should be pointed out that Rice's capacity for rebellion and risk-taking were qualities that The Globe took on board in their recruitment of her for the role. Likewise, executive board members influencing the recruitment of Rice would have been aware of the popularity and fan base enjoyed by Rice from her association with Kneehigh. Brand associations were formed between The Globe and

Kneehigh, with creative and economic ambitions being set in place to attract new audiences, but also drawing fans of Rice and Kneehigh to this venue.

It was within this theatrical landscape Rice developed her own theatre company, Wise Children, which has been awarded National Portfolio status from the Arts Council England. The name, Wise Children, is in acknowledgement of Rice's love for Angela Carter's novel *Wise Children*. Carter's work often explores feminist versions of fairy tales, developing feminist heroines. The same-titled first production was due to be performed at the National Theatre, then the Globe, instead it was created as a performance for her own company in 2018. The company is based in Bristol, where Rice has lived for over eight years, and despite a partnership with the Old Vic London, she has expressed a commitment to remain in the South West of the country.[15] The company has eleven core members (including Rice). A number of company members have formerly worked with Kneehigh such as; Simon Baker as technical director, Etta Murfitt as Choreographer and Ian Ross as musical director. As commented by Lyn Gardner, the formation of Wise Children is 'in effect the creation of a new family'[16]. The company also has an associative education programme: the School for Wise Children, developing skills for a career within the performing arts. This sense of family has been described in Kneehigh, and as part of a theatrical tree between Kneehigh and Wise Children, connections have been maintained in the company's first three productions, which will now be discussed.

Wise Children (2018)

The production was an adaptation of an Angela Carter novel on tour nationally between 2018-19. Many key members from Kneehigh worked with Rice on this production; Mike Shepherd, who performed as Peregrine Hazard, as well as Patrycja Kujawska, Melissa James and Etta Murfitt.

The production received a range of favourable reviews from three to five stars. Kate Kellaway, writing for *The Guardian* awarded this production five stars in her review, stating that Angela Carter herself would be 'bowled over by this life-enchanting, brilliantly uninhibited, all-singing and dancing (and let's not forget the incontinent talking) adaptation'[17]. Notably, Kellaway observed the productions 'blind casting', celebrating 'the theatrical idea of identity as provisional'[18]. In this capacity, the production allowed for fluid changes in sex, race and age to occur, suggesting that the managers of the Globe would be 'kicking themselves' over this 'phoenix of a show'[19]. Such a glowing review would have been welcomed by Rice as a vindication of her experiences at the Globe and as a celebration of her successful creative choices as a director.

Four-star reviews were also awarded by a number of publications. *The Stage* considered it a messy, but none-the-less joyous 'love letter to theatre'[20]. A second review for *The Guardian* described the production as a 'spectacular show', stating 'Rice's relaunch is a splashy one, celebrating the sheer razzle-dazzle of a life in theatre'.[21] The *Evening Standard, Time Out,* and *The Times* also rated the production with four stars, whilst the review in *WhatsOnStage* provided three stars, stating that the production did not compare as favourably to Rice's other shows.[22]

As validation and promotion for her new company, this production and resulting reviews would have been important, particularly in balancing the criticism directed towards Rice during her employment at The Globe. As a launch for what Wise Children could offer theatrically, the above reviews provided critical acclaim. In further validation of the success of this production, a recorded live production was aired on the BBC in May 2020 and was available on BBC iPlayer for a month after. Having watched this recording, my attention was drawn to the introduction to the production and Rice's new company. Rice was cited as an acclaimed British director in her own right, with the description of Wise Children based on her own theatrical reputation, rather than her associations with Kneehigh. Although Kneehigh was mentioned, Rice's own directorship was placed at the forefront.

Having seen a number of Rice's directed shows for Kneehigh, the work was characteristic of many of Kneehigh's performances, sharing similarities with *Nights at the Circus (2006).* This production was the first Angela Carter adaptation for Rice during her time with Kneehigh. As described before, physical theatre and movement were prevalent. In the case with *Wise Children,* the lead characters displayed expressiveness through dance, in contrast to acrobatics in *Nights at the Circus.* Both productions had narrator figures speaking directly to the audience in addition to a comedic stand-up act. In fact, *Wise Children* displayed many of the performance elements commonly found within a Kneehigh show. This is understandable given the amount of time Rice has worked with Kneehigh; her development as a director entwined with her career with the company. In contrast to a radical redesign of the 'brand' in pursuit of reinvention, Rice's company, Wise Children, shares many favourable commonalities with Kneehigh.

Despite a brief mention of the company within the video introduction for the live recording, the support from Kneehigh within *Wise Children* was clearly apparent. Connections between Rice, Wise Children and Kneehigh stand to be highly beneficial. Rice has a highly favourable theatrical history for adaptation with Kneehigh and some successes with the Globe. Kneehigh and their associated artists would benefit from working with another company, very much in keeping with the Kneehigh theatrical formula: one shaped by Rice (as well as Shepherd, Mitchell and Grose) during her formative years as a director. Whilst Wise Children as a company is still in its infancy, comparisons have been made with Kneehigh. Using the same Kneehigh cast and crew encourages familiar branding associations. Further production work from Wise Children is needed in order to evaluate its own brand identity and to consider how their theatrical style differs from that of Kneehigh. In contrast, the airing of this production affirmed Rice's own brand as an established contemporary British director on the BBC.

Malory Towers (2019)

Malory Towers was the second literary adaption for the company, this time taken from a series of books by Enid Blyton, written between 1946 and 1951. The story centres around a boarding school for girls relocated to Cornwall during WW2, following the main protagonist Darrell Rivers and her adventures. Rice stated that the Malory Towers series is 'radical to its bones', encompassing themes of friendship, bullying and post-war trauma[23]. In terms of contemporary appeal, Akbar stated in her review that although it maintained its period setting, it is framed by the present day with characters in 'contemporary dress, some holding mobile phones'[24]. In terms of branding, Akbar acknowledged that this adaptation had been given the 'Rice makeover', featuring 'cabaret, with song, dance, hints of camp and a preoccupation with theatrical artifice'[25]. Emerging in this second production was a description by a theatrical reviewer attempting to define Rice and/or Wise Children's theatrical style, using adjectives that have been used in the appraisal of Kneehigh production work.

Interestingly, the diversity of casting in terms of race and gender (embracing non-binary performers) was acknowledged. Likewise, a feminist narrative was perceived with what Akbar cited as a celebration of 'girlhood' and 'strong women', providing 'Malory Towers its most contemporary resonance'[26]. Immersive elements were described with the use of the foyer to extend the world of the play, audience interactions were highlighted as examples of total theatre. Similar descriptors have been used for Kneehigh's theatricality as seen in *Brief Encounter*. Akbar awarded this production five stars, contributing to the theatrical excellence established so far with *Wise Children*.

Lilith Wozniak's review for *Exeunt* was more critical, finding the contemporary framing of the production 'awkward' and 'stilted', with elements of the performance feeling 'subdued' and 'restrained'[27]. Questions were asked whether this was to do with the form of the book, and how this was realised as a script, suggesting the script doesn't do 'enough' to transform the 'episodic vignettes of a book' into a live show[28]. However, Wozniak concedes the 'broadly-drawn look at modern youth' within the 1940s, is 'full of the ingredients that make Emma Rice's shows so frequently exciting'[29]. Lilley, in her work discussing adaptation, commented on the recognition from the audience, assuming 'playful intertextual references' which are 'often subverted and reversed'[30]. Likewise, this subversion can be not only applied to the source material, but to the 'genre and historical context that the originals are embedded in'[31]. In the case of Malory Towers, a production that was advertised as being suitable for children, Rice's adaptation attempted subversion as a way of linking contemporary society with that of the 1940s. For Rice's age demographic, this time period would have familiar childhood connotations; for a much younger cohort, Rice felt that a 'bridge' was needed to make the material relatable to a contemporary children's audience. Despite the show not quite 'hitting its stride till the second act', positive elements were still observed in the work[32].

The review for *The Telegraph* was less complimentary about the production (awarding it two stars), forming links between the subject matter and *Harry Potter*. Despite the lack of spells and predominance of male characters (commonly found within Hogwarts), Dominic Cavendish observed a Cornish boarding school setting as described in the original book series, sharing commonalities with *Harry Potter*. Although Wise Children are established in Bristol, Cornish inspiration and connections familiar with Kneehigh are presented. Similar to the Potter series, Enid Blyton books were a part of children's popular culture, with Cavendish questioning why they haven't been adapted previously. As stated by Cavendish: 'The prospects of success here looked good: after years running Kneehigh theatre, Emma Rice's association with Cornwall runs deep as a tin mine; and her forte is the playful antic, in touch with her inner child'[33].

In his critique, Cavendish questioned Rice's skills as an adaptor, in contrast to her proved artistry and success as a director, suggesting a reliance on atmosphere in place of drama[34]. Similar to Wozniak's review, Cavendish argued that the contemporary framing device was 'redundant', with a lack of action and 'incidental detail', replaced instead with 'pace-slowing songs'[35]. Cavendish concluded that he found the 'sweetness' of the material unpalatable, indicating that this source material did not serve Rice well: 'Rice has been at her best when she has married her theatrical reveries to substance'[36]. The feminist narrative of 'spirited girlhood' was not considered inspiring enough to hold attention. This is an argument that has prevented many projects with a female centric plot and casting being made in the creative industries. Criticism can be perceived in a male reviewer as suggesting a lack of interest in the 'spirited girlhood' theme, whilst the female reviewers included in this study did not raise this as a concern. What has been exposed by Cavendish is a reflection on the adaptation process and whether it was 'successful' in 'subverting' the material for a modern audience. A consideration of what can be successfully adapted for the theatre is an issue raised by Cavendish's review.

Rice had experienced resistance before when she was with Kneehigh for adapting well-known material as illustrated by *A Matter of Life and Death* and *Brief Encounter*. In relation to these productions, some of the strongest arguments were formed against the transformation from one medium to another. Cavendish raises another tension, highlighting the selection of material, ill-served by Rice's theatrical adaptive style. Although I have not seen this production within the framework of my experiential archive, I have observed Cavendish's critique of Kneehigh's and Rice's work on a number of productions. Of course, this provides alternative voices, some of which are critical of the work and the company, offering a multi-layered reflection.

Romantics Anonymous (2017 and 2019-20)

Romantics Anonymous was originally a production performed as Rice's last show at the Globe, and despite the differences between the two parties, was perceived to be a fitting 'swansong'. The production was based on the French film *Les Émotifs Anonymes* (2010), realised as a musical (or as described by Gardner as a play with songs), composed by Michael Kooman, with lyrics by Christopher Dimond[37]. Featuring an examination of love and loss, the 2017 production was received favourably, with the added context of Rice's 'premature' departure: 'It's all the more bittersweet, because witty stagecraft combined with an ability to tug at the heartstrings is a reminder of what a great and distinctive talent the Globe is losing'[38]. In contrast to *The Umbrellas of Cherbourg* (another adaptation of a French film), this production enjoyed positive reviews and was reprised in 2020 for a second tour. The themes and cultural references connected to love and introversion within this production (such as self-help books and the difficulties of modern-day dating) were more contemporary and appealing to a wider audience. As described by Gardner, the production contained more dramatic content (with songs) than *The Umbrellas of Cherbourg*, with dialogue sung throughout. Gardner concluded her four-star review, stating that the production signalled to the Globe that Rice was 'unbowed' by her experience, making a strong theatrical platform to launch Wise Children.

This was pivotal for Rice, as indicated by Gardner, as a theatrical validation of her artistic choices as she transitioned to her new company. Although this was not a Wise Children's production (it became so in 2019-20), it acted as an advertisement for the company, strengthening Rice's brand association (having been destabilised by the Globe). Given Rice's difficulties with the theatre, Rice needed this production to repair the damage the former negative experience had induced.

Rice reprised *Romantics Anonymous* in 2019-20 and offered the chance for non-London theatregoers to experience this 'emerging classic' on tour. Following Kneehigh's global ambitions, tours were booked around America in the spring and summer of 2020. The review in Theatre Weekly awarded the production five stars. It noted that other national newspapers had similarly awarded four or five-star reviews, respectively: 'a rare accolade in itself' and displaying the 'universality' of its appeal[39]. Richard Jones also highlights the historical context of the production, stating the circumstances of the original production and reiterating (as Gardner) that this was an artistic loss for the Globe, with Rice's abilities for bringing together 'the best theatrical talent around'[40]. *Musical Theatre Review* formed positive connections with other material dealing with chocolate and love (*Willy Wonka* and *Chocolat*). Jones, like Gardner, pointed out Rice's 'acrimonious' parting with the Globe, highlighting the successful run at the Bristol Old Vic and the upcoming international tour.

Rice's first three productions with Wise Children have been successful in attracting audiences, achieving highly favourable reviews and securing international links to tour. This mirrored Kneehigh's successful global model, whilst enjoying favourable links with the company. Cavendish, in his review of *Malory Towers,* makes critical references to Rice's selection of stimuli and her ability for adaptation in contrast to direction. In defence, Rice still appears to engage with material she wishes to tell a story with through theatre. Highly positive reviews and strong audience attendance indicate spectators are interested in seeing her adaptation and directorial skills are work: the Rice brand of storytelling. The transition away from Cornwall could be observed as necessary. Rice has relocated to Bristol, and therefore can no longer claim Cornish residency or identity. In this capacity, Rice has undergone a personal reinvention, facilitating an artistic one. Rice may not wish to compete with Kneehigh, so by placing geographical distance between both companies, she has tempered any negative comparisons that could be drawn if Wise Children were also based in Cornwall. Cavendish, in his review of *Malory Towers,* observed the influence of Cornwall on Rice's artistic sensibilities. Like other artists emerging from old associations to new independent work, influences will still be perceived. Wise Children is still in its infancy as a theatre company, Rice embarking on the 'cartography style' construct of cultural identity I have previously debated. 'Brand Kneehigh' and Wise Children theatre company share key elements in relation to directorship and personnel. The company is branded as Rice's theatrical vehicle, with literary and filmic adaptation as the principal driver for stimuli, in contrast to Kneehigh's selection of fairy tales, myths and legends.

Kneehigh and Carl Grose (after Rice's Departure)

As I have discussed earlier, during the transitionary period of Rice leaving for the Globe, Kneehigh sought a new artistic director with Carl Grose being appointed in 2018. Carl Grose was a safe and well-established choice, working with the company over many years as a scriptwriter and actor. Recalling his first experiences with the company:

> I've been a life-long fan of Kneehigh since the first time I saw them at the age of thirteen. I was instantly inspired and immediately obsessed. I wanted to make theatre like them. So it is a strange thrill and a somewhat surreal honour to announce that I will be joining artistic director <u>Mike Shepherd</u> as deputy Artistic Director as of November. [41]

The news desk at Broadwayworld.com reflected that this was 'a natural step' for the company, given Grose's history and love for Kneehigh. Grose continued by stating that 'over the past six years Mike and I have already been exploring a new way of working', giving examples of productions mirroring this 'new way of working' such as *Dead Dog in a Suitcase, Tin Drum* and *Ubu Karoke*[42]. I have selected these productions in order to consider the impact of Grose's artistic direction (shared with Shepherd) and to analyse the work since Rice's departure.

Grose did not explicitly provide details on what these 'new ways of working' are but commented that, through his joint directorship with Shepherd, they intend to build on their relationship and continue to tell stories (Broadway world 1). Creatively, Grose has been a key creative figure in many successful Kneehigh productions with writing credits for; *Dead Dog in a Suitcase, The Tin Drum, Ubu Karoke, Tristan & Yseult, Bacchae, Blast! Wagstaffe the Wind-up Boy, Cymbeline, Hansel and Gretel* and *The Wild Bride.* From this extensive list, creative connections are firmly displayed. Just as Rice has been recognised for her directorship in 'Brand Kneehigh', Carl Grose should also enjoy similar associations through his scripted work and adaptations. Grose is as firmly intertwined within the Kneehigh brand as Mitchell (for his site-specific work and landscape theatre), Shepherd and Rice. The next section will consider the productions under the influence of Grose's joint artistic directorship.

The Tin Drum (2017)

This production (directed by Mike Shepherd) was the first under Grose's new role, with a script adapted by Grose from Günter Grass's novel of the same name. As with the other productions discussed in this section, there was a move away from fairy tales to exploring classic literature with political and social themes. Rice had always asserted that love has been a reoccurring motif for the company. The narratives of love were explored through romantic and familial relationships, on a 'local' level. Through the selection of material from Shepherd and Grose's new artistic directorial partnership, love was explored from a social and 'global' standpoint. In the case of *The Tin Drum*, the 'love' (or lack of love) inherent in humanity was explored in social and politically charged situations.

The theatrical style of *The Tin Drum* featured familiar associative elements such as puppetry (continuing the influence from their former working relationship with the Little Angel Theatre Company), music and 'cabaret' performance. Although the production was an adaptation of a novel, Catherine Love observed Kneehigh seizing 'on the novel's folk-tale qualities' in order to make 'an allegory for conflict', by considering life in Danzig before, during and after the second world war[43]. Love stated that despite the seriousness of the subject matter, Kneehigh can still apply their 'brand' of childlike invention with 'mischievous comedy buried amid the rubble of war'[44].

Using a puppet to portray the lead character, Oskar (operated by Sarah Wright), allowed for a stark contrast to be made between him (forever young due to a chronic condition) and the rest of the production.

> The austerity of his appearance is at sharp odds with the colour and chaos everywhere else: a single point of unchanging focus in a fast swirling world. He's an odd, unsettling figure, childishly petulant in some ways yet disturbingly mature in others. As often with puppets, it's astonishing how much can be read upon his fixed wooden features. [45]

Arguably, the otherworldly look of Oskar contributed to the folk-tale quality characteristic to Kneehigh's work. Love opined that the production was 'shape-shifting' and undecided artistically: 'It's not quite musical, not quite opera, not quite play'[46]. Love also stated that because of the 'chaotic' nature of the production through the combination of music and fast pace (in order to condense Grass's novel to under two hours), dialogue and lyrics were skimmed past and hard to hear. I also experienced this in my spectatorship, attributing it to the acoustics within Shoreditch Town Hall.

The review for *Exeunt Magazine* indicated similar perceptions of a vibrant, yet aimless production. Wozniak considered that despite the loud bangs and explosions, the performance failed to generate excitement or fully connect with the audience. A detachment or 'alienation' is cited, caused by the play being almost entirely sung which 'should hook into the audience's emotions, but most of the time it only serves to push us further away'[47]. In contrast, this described alienation worked well for puppet Oskar 'watching the adults from the sidelines with bemusement, an intriguing detachment'[48].

Other distancing elements came from the microphone usage of the performers, used to generate a 'popstar-like' effect, particularly in the dictator's portrayal, described by Wozniak as a 'Madonna/Lady Gaga-esque Hitler figure'[49]. This use appeared to make a commentary of celebrity, but according to Wozniak, never fully 'coalesces'. The structure of the play itself was additionally cited as problematic, contributing to this disconnection: the scenes were episodic, making it difficult to 'invest' in the action and the characters.

Part of the production's inconsistency was the placement of scenes creating a jarring effect on the emotional tone of the performance. Wozniak perceived Kneehigh's ability to combine light and dark and 'poignancy and ridiculousness' as one of Kneehigh's strengths[50]. However, this was not successfully achieved within *The Tin Drum*.

> Here, it just seems odd. *The Tin Drum* has successful moments of both mysterious uncanniness and warm familial storytelling, but often settles into an unhappy medium, where we are told exactly what is happening, but still feel separated from it. [51]

Wozniak observed moments of 'genius' in the production. However, the wider political context of fascism was superficially explored with Wozniak preferring an examination of Oskar's parents 'love triangle' relationship, rather than 'the Nazi drama at the forefront of the play'[52].

The review in *The Telegraph* offered further critique, awarding the production two stars. Cavendish commented on the confusing nature of Grose and Shepherd's adaptation and described being 'almost bludgeoned by the musical barrage'[53]. Sharing similar observations to Wozniak, Cavendish perceived the production as chaotic and frantic: 'A playground riot of a show'[54]. I considered my spectatorship in similar terms. Because of the rushed nature of the performance, I could not fully hear the performers. Initially blaming the Shoreditch Townhall venue (this was the first time I had attended a performance there), I could not connect or care about the characters, and like Wozniak, wished for a more personal, 'localised' approach to the material.

In contrast, reviews in *The Guardian* and *Timeout* were more favourable, with Clapp for *The Guardian* stating: 'this is Kneehigh company at its best'[55]. While Clapp described some confusion within its storytelling, the recognisable qualities of Grose's prose were still evident. *Timeout* gave the production four stars, describing it as 'unsettling and magical', whilst conceding that the production would enjoy a mixed reception as a 'dark dose of theatrical Marmite'[56]. Saville observed the connotation with new wave-era *Top of the Pops* and Weimar cabaret in a postmodern mix of cultural semiotics: 'Performers break scenes to sing soul baring torch songs with synth-pop accompaniment'[57].

In contrast to Rice's first productions with Wise Children, there appeared to be much less emphasis on Grose's premiership as artistic director. Grose has been connected with Kneehigh for many years, with his contributions being at the forefront of the company's theatrical style. For Rice the stakes were higher by showcasing the material of a new theatre company. In the case of Grose, there was a sense of a natural continuation of the Kneehigh brand, with a slight revision of artistic direction. The reviews for Grose's first production as Artistic Director were varied, owing more to the problematic nature of adapting a novel. However, the theatrical development of *The Tin Drum* through sung dialogue and microphone use contributed to causing confusion and a lack of engagement.

Dead Dog in a Suitcase and Other Love Songs (2014 and 2019)

This is a production I experienced in the Asylum in 2014 and at the Lyric Hammersmith in 2019 (both directed by Mike Shepherd) and it holds a unique place within my experiential archive. The production at the Asylum premiered the work in Cornwall before it was taken on tour nationally. In contrast to the previous summer season production of *Steptoe and Son* (2013): a production that ambitiously adapted three episodes of the same-titled British TV show with mixed responses, I hoped for a return to the qualities of work I had enjoyed with *Tristan and Yseult, Cymbeline* and *The Wooden Frock.* I was not disappointed, experiencing a production (mirroring a number of theatrical reviews) using music, movement, and puppetry in an inventive and exciting adaptation of *The Beggars Opera*.

As observed by Hickling in his review for *The Guardian*, Kneehigh had reworked the play with ska and dubstep music, contemporary dialogue and costumes. By doing so, Hickling observed that the inclusion of contemporary culture (through ska and dubstep), had the effect of making the work 'curiously timeless'[58]. It also follows the cyclical nature of adaptation and storytelling, with each version adding new qualities and contexts, contributing to the 'timelessness' commented on by Hickling. The inventive use of puppetry was noted, with a description of a corpse dog puppet discovered in a suitcase with flies buzzing around it on attached wires. I would add that this adaptation was in keeping with the theatrical style of 'Brand Kneehigh', but also fit within the environment of the Asylum: establishing fun and entertainment during the summer season.

As described previously in Chapter 6, the environment of a circus tent has its own unique qualities, so too does the Asylum venue. In addition to the 'magical' nature of the tent appearing to be bigger on the inside with a panoramic configuration of the stage, the light canvas material allowed for the transition of day to night, contributing to the atmosphere of the performance. Unlike the thick canvas material of a traditional circus tent, coated to obscure daylight, the Asylum used white material allowing natural light to enter the venue. As a spectator, I found that the diminishing daylight replaced by theatrical lighting induced a feeling of transition from the outside world into the world of the play. Evening performances at the Asylum were usually scheduled for 8pm, factoring in summer daylight hours, as it was potentially impractical to start performances much earlier. Although the above transitional effect described may not be intentional, I found it to be a 'magical' experience unique to seeing the performance at the Asylum in contrast to other venues.

Returning to Hickling's review, observations are made about the 'success' of Kneehigh's adaptations: "As such, the company's choice of subject tends to fall into two categories: those that suit such a highly evolved house style and those that don't"[59]. Kneehigh's 'house style' has been critiqued in *Cymbeline* and *A Matter of Life and Death*, whilst praised in *Tristan and Yseult* and *The Red Shoes*. In contrast, the company received both praise and critique for *Brief Encounter*. Hickling commented that the adaption process of *The Beggar's Opera* in this production was a success, creating a new 'urban myth'[60]. According to Hickling, through the use of ready-made songs and ballads by Composer Charles Hazelwood, a 'jukebox musical' had been created, contributing to the cultural context within the production. In this capacity, new associations were formed between the past and the present: 'bawdy 18th-century airs and catches share a direct bloodline with ska, grime and dubstep'[61]. This production enjoyed highly favourable commentary, becoming a part of the 'canon' of Kneehigh 'classics', reprised again and again.

Dead Dog in a Suitcase (and other love songs), was reprised in 2019, with many of the same performers involved. Teresa Guerreiro, in her review, awarded the production four stars, stating positively that it contained many of Kneehigh's 'trademark theatrical devices: energetic acting, music, dancing, puppetry and an entirely original take on its subject'[62]. Guerreiro also merited the production for its 'social criticism', citing Grose's notes within the programme, wishing to consider the social questions posed by John Gay (original writer of *The Beggars Opera*). In contrast to reviews for *The Tin Drum*, the social and political debates within this production are clearer, offering depth and layers for consideration or as stated by Guerreiro, 'food for thought'[63].

Other reviews for the production also gave positive commentary. Tristram Fane Saunders review for *The Telegraph* afforded the production five stars, highlighting the 'localised' semiotics of Punch and Judy and the British seaside.

> *Dead Dog in a Suitcase (and other love songs)* is an end of the pier puppet show writ large, relentlessly cartoonish in its slapstick violence and amorality. It left me grinning from ear to ear. [64]

Cornwall is also part of the British seaside, with a heritage reminiscent of Saunders descriptions. *The Standard* reviewed the production favourably, commenting on Kneehigh's ability to transform *The Beggar's Opera*, exposing the criminal machinations of the modern world[65]. All commentators observed its relevancy, cleverly drawing links between the source material and contemporary culture, and in terms of 'Brand Kneehigh', generating another classic production, eligible for reprisal in the future for both national and international tours.

Kneehigh's Ubu! A Singalong Satire (2019)

The most recent Kneehigh production I have attended was *Ubu* (directed by Carl Grose) in December 2019. My 'itinerant' spectatorship began in seeing marketing campaigns promoting it as an adaptation of Alfred Jarry's *Ubu Roi*. It helped in forming associations of this play through my earlier education in theatre studies, knowing this was a classic production, studied on a number of educational syllabuses. Other preconceptions were influenced by spectators who had already seen the production, informing me that the performance was in the style of karaoke. Associations with karaoke as entertainment involving music and audience participation were clear, giving rise to a curiosity as to how Kneehigh would incorporate this into a political drama. In fact, karaoke is a clear example of globalised leisure, originating in Japan and rapidly (through globalisation) becoming a popular form of entertainment throughout the globe.

Using karaoke as an immersive tool established an immersive experience and was different from the audience participation Kneehigh has previously instigated in other performances. The production featured a contemporary script by Grose, punctuated with contemporary pop music, generating another jukebox musical. A screen with subtitles projected song lyrics, with the audience encouraged to sing along with the cast. The audience configuration was set up like a gig or concert, with most people standing and people again were encouraged to move around the area, having the freedom to buy refreshments (stalls were set up selling a range of drinks at the back of the auditorium). A new interval format was introduced with three short breaks (or 'pit stops') of five minutes allowing audience members to either purchase a drink or visit the bathroom.

Political references were modernised, with the use of social media platforms allowing for another layer of connection with the audience. The fact that the performance I attended was just before the general election added further social and political context by reinforcing the politically subversive message inherent within the plot and Kneehigh's version. Within my experience of the production, I found the performances highly animated and energetic, and despite the serious nature of the political debate on offer, very reminiscent of a pantomime. Kneehigh has previously produced pantomime style shows, performing them during the Christmas period. These have included; *Hansel and Gretel*, *Rapunzel*, and *Midnight's Pumpkin* (a more light-hearted and pantomime version of Cinderella – in contrast to the darker overtones of *The Wooden Frock* which explores incest and abusive relationships).

The construction of props was much more simplistic and cartoon-like, lacking the sophistication of the props seen in the production *Dead Dog in a Suitcase*. A ghost character was created by a white paper bag labelled 'Ghost' (with a hole cut in the middle), placed over an actor's head, evoking a rustic village hall charm. A giant bomb decorated with a black and white spiral was thrown around the stage like a giant beach ball. The motif of the 'Tim Burton-esque' black and white spiral was repeated throughout the set, reinforcing the cartoon style aesthetic. The performer's costumes and make-up were equally clown-like and exaggerated; with a mop head used as Ubu's hairpiece, and a spiral 'Madonna-like' pointed bra worn by Shepherd playing Ubu's wife.

The relaxed gig like atmosphere of the production, in addition to the comedic and 'homemade' quality of the props, added to the entertainment factor encouraged by Kneehigh. As outlined above, a jukebox musical was developed to punctuate scenes in the play, performed by a live band, with lyrics projected to create the karaoke component of the play. Popular songs from the twentieth and twenty-first century were performed such as Britney Spears' *Toxic,* David Bowie's *Heroes* and Survivor's *Eye of the Tiger.* Kneehigh placed the emphasis on the audience to accompany the band, contributing greatly to the atmosphere of the production. In the latter part of the performance, an Olympics style game show was set up with audience members competing against one another. The activities were reminiscent of children's party games, embraced and executed with enthusiasm by most audience members.

In the production of *Ubu,* Kneehigh had created a distinct form of entertainment and performance experience. Generated in this performance was a fusion of theatre, concert, karaoke and gameshow. The format of having the audience standing (replicating concerts), encouraged flexibility and fluidity, as it allowed for audience members to move around the space, but to also engage in the karaoke format to sing and dance. Although the show lasted two hours (beyond the average length of a concert), encouraging the audience to be more active and participatory did not tax the audience physically. At the very end of the production, while the Kneehigh band were performing the Lou Reed song *Perfect Day*, the audience were complicit in condemning Ubu by pointing an accusatory finger at him during the repeated phrase: 'you're going to reap just what you sow'. Within that action, the cast was encouraging everyone to unify as a political force against Ubu's dictatorship. Holly Williams, in her review for *The Independent* also found this to be an evocative moment within the production: 'It sends a shiver through the tent on a warm night. It is a reminder to speak truth to power; a reminder that our voices, together, really can be louder'[66]. The subtitles projected on screens above the seated audience area reinforced the positive possibilities for political change.

Although *Ubu* had started out as a pantomime, the play progressively revealed its political core, making this production, in contrast to the other plays performed under Grose's artistic directorship, more politically direct and active. This 'singalong' satire, in contrast to other political/social plays like *Blast* and *Quicksilver*, was much more global in scope, considering political machinations from around the world (mixed with references to the EU and Brexit). In the final moments of the production, Kneehigh reached out to the audience (and in a Brechtian capacity), imploring them to consider the political landscape and make changes.

Lyn Gardner, writing for *Stagedoor,* considered that *Ubu* displayed Kneehigh's 'trademark' performance style, stating that a feeling of inclusion was successfully achieved 'because the company treats its audience with real generosity'[67]. As a spectator, I experienced this atmosphere with the audience becoming the citizens of the fictional town of Lovelyville. Gardner was also in praise of the work of Charles Hazelwood, weaving familiar songs into the performance, driving the action of the play. A noted comedic highlight featured an assassination accompanied by The Carpenters' song *Close to You*. Gardner, similarly, watching this production as I did in the run-up to the UK General Election, felt the political attack on right-wing politicians such as Donald Trump and Nigel Farage 'not quite savage enough'[68]. Partly this was because of the portrayal of the Ubu's, representing the likes of Trump and Farage, as bumbling, outrageous, yet likeable fools: 'As an audience you are put in the odd position of obviously wanting to boo the Ubu's but also finding them the most interesting people on stage'[69]. Arguably this fulfilled the function of the play (embedded within the title) as satire; despite its lack of 'savageness', a critical gaze of these fascist dictators was still established.

Kate Wyver, also reviewing for *The Guardian* was more critical in her appraisal of the production, finding the improvisational style of the production as 'thrown-together', losing the power to fully consider the 'current political situation' with depth[70]. Highlighting a similar analogy to Gardner, Wyver felt the political message was weakened by the pantomime theatrics employed, finding this element superficial and crowd-pleasing.

> Kneehigh are best at causing chaos and it would be churlish not to note that the school groups seemed to have a ball as their classmates are chosen for the mid-show games and fights, lapping up the double entendres and swaying along to the slower songs. [71]

Despite Kneehigh's attempts at generating entertainment, Wyver found the 'sense of hope' created at the end through the removal of the Ubu dictatorship overshadowed by the production's slapstick comedic style.

The Independent, reviewing the production in the Asylum, observed Kneehigh's comedic combination of power and populism with 'mass karaoke'[72], and a globalised form of entertainment. Hazelwood commented on the intended effect (again mirroring the Three Islands Project) as fitting in with the branded world of the Asylum: 'It should feel a bit like being at a festival - bellowing your lungs out to whatever is playing'[73]. Williams commented on the atmosphere of her spectatorship, showing Kneehigh's success in creating vibrancy and fun: 'This is theatre as a good night out; it's a gig, a knees-up'[74]. A return to the company's 'roots' was also observed, with Shepherd stating he was keen to get back to improvised work[75]. Grose reinforced this stating: 'It's a rough, very spontaneous event. The exciting thing about improv is getting yourself into the s*** - that's where the magic happens'[76]. Taken in by the entire experience of the performance, Williams described her own itinerant spectatorship:

> I watch one warm evening in early August, adding to the south coast of <u>Cornwall</u>'s heaving hordes of tourists. After an afternoon spent strolling around the walled gardens and lush, sub-tropical jungled valleys of the Lost Gardens of Heligan, I follow its snaking pathways to a field where the Asylum sits, the dome squatting in front of a stunning view out to sea. The whole thing, frankly, seems charmed. [77]

Further descriptions from Williams reflected that the rest of the audience were also affected by this 'charm': 'a mixture of tourists and Kneehigh diehards, they're all up for it'[78]. Within that statement, Williams succinctly communicated the appeal of 'Brand Kneehigh', illustrating Pine and Gilmore's 'experience economy'.

Williams wrote the review during the premiere of the production at the Asylum. As part of her review, they invited her to an after-show party at the rehearsal barns in Gorran Haven to celebrate this new play.

> There are great pots of food and crates of drinks; outside a bonfire flickers, and someone points out the Milky Way to me overhead. You don't get that at an opening night party in the West End. [79]

This memorable experience continued her spectatorship, with her documenting the experiences in her review. It created a distinctive form of spectatorship, something that is part of the Kneehigh brand in their devising and rehearsal work, but also in keeping with the localised elements (as indicated in the quote above) specific to the Gorran Haven barns.

In the third and most recent production under the Grose and Shepherd artistic directorship, the Kneehigh brand has continued a positive trajectory, bypassing any concerns over Rice's departure. Grose as a long-standing collaborator was an assured choice, facilitating a focus on political drama, redefining them as folktale analogies. In contrast to the 'universality' of love and loss, as explored during Rice's tenure, there was a more social, global gaze through Grose's adaptations; a gaze shifting again from the local to the global. Paradoxically, this comes at a major time in British politics, with a redirection from global to localisation evident through Brexit. A direction mirrored by the majority vote to leave the EU in Cornwall: but not shared by Shepherd and Kneehigh.

Kneehigh and Brexit

On the 24 June 2016, when the British voted in favour of leaving the EU, Kneehigh shared their thoughts on the referendum through a Facebook post. Placing a picture on Facebook entitled, 'Dark Times' by Daryl Waller (their associate artist and illustrator since 1999), the company wrote alongside this bleak image: 'This is now, this is it...'[80]

Fig. 7-5. Kneehigh Facebook Post, June (2016)

Although not outwardly citing the EU referendum as the direct subject for commentary, we can assume this was the case. On a day that affected the British public and divided opinion, such a post, would be linked to this momentous event. In sharing this image, and with a short but concise statement attached, Kneehigh declared their allegiance to remain part of the EU and their opinion that 'dark times' would lie ahead as a consequence of leaving this alliance.

Shepherd, in an interview with *The Guardian* in 2017, revealed that he 'despaired of Cornwall recently – the fact it voted Ukip, then Brexit', and that he had moved back to London 'a few years ago'[81]. Trueman's article referred to Cornwall as Kneehigh's home. This is still the case, despite Shepherd's relocation. Shepherd has been fundamental to the creation and success of Kneehigh and arguably part of the brand. Shepherd's opinions of Cornwall and Brexit present another tension within the local and global dichotomy. However, 'Brand Kneehigh' is separate from Shepherd, and now from Rice; still connected, but enjoying its own identity. Its home is still in Cornwall, with work originating and being devised or adapted there, even if Shepherd now lives in London and Rice in Bristol.

Many others shared a negative perception of Brexit and its effect in the creative industries, according to Georgina Snow, writing for *The Stage*. Referring to a survey conducted by the Creative Industries Federation earlier on in the 2016, Snow cited 96% of its members wishing to stay in the EU[82]. Snow presented the reasons for this vote included access to EU funding and free movement of talent - factors which Kneehigh has enjoyed throughout its career. As results of the voting demographics revealed in the news, what emerged in Kneehigh's home county of Cornwall was a desire to no longer be part of Europe or the EU collective. This was surprising given the financial investment the EU supplied the county, with £2.5bn donated by EU funds and a combination of public/private investment since 2000, lasting until 2020.[83]. The county of Cornwall is one of the poorest areas in Europe, due to the decline of the fishing, farming and mining industries, and attracted large amounts of EU money to regenerate the area. This had given rise to ventures such as the Eden Project and support of the Cornish theatre scene.

The economic factors concerning Cornwall and its effect on Kneehigh's creative ambitions are direct issues now facing the county due to Brexit. Anne Carlisle, Falmouth University's Vice-Chancellor, expressed her support for remaining, mindful of the funds invested by EU for developing both the Falmouth and Exeter campuses. Carlisle suggested that Cornwall was on 'the edge geographically' and it is important for it to be part of something 'bigger such as the EU'[84]. However, some local Cornish residents interviewed commented that they had not benefitted from this funding, stating that it was 'just about impossible to get a good job here'[85]. Not all those interviewed felt the same way, presenting a polarisation of views around this complex situation. Hotel owner, Ameena Williams, was concerned that the vote will put off foreign tourists, stating the vote was based on a nostalgic view of England, and a national identity that no longer exists: 'They think we can go back to the days of Churchill and tea on the lawn. Those days have gone'[86]. Dr Merv Davey voiced similar opinions to Mike Shepherd, that Cornwall has strong connections with Europe, while mainland England (particularly London) neglect and forget about the needs of this county.

'They have never been bothered about Cornwall', he said. And it was not just about the money. 'Cornwall has got very strong cultural links with

Europe, especially Brittany. Suddenly we're not European anymore and that
horrifies me,' said Davey. [87]

Despite fears of leaving the EU, the vote to leave offered the opportunity to
create a new power structure, developing industries (including fishing) that
the EU previously sanctioned against. This freedom of expression over
space and place has also been felt by Kneehigh, encouraging them in their
development of the Asylum. The Asylum utilised the strengths of
globalisation and localism through cultural exchange, in creating a branded
space with international influences. It is as an act of rebellion, likened to
Brexit, wishing to reclaim a sense of identity and space, withdrawing from
the homogenising effects of globalisation.

Kneehigh worked hard to develop a career that is successful in their
birthplace and 'spiritual' home of Cornwall, at the same time achieving
theatrical acclaim nationally and internationally. They have prided
themselves and the Cornish community as being 'outward looking', rather
than parochial through evolving notions of cultural identity and feelings of
being disenfranchised from mainstream English politics, economics and
society. Despite their ambitions and the pride the Cornish county has
expressed at the global success of Kneehigh, the community supported
others in the country by voting for Brexit. This raised difficult questions for
Kneehigh, a company with global ambitions, who developed projects that
could work internationally to secure Arts Council and British Council
funding. They are a company who supported and sponsored overseas artists,
providing them with an opportunity to work and share their creative practice
in the UK. The multitudinous factors affecting the events of the EU
referendum are factors that Kneehigh had been 'wrestling' with since their
beginnings in 1980: concerning Kneehigh's place in the world and their
identity within their 'home'.

This text has presented these issues and tensions, exploring Kneehigh's
ways of navigating around them, but as with the EU referendum, it does not
and cannot offer solutions. The questions raised are concerns being debated
on a global platform. Larry Elliot, journalist and economics editor for *The
Guardian,* presented the UK's vote to leave as a rejection of globalisation,
showing that votes were used to voice dissonance against an unfair
economic global system.

Now we have Britain's rejection of the EU. This was more than a protest
against career opportunities that never knock and the affordable homes that
have never been in place for the last three decades. [88]

Further on in this article, Elliot becomes much more prosaic about this vote as a way of protest, citing those accountable for this imbalance and the failure of globalisation.

> An increasing number of voters believe there is not much on offer from the current system. They think globalisation has benefited a small privileged elite, but not them. They think it is unfair that they should pay the price for bankers' failings. They hanker after a return to security that the nation state provided, even if that means curbs on the core freedoms that underpin globalisation, including the free movement of people. [89]

The latter part of Elliot's statement instigated the debate concerning the perceived strength of national identification and parochial boundaries protecting local needs, ideas and opinions. Elliot supported a global sceptic view which he asserted is shared by 'large numbers of people across Europe', which regards a flexible globalised economy as unworkable. Kneehigh might argue otherwise, wishing to stay connected with the rest of the world through their Facebook post, growing their company through this very flexible, global business model.

Closure of Kneehigh

On 3rd June 2021 Kneehigh announced its closure via social media and through a post on their website. Reactions from supporters, artists, journalists, and researchers ranged from shock and disbelief to heartbreak, observing the devasting loss of a 'theatrical superpower':[90]

> Someone just tweeted me that it's like the death of David Bowie "times 50" – that's how devastated people are by the shock news that Cornwall's Kneehigh Theatre is being wound up after 40 glorious years.[91]

Piecing together the circumstances and events culminating in its closure, a range of influences are displayed. Revealed within an article by BBC news are financial difficulties sustained during the pandemic, which the company were hopeful to resolve. However, the company had lost £140,000 in April 2020 (as per the company's accounts listed for that year and despite receiving the Culture Recovery Fund), a month after the country was plunged into its first Covid-19 lockdown. Based on the recovery fund, Kneehigh were hoping to reinvent itself after incurring losses suffered due to the pandemic, which has left the company in a vulnerable and precarious position.[92] In response the company had refocused energies to consider and revise its business operating model, with a focus on their creative spaces such as the Asylum and their rehearsal barns as central to this new outlook.

Having an enforced break due to the pandemic, the company had created a recorded short performance The *Neon Shadow* airing on YouTube in August 2020. This was followed by *Random Acts of Art* in May 2021, a series of site-specific performances and installations around Cornwall to celebrate Kneehigh's 40th anniversary. Speaking to local newspaper *Cornwall Live*, Phil Gibby, arts council area director for the South West, acknowledged the sad news of Kneehigh's 'final chapter', but conceded that this was the best course of action as recommended by the trustees of the company, based on the given circumstances.[93]

In the company's own statement, is a transparent reflection on the recent changes in artistic leadership, questioning whether Kneehigh could 'sustain their vision going forward'.[94] Likewise, Mike Shepherd standing down as artistic director was a seismic change for the company, instigating the winding down of the company. Shepherd announced his departure on 16th May 2021, two weeks prior to Kneehigh's closure. Writing for *The Guardian,* Damien Gayle's headline signposts the changes in artistic leadership as a major catalyst, although the article does not contribute any further insight into this event than has already been provided by Kneehigh's official statement.[95]

Taking on board the research and observations of this book, Kneehigh have previously experienced a similar critical juncture and survived. In this instance, having the founding member and artistic director leave, at a time when the company have faced an unprecedented break in performance work and revenue, proved too challenging for the company to continue. How much a key figure is intrinsic to the brand and continuation of the company is a pertinent factor; a factor proving to be intractably linked to Kneehigh and its survival. Arguably, Mike Shepherd 'is' Kneehigh, with Emma Rice experiencing similar associations during her time with the company. Both artistic directors have been part of 'Brand Kneehigh' in addition to shaping its theatrical style. Despite concerns over the impact of Brexit and potential withdrawal of funding for the Cornish County, artistic leadership and Covid 19 have had a greater and more sustained influence. The county had received substantial funding from the EU, as it is one of the most economically deprived areas in the UK and there is still an ongoing question on how theatre in Cornwall will survive and thrive after losing this funding initiative. Due to their closure, we will not be able or observe whether Kneehigh's opinions on the globality of Cornish identity will change due to the impact of this referendum result. However future research could explore the development of Wise Children, noting the emergence of their theatrical brand and the evolutionary nature of their relationship with Kneehigh.

To conclude, this book has established the Asylum's development as a rehearsal/performance space, as a 'flagship' for the Kneehigh Brand, and as Kneehigh's home. The Asylum was a place to nurture Kneehigh's ambitions, provide a solution to their survival, and balance local and global tensions. Despite Kneehigh's closure, the company have created a theatrical brand spanning 40 years, with an artistic legacy continuing with Wise Children. Their eclectic theatrical style and focus on storytelling and reinvention has gained many followers, making an important contribution to the British contemporary landscape theatrical landscape.

Notes

[1] Rice, E. Post Talk for *Rebecca*, Birmingham Rep, 2016.

[2] Wiegand, C. "Shakespeare's Globe appoints Emma Rice of Kneehigh as new artistic director", *The Guardian,* 1st May 2015-Pg.1.

[3] Gardner, L. *The Guardian,* 1st May 2015.

[4] Kellaway, K. "Emma Rice: 'I don't know how I got to be so controversial'", *The Observer,* 1st June 2018, Pg-2.

[5] Young, I. "Shakespeare's Globe: The real-life drama that led Emma Rice to quit", *BBC News,* 19th April 2017.

[6] Young, I. "Shakespeare's Globe: The real-life drama that led Emma Rice to quit", *BBC News,* 19th April 2017.

[7] Young, I. "Shakespeare's Globe: The real-life drama that led Emma Rice to quit", *BBC News,* 19th April 2017.

[8] Young, I. "Shakespeare's Globe: The real-life drama that led Emma Rice to quit", *BBC News,* 19th April 2017.

[9] Brown, M. "Shakespeare's Globe board did not respect me, says artistic director", *The Guardian,* 19th April 2017.

[10] Singh, A. "Emma Rice: it was a mistake for Shakespeare's Globe to hire me", *The Telegraph,* 18th December 2017.

[11] Brown, M. "Shakespeare's Globe board did not respect me, says artistic director", *The Guardian,* 19th April 2017.

[12] Kellaway, K. "Emma Rice: 'I don't know how I got to be so controversial'", *The Observer,* 1st June 2018, Pg-1.

[13] Kellaway, K. "Emma Rice: 'I don't know how I got to be so controversial'", *The Observer,* 1st June 2018, Pg-3.

[14] Singh, A. "Emma Rice: it was a mistake for Shakespeare's Globe to hire me", *The Telegraph,* 18th December 2017.

[15] Kellaway, K. "Emma Rice: 'I don't know how I got to be so controversial'", *The Observer,* 1st June 2018, Pg-5.

[16] Gardner, Lyn. "Emma Rice: Directing Theatre... and Being Fearless", *Digital Theatre Plus.*Pg-3.

[17] Kellaway, K. "Wise Children review – Emma Rice's joyous Angela Carter adaptation", *The Guardian*, 21st October 2018.

[18] Kellaway, K. "Wise Children review – Emma Rice's joyous Angela Carter adaptation", *The Guardian*, 21st October 2018.

[19] Kellaway, K. "Wise Children review – Emma Rice's joyous Angela Carter adaptation", *The Guardian*, 21st October 2018.

[20] Tripney, The Stage, "Wise Children" Review. 2018.

[21] Akbar, A. "Malory Towers review – Emma Rice takes Blyton to the top of the class", *The Guardian*, 26th July 2019.

[22] Wood, A. "Did critics think Wise Children was a smart act?", *WhatsOnstage.com*, 19th October 2018. Pg-2.

[23] Akbar, A. "Malory Towers review – Emma Rice takes Blyton to the top of the class", *The Guardian*, 26th July 2019.

[24] Akbar, A. "Malory Towers review – Emma Rice takes Blyton to the top of the class", *The Guardian*, 26th July 2019.

[25] Akbar, A. "Malory Towers review – Emma Rice takes Blyton to the top of the class", *The Guardian*, 26th July 2019.

[26] Akbar, A. "Malory Towers review – Emma Rice takes Blyton to the top of the class", *The Guardian*, 26th July 2019.

[27] Wozniak, L. "Review: Malory Towers at The Passenger Shed, Bristol", *Exeunt Magazine*, 19th July 2018. Pg-2.

[28] Wozniak, L. "Review: Malory Towers at The Passenger Shed, Bristol", *Exeunt Magazine*, 19th July 2018. Pg-4.

[29] Wozniak, L. "Review: Malory Towers at The Passenger Shed, Bristol", *Exeunt Magazine*, 19th July 2018. Pg-3.

[30] Lilley, H. "Kneehigh's Retellings", Reilly, K (ed). *Contemporary Approaches to Adaptation in Theatre,* Palgrave Macmillan*,* 2018. Pg-13.

[31] Lilley, H. "Kneehigh's Retellings", Reilly, K (ed). *Contemporary Approaches to Adaptation in Theatre,* Palgrave Macmillan*,* 2018. Pg-13.

[32] Wozniak, L. "Review: Malory Towers at The Passenger Shed, Bristol", *Exeunt Magazine*, 19th July 2018. Pg-5.

[33] Cavendish, D. *The Telegraph*, "Malory Towers, Bristol Passenger Shed, review: not quite a ripping yarn", 27th July 2019. Pg-1.

[34] Cavendish, D. *The Telegraph*, "Malory Towers, Bristol Passenger Shed, review: not quite a ripping yarn", 27th July 2019. Pg-2.

[35] Cavendish, D. *The Telegraph*, "Malory Towers, Bristol Passenger Shed, review: not quite a ripping yarn", 27th July 2019. Pg-3.

[36] Cavendish, D. *The Telegraph*, "Malory Towers, Bristol Passenger Shed, review: not quite a ripping yarn", 27th July 2019. Pg-4.

[37] Gardner, L. "Romantics Anonymous review – Emma Rices's Charming Globe swansong", *The Guardian,* 31st October 2017. Pg-1.

[38] Gardner, L. "Romantics Anonymous review – Emma Rices's Charming Globe swansong", *The Guardian,* 31st October 2017. Pg-1.

[39] Jones, R. "Review: Romantics Anonymous at Bristol Old Vic", *TheatreWeekly.com.* 23rd January 2020. Pg-1.

[40] Jones, R. "Review: Romantics Anonymous at Bristol Old Vic", *TheatreWeekly.com.* 23rd January 2020. Pg-2.

[41] Broadway World. "Carl Grose To Become Deputy Arstistic Director At Kneehigh", *broadwayworld.com*, 24th October 2018. Pg-1.

[42] Broadway World. "Carl Grose To Become Deputy Arstistic Director At Kneehigh", *broadwayworld.com*, 24th October 2018. Pg-1.

[43] Love, Catherine. "The Tin Drum review – Kneehigh turn Grass's fable into chaotic cabaret", *The Guardian,* 6th October 2017, Pg-1.

[44] Love, Catherine. "The Tin Drum review – Kneehigh turn Grass's fable into chaotic cabaret", *The Guardian,* 6th October 2017, Pg-2.

[45] Love, Catherine. "The Tin Drum review – Kneehigh turn Grass's fable into chaotic cabaret", *The Guardian,* 6th October 2017, Pg-2.

[46] Love, Catherine. "The Tin Drum review – Kneehigh turn Grass's fable into chaotic cabaret", *The Guardian,* 6th October 2017, Pg-2.

[47] Wozniak, L. "Tin Drum Review", *Exeunt Magazine,* 2017. Pg-3.

[48] Wozniak, L. "Tin Drum Review", *Exeunt Magazine,* 2017. Pg-2.

[49] Wozniak, L. "Tin Drum Review", *Exeunt Magazine,* 2017. Pg-4.

[50] Wozniak, L. "Tin Drum Review", *Exeunt Magazine,* 2017. Pg-4.

[51] Wozniak, L. "Tin Drum Review", *Exeunt Magazine,* 2017. Pg-5.

[52] Wozniak, L. "Tin Drum Review", *Exeunt Magazine,* 2017. Pg-5.

[53] Cavendish, D. *The Telegraph,* "My does this show bang on - Tin Drum Review", 15th November 2017. Pg-2.

[54] Cavendish, D. *The Telegraph,* "My does this show bang on - Tin Drum Review", 15th November 2017. Pg-3.

[55] Clapp, S. "The Tin Drum review – a banging hit", *The Guardian,* 15th October 2017. Pg-1.

[56] Saville, A. "The Tin Drum Review", *Timeout,* 11th December 2017. Pg-1.

[57] Saville, A. "The Tin Drum Review", *Timeout,* 11th December 2017. Pg-1.

[58] Hickling, A. "Dead Dog in a Suitcase review – madcap mastery and jukebox hijinks", *The Guardian,* 1st July 2014. Pg-1.

[59] Hickling, A. "Dead Dog in a Suitcase review – madcap mastery and jukebox hijinks", *The Guardian,* 1st July 2014. Pg-1.

[60] Hickling, A. "Dead Dog in a Suitcase review – madcap mastery and jukebox hijinks", *The Guardian,* 1st July 2014. Pg-1.

[61] Hickling, A. "Dead Dog in a Suitcase review – madcap mastery and jukebox hijinks", *The Guardian,* 1st July 2014. Pg-2.

[62] Guerreiro, T. "Kneehigh, Dead Dog in a Suitcase Review", *Culture Whisper,* 24th May 2019. Pg-1.

[63] Guerreiro, T. "Kneehigh, Dead Dog in a Suitcase Review", *Culture Whisper,* 24th May 2019. Pg-4.

[64] Saunders, T.F. "Dead Dog in a Suitcase (and other love songs) review: Kneehigh turn The Beggar's Opera into an uproarious Punch and Judy show", *The Telegraph,* 24th May 2019. Pg-1.

[65] Mountford, F. "Dead Dog in a Suitcase (and Other Love Songs) review: London's underbelly dragged into the modern world", *London Evening Standard,* 28th May 2019. Pg-1.

[66] Williams, H. "Singing truth to power: How Kneehigh's new show uses mass karaoke to topple a dictator", *The Independent,* 7th August 2018. Pg-7.

[67] Gardner, L. "Kneehigh's Ubu! A Singalong Satire", *Stagedoor,* 9th December 2019. Pg-1.

[68] Gardner, L. "Kneehigh's Ubu! A Singalong Satire", *Stagedoor,* 9th December 2019. Pg-3.

[69] Gardner, L. "Kneehigh's Ubu! A Singalong Satire", *Stagedoor,* 9th December 2019. Pg-4.

[70] Wyver, K. "Kneehigh's Ubu! A Singalong Satire review – karaoke hell", *The Guardian,* 13th December 2019. Pg-1.

[71] Wyver, K. "Kneehigh's Ubu! A Singalong Satire review – karaoke hell", *The Guardian,* 13th December 2019. Pg-2.

[72] Williams, H. "Singing truth to power: How Kneehigh's new show uses mass karaoke to topple a dictator", *The Independent,* 7th August 2018. Pg-3.

[73] Williams, H. "Singing truth to power: How Kneehigh's new show uses mass karaoke to topple a dictator", *The Independent,* 7th August 2018. Pg-3.

[74] Williams, H. "Singing truth to power: How Kneehigh's new show uses mass karaoke to topple a dictator", *The Independent,* 7th August 2018. Pg-4.

[75] Williams, H. "Singing truth to power: How Kneehigh's new show uses mass karaoke to topple a dictator", *The Independent,* 7th August 2018. Pg-4.

[76] Williams, H. "Singing truth to power: How Kneehigh's new show uses mass karaoke to topple a dictator", *The Independent,* 7th August 2018. Pg-4.

[77] Williams, H. "Singing truth to power: How Kneehigh's new show uses mass karaoke to topple a dictator", *The Independent,* 7th August 2018. Pg-5.

[78] Williams, H. "Singing truth to power: How Kneehigh's new show uses mass karaoke to topple a dictator", *The Independent,* 7th August 2018. Pg-5.

[79] Williams, H. "Singing truth to power: How Kneehigh's new show uses mass karaoke to topple a dictator", *The Independent,* 7th August 2018. Pg-6.

[80] Kneehigh Facebook Post, June 2016.

[81] Trueman, M. "The church of the lost cause: inside Kneehigh's wild Cornish home", *The Guardian,* 18th September 2017, Pg-2.

[82] Snow, G. *The Stage,* "Brexit: what does it mean for the arts?", published 24.06.2016. Pg-2.

[83] Morris, S. *The Guardian,* "Cornwall fears loss of funding after backing Brexit", published 26.06.2016. Pg-1.

[84] Morris, S. *The Guardian,* "EU cash flows to Cornwall, but many want to leave", published 13.06.2016. Pg-3.

[85] Morris, S. *The Guardian,* "Cornwall fears loss of funding after backing Brexit", published 26.06.2016. Pg-2.

[86] Morris, S. *The Guardian,* "Cornwall fears loss of funding after backing Brexit", published 26.06.2016. Pg-2.

[87] Morris, S. *The Guardian,* "Cornwall fears loss of funding after backing Brexit", published 26.06.2016. Pg-3.

[88] Elliot, L. *The Guardian,* "Brexit is a rejection of globalisation", published 26.06.2016. Pg-1.

[89] Elliot, L. *The Guardian,* "Brexit is a rejection of globalisation", published 26.06.2016. Pg-2.

[90] BBC. *BBC News*, "Cornwall 'theatrical superpower' Kneehigh to 'wind down'. 3rd June 2021.Pg-1.

[91] Trewhela, L. *Plymouth Live,* "Why no more Kneehigh Theatre is devasting for Cornwall", 1st April 2022. Pg-1.

[92] Vergnault, O. *In Your Area,* "Kneehigh Theatre to reinvent itself and thrive again thanks to Government recovery fund", 19th October 2020.

[93] Becquart, C. *Cornwall Live,* "Kneehigh Theatre is closing permanently", 21st June 2021.

[94] BBC. *BBC News*, "Cornwall 'theatrical superpower' Kneehigh to 'wind down'. 3rd June 2021.Pg-2.

[95] Gayle, D. *The Guardian,* "Kneehigh theatre to close after 'changes in artistic leadership", 3rd June 2021.

APPENDIX A

PRODUCTIONS

Kneehigh Productions
(Mike Shepherd forms Kneehigh)
1980-1989
1980 - The Adventures of Awful Knawful
1981 - Mr Corbett's Ghost
1982 - The Labyrinth
1982 - Around the World in Eighty Days [Minutes]
1983 - The Golden Pathway Annual
1983 – Skungpoomery by Ken Campbell
1984 - The Jungle Book
1985 - Further Adventures of the Three Musketeers by Steve Betts
1985/6 - Tregeagle [2nd version]
1986 -Fools' Paradise
1987 - Cyborg by John Downie
1988 - Sun and Shadow by Stuart Delves
1989 - Tregeagle [3rd version]

1990 - 1990
1990 -Ting Tang by Nick Darke
1990 – Tinderbox by Charles Causley
1991 - Peer Gynt
1992 - Ship of Fools
1993 – Windfall [Very Old Man with Enormous Wings reworked]
1993 -Danger My Ally by Nick Darke
1994 -The Bogus by Nick Darke
1994 - Ravenheart
1994/5 -The Ashmaid

(Bill Mitchell is appointed Joint Artistic Director)
1995 - The King of Prussia by Nick Darke
1996- Tregeagle [4th version]
1997- Arabian Nights

1998 -The Riot by Nick Darke
1999 -The Itch by Emma Rice

2000 - 2020
2000- The Red Shoes by Emma Rice
2001 -Cry Wolf
2002- Pandora's Box by Margaret Wilkinson

(Bill Mitchell stands down as Joint Artistic Director)
(Emma Rice is Appointed Joint Artistic Director)
2003/4 - Tristan and Yseult by Carl Grose and Anna Maria Murphy
(Minack Theatre)
2004 -The Wooden Frock by Tom Morris

(Bill Mitchell leaves Kneehigh to focus on Wildworks Theatre)
2005 - Tristan and Yseult
2005 -The Bacchae by Carl Grose and Anna Maria Murphy
2006 - Nights at the Circus by Tom Morris
2006 – Cymbeline by Carl Grose
2006 - Rapunzel
2007 - A Matter of Life and Death
2007 - Brief Encounter by Emma Rice
2008 -Don John
2009 - Hansel and Gretel by Carl Grose
2010 - Blast!
2011- The Wild Bride
2011 - Wah! Wah! Girls
2011 - The Umbrellas of Cherbourg
2012 - Midnight's Pumpkin
2013 - Steptoe and Son
2013 – Brief Encounter (Australia and USA Tour)
2014 - Dead Dog in a Suitcase by Carl Grose
2014 - Noye's Fludde by Benjamin Britten (opera)
2015 - Rebecca
2016 -The Flying Lovers of Vitebsk by Daniel Jamieson
2016 – FUP adapted by Simon Harvey
2016 - 946: The Amazing Story of Adolphus Tips adapted by Michael
Morpurgo and Emma Rice

(Emma Rice Leaves Kneehigh to join The Globe as Artistic Director)
2017 – The Tin Drum
2017 – Tristan and Yseult (Minack Theatre)
2018 – Kneehigh's Ubi

(Carl Grose is appointed Deputy Artistic Director)
2019 - Dead Dog in a Suitcase
2019 – The Dancing Frog
2019 – Kneehigh's Ubi (Asylum & National Tour)

SCHOOL SHOWS INCLUDED:
- Who Stole the Sun?
- Trelumpkin and Trebumpkin
- Stig
- Footprints 1
- The Very Old Man with Enormous Wings
- Poetry in Action
- Rare Earth and Rubbish (with Belgrade Theatre)

BIBLIOGRAPHY

A&B, *Arts and Business News*, "Eden Project and Kneehigh Theatre have been shortlisted for an Arts and Business Award 2002", published 15th Oct 2002.

Ahmad, Nick. "It's all about telling a story", *Yorkshire Post (North Yorkshire Edition)*, published 29th Sep 2004.

Aird, W.M. *The English Historical Review,* Vol. 116, No.465, Feb 2001, 184-185 Oxford University Press.

Akbar, A. "Malory Towers review – Emma Rice takes Blyton to the top of the class", *The Guardian*, 26th July 2019, <https://www.theguardian.com/stage/2019/jul/26/malory-towers-review-emma-rice-enid-blyton-passenger-shed-bristol>. (accessed 22/02/2020).

Allain, Paul. "The Archive", *Contemporary Theatre Review,* 25:1, 32-35, 2015. <http://dx.doi.org/10.1080/10486801.2015.992233>.

Armitstead, C. "A matter of life, death and two different endings", *Guardian Unlimited: Arts blog – theatre,* <http://blogs.guardian.co.uk/theatre/2007/05/a_matter_of_life_death_and_alt.html> Published 25/05/2007.

Armitstead, C. "Into the afterlife", *The Guardian,* <http://arts.guardian.co.uk/print/0,,329811516-123425,00.html> Published 07/05/2007.

Arts Council England, *Appraisal process for Grants for the Arts,* information sheet. <http://www.artscouncil.org.uk/sites/default/files/download-file/Appraisal_process_for_Grants_for_the_Arts_AUG2016.pdf > (accessed 12/03/2017).

Arts Council, S. "Moulding a different view of the Clay", *The Western Morning News,* published 1st August 2000.

Bassett, K. "A Very Old Man With Enormous Wings, South Quay, Hayle", *The Independent,* published 2nd Aug 2005.

Bassett, K. "A Matter of Life and Death", *The Independent,* <http://www.independent.co.uk/arts-entertainment/theatre/reviews/a-matter-of-life-and-death > Published 13th May 2007.

Barnett, David. "Political theatre in a shrinking world: René Pollesch's postdramatic practices on paper and on stage", *Contemporary Theatre Review,* 16:01, 31-40, 2006 DOI: 10.1080/10486800500450957.

BBC Homepage England. Reviews "Kneehigh has wings" *Three Islands Project Hayle, Penwith, Cornwall,* 3rd Aug 2005.

BBC. *BBC News,* "Cornwall 'theatrical superpower' Kneehigh to 'wind down'. 3rd June 2021.

Becquart, C. *Cornwall Live,* "Kneehigh Theatre is closing permanently", 21st June 2021.

Bell, Susan. "Twenty Five Years of Footsbarn - 1971-1996, *Contemporary Theatre Review,* 8:2, 83-93, DOI: 10.1080/10486809808568514 <http://dx.doi.org/10.1080/10486809808568514>.

Belshaw, T. *Sheffield Star*, "The Riot", published 8th March 2000, Kneehigh Archive, Falmouth University.

Benedict, D. "A Matter of Life and Death", *Variety*, Published 18/03/2008.

Bettelheim, B. *The Uses of Enchantment - the meaning and importance of fairy tales,* Penguin Books, UK, 1976. Pg.3 – 310.

Bhabha, Homi. K. *The Location of Culture,* Routledge, 1994. Ebook. 14-359.

Billington, M. *The Guardian,* "Brief Encounter", 18/02/2008 <https://www.theguardian.com/stage/2008/feb/18/theatre1>.

Blackmore Vale Magazine 2001, "Wolf, Kneehigh Theatre on tour", *Blackmore Vale Magazine,* Published 02/02/2001.

British Council, *General Report Cymbeline*, Kneehigh Archive, Falmouth University. 2008.

British Council, *Kneehigh Theatre*, Theatre and Dance, <https://theatreanddance.britishcouncil.org/artists-and-companies/k/kneehigh-theatre/> (accessed 18/07/2018).

Broadway World. "Carl Grose To Become Deputy Arstistic Director At Kneehigh", *broadwayworld.com*, 24th October 2018, <https://www.broadwayworld.com/westend/article/Carl-Grose-To-Become-Deputy-Arstistic-Director-At-Kneehigh-20181024 > (accessed 24/02/2020).

Brown, M. "Shakespeare's Globe board did not respect me, says artistic director", *The Guardian,* 19th April 2017, <https://theguardian.com/stage/2017/apr/19/shakespeare-globe-board-did-not-respect-me-says-artistic-director-emma-rice> (accessed 22/02/2020).

Burke, Peter. *Cultural Hybridity*, Policy Press, Cambridge, UK. 2009.

Butler, J. "Plunge into show's heart", *Three Islands Project Hayle, Penwith, Cornwall,* 2005.

Cavendish, D. *The Telegraph*, "The short hop from old barn to Broadway", V&A Theatre Archive, Published 2nd August 2010.

Cavendish, D. *The Telegraph*, "Malory Towers, Bristol Passenger Shed, review: not quite a ripping yarn", 27th July 2019, <https://telegraph.co.uk/theatre/what-to-see/malory-towers-bristol-passenger-reviewnot-quite-ripping-yarn/ >.

Cavendish, D. *The Telegraph,* "My does this show bang on - Tin Drum Review", 15th November 2017.

Chan, K.B. and Peverelli, P. "Cultural Hybridization: A Third Way Between Divergence and Convergence", *World Futures,* 2010, 66:3

Cheal, D. *The Telegraph,* "Brief Encounter", 09/02/2008. https://www.telegraph.co.uk/culture/theatre/drama/3671045/Brief-Encounter-I-want-people-to-laugh-and-cry.-Thats-our-job.html.

Clapp, S. "Coming to a clay-pit near you", *The Guardian,* 2001, Kneehigh Archive, Falmouth University.

Clapp, S. "The Tin Drum review – a banging hit", *The Guardian,* 15th October 2017, <https://www.theguardian.com/stage/2017/oct/15/the-tin-drum-everyman-liverpool-banging-hit >. (accessed 22/02/2020).

Clayton, Emma "Experienced troupe dress to impress", Telegraph & Argus, published 23rd Jan 2004.

Coleman. *Tristan and Yseult Program*, Kneehigh Theatre Company. 2005.

Coombs, Anna. *Hall for Cornwall, View from the Edge, March - May 2002, Audience Development Delivery Report.* May 2002.

Costa, M. *The Guardian G2,* "Arts: Theatre: Troupe therapy: Kneehigh", Published 2008, < http://lexisnexis.com/uk/nexis> (accessed 08/01/2012).

Costa, M. *The Guardian,* "Musicals we love: The Umbrellas of Cherbourg, Published 31st March 2014,
< https://www.theguardian.com/stage/2014/mar/31/musicals-the-umbrellas-of-cherbourg > (accessed 11/04/2017).

Cornwall County Council Application 1996-97, Kneehigh Theatre, Kneehigh Archive Falmouth University.

Cornwall County Council, *Kneehigh Theatre Application (1996-97),* Kneehigh, Archive, Falmouth University.

Cornish Guardian, "Kneehigh takes the lid off a brand new production", published 11/04/02.

Cornwall Venues: Trevarno, Heligan, Trelissick Summer 2000 Merged Audience Survey Results 26/9/00, Kneehigh Theatre.

Cummings, Neil. & Lewandowska, Marysia. "From Enthusiasm to the Creative Commons." *The Archive.* Ed. Charles Merewether. Whitechapel Gallery Ventures: London, UK, 2006. 149-153.

Dan, Catlin. & Kiraly, Josef. "Politics of Cultural History." *The Archive.* Ed. Charles Merewether. Whitechapel Gallery Ventures: London, UK, 2006. 113-116.

Delanty, G. "Cultural diversity, democracy and the prospects of cosmopolitanism: a theory of cultural encounters", *The British Journal of Sociology,* Vol 62, Issue 4, 2011.

Derrida, Jacques. *Archive Fever - A Freudian Impression,* The University of Chicago Press: Chicago, USA, 1996. 2-111.

Dibdin, T. "Critics' hit parade", *The Stage Edinburgh Preview 2001 ,*2001.

Dickson, A. "World Shakespeare festival: around the Globe in 37 plays", *The Guardian,* published 20th April 2012
<https://www.theguardian.com/stage/2012/apr/20/world-shakespeare-festival-globe-theatre-rsc> (accessed 12/03/2017).

Dorney, Kate. "Archives", *Contemporary Theatre Review,* 23:1, 8-10, 2013. http://dx.doi.org/10.1080/10486801.2013.765101.

Dorney, Kate. "Chapter 5 - Touring and the Regional Repertoire: Cheek By Jowl, Complicite, Kneehigh and Eastern Angles", ed. Dorney, Kate & Merkin, Ros. *The Glory of the Garden English Regional Theatre and The Arts Council 1984 - 2009,* Cambridge Scholars Publishing, 2010. 103-124.

Doubtful Island, Assorted dates in April Overall Statistics, Audience Survey Results, 24/4/99, Kneehigh Theatre.

Doubtful Island, Programme, Kneehigh Theatre, Kneehigh Archive Falmouth University, September 1999.

Dreyblatt, Arnold. "Questionnaire 2." *Performance Research: On Archives and Archiving.* Ed. Gough, Richard. & Roms, Heike. *Vol 7. No.*4, Routledge, Dec 2002. 48-49.

Dyer, J. *The West Briton Redruth, Camborne & Hayle Edition,* "All Hayle the Kneehigh Lot", *Three Islands Project Hayle, Penwith, Cornwall,* "A Very Old Man with Enormous Wings – Evaluation Report", published 28th July 2008.

Editorial, *The Guardian,* "The Guardian view on UK theatre: on the brink", published 20.05.2020 <https://www.theguardian.com/commentisfree/2020/may/20/the-guardian-view-on-uk-theatre-on-the-brink?CMP=Share_iOSApp_Other >

Elliot, L. *The Guardian,* "Brexit is a rejection of globalisation", published 26.06.2016 <https://www.theguardian.com/business/2016/jun/26/brexit-is-the-rejection-of-globalisation>.

Erenstein, Robert, L. "From Filth-ridden and Venal Folk to National Cultural Heritage: Street Theatre as an Export Product", *Maske und Kothum,* vol 33, 1-2, p23-28, June 1987. <DOI: 10.7767/muck.1987.33.12.23>.

Exeter Phoenix. *Interview with Theatre Alibi Artistic Director Nikki Sved,* 28th January 2014. <https://www.exeterphoenix.org.uk/interview-with-theatre-alibi-artistic-director-nikki-Sved/>.

Feasibility Study Report June 1997, Kneehigh Theatre.

Featherstone, Mike. *Global Culture: Nationalism, Globalisation and Modernity,* Sage Publications, 1997, Ebook.

Feaver, J. *The Spectator,* "Magical mystery tour: Jane Feaver goes behind the scenes with Kneehigh, a theatre company with an international reach that remains resolutely close to its Cornish roots", published July 23rd 2011.

Ferguson, F.S. *Technology and Culture,* Vol. 10, No. 3, July 1969, 449-452 The John Hopkins University Press.

Fischer-Lichte, E. *The Show and the Gaze of Theatre – A European Perspective,* University of Iowa Press, 1997.

Freshwater, H. *Theatre and Audience,* Palgrave MacMillan, UK, 2009.

Foucault, Michel. *The Archaeology of Knowledge,* Routledge, 1989. 146-147.

Foucault, Michel. "The Historical a priori and the Archive." *The Archive.* Ed. Charles Merewether. Whitechapel Gallery Ventures: London, UK, 2006. 26-30.

Freud, Sigmund. "A Note upon the Mystic Writing-Pad." *The Archive.* Ed. Charles Merewether. Whitechapel Gallery Ventures: London, UK, 2006. 20-24.

Fun Palaces. <http://funpalaces.co.uk> (accessed 17/03/2018).

Gardner, Lyn. "Emma Rice: Directing Theatre... and Being Fearless", *Digital Theatre Plus,* <https://www.digitaltheatreplus.com>, (accessed 22/02/2020).

Gardner, L. "Kneehigh's Ubu! A Singalong Satire", *Stagedoor,* 9th December 2019, <https//stagedoorapp.com/lyn-gardner/review-kneehighs-ubu-a-singalong-satire?ia=336> (accessed 22/02/2020).

Gardner, L. "Romantics Anonymous review – Emma Rices's Charming Globe swansong", *The Guardian,* 31st October 2017, <https//www.theguardian.com/stage/2017/oct/31/romantics-anonymous-review-sam-wanamaker-playhouse>, (accessed 22/02/2020).

Gardner, Lyn. "The Guide: Manchester Festival", *The Guardian – Magazine Supplement,* 2009, <http://www.lexisnexis.com/uk>

Gardner, L. "We like our plays to be foolish", *The Guardian,* published 2005.

Gatti, T. "Where theatres wild things are", *The Times,* published 24th July 2010 <http://www.lexisnexi.com/uk/nexis> (accessed 08/01/2012).

Gayle, D. *The Guardian,* "Kneehigh theatre to close after 'changes in artistic leadership", 3rd June 2021.

Ghost Nets 2 Return to Paradise, Audience Survey Results 17/9/99, Kneehigh Theatre.

Giannachi, Gabiella. *Contemporary Theatre Review,* "Exposing globalisation: Biopolitics in the work of critical art ensemble", 16:01, 41-50, 2006, DOI: 10.1080/10486800500450973.

Gilbert, H. *In the Balance, Indigeneity, Performance, Globalization* Liverpool University Press, UK. 2017. 1-316.

Gilbert, H. & Lo, J. *Performance and Cosmopolitics – Cross-Cultural Transactions in Australasia,* Palgrave MacMillan, UK. 2009. 1-256.

Gilbert H. & Tompkins, J. *Post-Colonial Drama – Theory, Practice, Politics,* Routledge, UK. 2002. 1-355.

Gillespie, K. & Hennessey H.D. *Global Marketing,* South-Western, Cengage Learning, Third Edition, UK, 2011, 1-295.

Gilmore, J.H. & Pine, B.J. *Authenticity what consumers really want,* Havard Business Press, USA. 1-191. 2007.

Gillinson, M. "Punchdrunk's Sleep No More: is this a sell-out which I see before me?", *The Guardian,* 2012, <http://www.guardian.co.uk/stage/theatreblog/2012/feb/06/punchdrunk-sleep-no-more-commercial>.

"Global Cornwall", *The Asylum*: Truro, Cornwall, Kneehigh Theatre, 12th Aug. 2012.

Green, Renee. "Survival: Ruminations on Archival Lacuna." *The Archive.* Ed. Charles Merewether. Whitechapel Gallery Ventures: London, UK, 2006. 49-55.

Gough, Richard. & Roms, Heike. Ed. *Performance Research: On Archives and Archiving Vol 7. No.*4, Routledge, Dec 2002. 3-128.

Govan, E., Nicholson, H. and Normington, K. *Making a Performance – Devising Histories and Contemporary Practices,* Routledge, Abingdon UK. 2007.

Grose, C. *Tristan and Yseult,* Oberon Modern Plays. UK. 2005.

Guerreiro, T. "Kneehigh, Dead Dog in a Suitcase Review", *Culture Whisper,* 24th May 2019, <https://www.culturewhisper.com/musicals/kneehigh_dead_dog_in_a_suitcae_lyric_hammersmith/13767 >, (accessed 22/02/2020).

Hall, Stuart. "The Local and The Global: Globalization and Ethnicity", *Culture, Globalization, and the World-System – Contemporary Conditions for the Representation of Identity,* editor Anthony D. King, University of Minnesota Press, 1997. *www.jstor.org/stable/10.5749/j.ctttsqb3.6* (accessed 17/10/2016).

Hards, S. "Kneehigh's Asylum at Carlyon Bay praised for boosting economy", *Cornwall Live,* 13th September 2019, <https://www.cornwalllive.com/whats-

on/whats-on-news/kneehighs-asylum-carlyon-bay-praised-3287343>, (accessed 07/03/2020).

Hards, S. "The inside story of iconic music venue Cornwall Coliseum three years after it was demolished", *Cornwall Live*, 8th April 2018, < https://www.cornwalllive.com/news/cornwall-news/inside-story-iconic-music-venue-1420997>, (accessed 07/03/2020).

Harvie, J. *Contemporary Theatre Review,* "Witnessing Michael Landy's Break Down: Metonymy, affect, and politicalised performance in an age of global consumer capitalism", 16:01, 62-72, 2006, DOI: 10.1080/10486800500451013.

Harvie, J. & Rebellato, D. *Contemporary Theatre Review,* "Editorial", 2006, 16:01, 3-6, DOI: 10.1080/10486800600630615.

Haydon, A. "Brief Encounter – Kneehigh at the Haymarket Cinema", *Postcardsgods.blogsot.com*, 20th February 2008, http://postcardsgods.blogspot.com/2008/02/brief-encounter.html.

Heddon, D. and Milling, J. *Devising Performance – a critical history*, Palgrave Macmillian, UK, 2006.

Hell's Mouth Site Specific - Hendra Pit 22 August - 2 Sept 2000, Tues-Sat Audience Survey Results 26/9/00, Kneehigh Theatre.

Hevva! Project Report, Kneehigh Theatre, 1999.

Hickling, A. "Dead Dog in a Suitcase review – madcap mastery and jukebox hijinks", *The Guardian,* 1st July 2014, <https://www.theguardian.com/stage/2014/jul/01/dead-dog-in-a-suitcase-review >, (accessed 22/02/2020).

Hiller, Susan. "Working Through Objects." *The Archive*. Ed. Charles Merewether. Whitechapel Gallery Ventures: London, UK, 2006. 41-48.

Hitt, M. et al. *The Global Mindset - Putting it All Together: So What is a Global Mindset and Why is it Important?* Emerald Insight, 2015. 1-216.

Holton, R. "Globalisation's Cultural Consequences", *Annals of the American Academy of Political and Social Science – Dimensions of Globalisation,* 2000, Vol 570.

Houseman, J. "Romantics Anonymous – Bristol Old Vic", *MusicalTheatre.com,* 26th January 2020, <http://musicaltheatre.com/romantics-anonymous-bristol-old-vic/>.

Hutera, Donald. "Camp followers of the bacchanal", *The Times,* published 5th Oct 2004.

Iball, Helen. "Dusting Ourselves Down." *Performance Research: On Archives and Archiving.* Ed. Gough, Richard. & Roms, Heike. *Vol 7. No.*4, Routledge, Dec 2002. 59-63.

Iezzi, T. "Punchdrunk's Felix Barrett Drops You In His Theater With No Directions Home.", *CoCreate*, 2012, <http://www.fastcocreate.com/1679201/punchdrunks-felix-barrett-brings-theater-to-life-literally>.

Inside Cornwall. "Crazy like a wolf", *Insider Info*, Dec/Jan 2001.

International Council on Archives. *Code of Ethics,* adopted by the General Assembly in its XIII session Beijing, China on 6th September 1996.

Jane, Sarah. Interview by Catherine Trenchfield. Kneehigh Archive, Falmouth University, Cornwall, UK, 12th Aug. 2010.

Jones, R. "Review: Romantics Anonymous at Bristol Old Vic", *TheatreWeekly.com*. 23rd January 2020, <https://theatreweekly.com/review-romantics-anonymous-at-bristol-old-vic/>.

Kabakov, Ilya."The Man Who Never Threw Anything Away." *The Archive*. Ed. Charles Merewether. Whitechapel Gallery Ventures, London, UK, 2006. 32-37.

Kellaway, K. "Emma Rice: 'I don't know how I got to be so controversial'", *The Observer*, 1st June 2018, <https://www.theguardian.com/stage/2018/jul/01/emma-rice-controversial-shakespeares-globe-wise-children> (Accessed 22/02/2020).

Kellaway, K. "Wise Children review – Emma Rice's joyous Angela Carter adaptation", *The Guardian*, 21st October 2018, <https://www.theguardian.com/stage/2018/oct/21/wise-children-old-vic-review-emma-rice-angela-carter> (Accessed 22/02/2020).

Kingfisher, Catherine. "Globalisation as Hybridity", *Globalisation and Women's Poverty*, editor Catherine Kingfisher, University of Pennsylvania Press, 2002.

Klein, Naomi. *No Logo*, Fourth Estate, 2010.

Kluszczysk, R.W. "Arts, Media, Cultures: Histories of Hybridisation", *Convergence: The International Journal of Research into New Media Technologies*, 2005, Vol. 11, No. 4.

Kneehigh Archive Press Cuttings 2012. Kneehigh Archive Falmouth University, 2012.

Kneehigh Report on the Debates on Cornwall and its Future November 1998.

Kneehigh Theatre. *Kneehigh Theatre Application to the Arts Council of England National Lottery Funding Capital Programme for Equipment October 1998 Reference 98-642*, Kneehigh Theatre.

Kneehigh Theatre Trust Limited 2001, Kneehigh Theatre, 2001.

Knight, David, B. "Extending the Local: The small town and globalization", *GeoJournal*, Vol. 45, No. ½, *Globalisation and Geography*, 1998, pp. 145-149.

Knowles, R. *Reading the Material Theatre*, Cambridge University Press, 2004.

Korff, Ruediger. "Encloses of Globalisation: The Power of Locality", *Dialectical Anthropology*, Vol. 27, No. 1, 2003, pp 1 -18,

Kuhn, Andrea, "Theatre, but more relaxed", *Western Morning News*, 30th November 2013.

Kuran, T. and Sandholm, W.H. "Cultural Integration and its Discontents", *The Review of Economics*, Vol 75, No. 1, 2008, Oxford University Press.

Laera, M. *Theatre and Adaptation: return, rewrite, repeat*, Bloomsbury, 2014.

Lam, S.K. "'Global corporate cultural capital' as a drag on glocalization: Disneyland's promotion of the Halloween Festival", Sage Journals, Vol 32, Issue 4, 2010, pp 631-648.

Legrain, Phillipe. *Open World: The Truth About Globalisation*, Abacus, 2007.

Lilley, H. "Kneehigh's Retellings", Reilly, K (ed). *Contemporary Approaches to Adaptation in Theatre*, Palgrave Macmillan, 2018.

Limited Trustee's Report and Accounts for the year ended 31st March 2001, Kneehigh Theatre Trust.

Lonergan, P. *Theatre and Globalisation – Irish Drama in the Celtic Tiger Era,* 2009.

Love, Catherine. "The Tin Drum review – Kneehigh turn Grass's fable into chaotic cabaret", *The Guardian,* 6th October 2017, <https://www.theguardian.com/stage/2017/oct/06/the-tin-drum-review-kneehigh-everyman-liverpool-gunter-grass>.

Mahoney, E. "A Very Old Man with Enormous Wings", *The Guardian,* published 29/07/2005.

Markwell, R. *Cymbeline Review,* BBC.CO.UK. <http://www.bbc.co.uk/bristol/content/articles/2006/10/19/kneehigh_feature.sh tml>.

Marketing Week, "Fantasy Brands; Courvoiser's escapist strategy that drive sales", 2011, <http://www.lexusnexis.com/uk>.

Marmion, P. *Kneehigh Archive,* "A local play, for local people…", 2005, Falmouth University.

McGinn, C. "Punchdrunk isn't just theatrical any more.", *Timeout London,* 2012, <http://www.timeout.com/london/theatre/article/2547/punch-isnt-just-theatrical-any-more>.

Media Release, "Quick Silver Underground – Special additional performance at Carnglaze caverns", Kneehigh Theatre, Published 10/03/2003.

Merewether, Charles. ed. *The Archive,* Whitechapel Gallery Ventures, London, 2006. 10-191.

Mlinar, Z. *Globalisation and Territorial Identities* (1992) Avebury Ashgate Publishing Limited, 1992.

Morris, S. *The Guardian,* "Cornwall fears loss of funding after backing Brexit", published 26.06.2016. <https://www.theguardian.com/uk-news/2016/jun/26/cornwall-fears-loss-of-funding-after-backing-brexit>.

Morris, S. *The Guardian,* "EU cash flows to Cornwall, but many want to leave", published 13.06.2016 <http://www.theguardian.com/politics/2016/jun/13/eu-cash-flows-to-cornwall-but-many-want-to-leave>.

Morse, O. "London saw it first this time!", *Cornish Guardian,* published 3rd February 2000.

Mountford, F. "A very good hair day", *Evening Standard,* published 23/12/2007.

Mountford, F. "Dead Dog in a Suitcase (and Other Love Songs) review: London's underbelly dragged into the modern world", *London Evening Standard,* 28th May 2019, <https://www.standard.co.uk/go/london/theatre/dead-dog-in-suitcase-theatre-review-a4152751.html>, (accessed 22/02/2020).

Moynagh, M. & Worsley, R. *Going Global – Key Questions for the 21st Century,* A&C Black Publishers, London. 2008.

Nash, J. "A lamb in wolf's clothing", *Blackmore Vale Magazine,* Published 02/02/2001.

National Theatre Archive, National Theatre, London, UK, 2014.

Nield, Sophie. *Contemporary Theatre Review,* "There is another world: Space, theatre and anti-capitalism, 16:01, 51-61, 2006,

DOI: 10.1080/10486800500451005

Notes for Students – The Umbrellas of Cherbourg, Kneehigh Theatre, 2011
<http://www.kneehigh.co.uk/userfiles/files/Umbrellas%20of%20Cherbourg%2
0-%20Notes%20for%20Students.pdf> .

Oddey, A. *Re-framing the Theatrical – interdisciplinary landscapes for performance,* Palgrave MacMillan, 2007.

Oddey, A. and White, C. *Modes of Spectating,* Intellect, Uni of Chicago Press. 2009.

Oyserman, D, Sakamoto, I. and Laiffer, A. "Cultural Accomodation: Hybridity and the framing of social obligation.", *Journal of Personality and Social Psychology,* Vol 74, No. 6. 1998.

Parker, S. "A World of Wonder", *Western Morning News,* published 20th Jan 2004.

Parker, S. *The Western Morning News 1st August 2000,* "Moulding a different view of the Clay", Published 1st August 2000.

Parker, S. *The Western Morning News,* "Play tells fishy story of a boy who wouldn't fit in", Published 25th September 2001.

Parker, S. "Tales of fish and fire, wolves and water", *Western Morning News,* published 18/6/02.

Parker, S. *Western Morning News,* "Yee-ha! Roll up for a real wild west panto", Published 26th November 2002.

Parker, S. *The Western Morning News Devon Edition,* "Kneehigh goes from Meva' to Manhattan", Published 7th August 2007.

Pearson, M. *Mickery Theater - an imperfect archaeology,* Amsterdam University Press, 2014. 1- 312.

Penlee Project ERDF BID Project Outline, Perfect Moment, Kneehigh Theatre, Feb 2001.

Pearson, Mike. and Shanks, Michael. *Theatre/Archaeology,* Routledge, London, 2001. Xiv – 54.

Pelaez Lyons, Andrea. *Interview by Catherine Trenchfield.* Personal interview recorded at West Thames College, Isleworth. 17th November 2011.

Phelan, Peggy. & Lane. J. Ed. *The Ends of Performance,* New York Uni Press, 1998. 8-80.

Phelan, Peggy. *Unmarked the Politics of Performance,* E Library, Routledge, 2005. 2-162.

Pine, Joseph. & Gilmore, James. *The Experience Economy: Work is Theatre & Every Business a Stage,* Harvard Business School Press, Boston, 1998.

Prance, G. "A Paradise for Economic Botanists: The Eden Project" *Economic Botany,* Vol. 56, No 3, Autumn 2002, 226-230, Springer on behalf of New York Botanical Garden Press.

Punchdrunk Theatre, *Temple Studios "The Drowned Man",* London, 2013-14.

Radosavljevic, Duska. "Chapter 4 Kneehigh Theatre", ed. Tomlin, Liz. *British Theatre Companies 1995 - 2014,* Bloomsbury, 2015, 155-177.

Rae, P. *Contemporary Theatre Review,* "Where is the cosmopolitan stage?", 16:01, 8-22, 2006, DOI: 10.1080/1048600500450841.

Ranciere, J. *The Emancipated Spectator,* Verso, UK, 2011.

Rebellato, Dan. *Theatre and Globalisation,* Palgrave MacMillan: Hampshire, UK. 2009.

Rebellato, Dan. *Contemporary Theatre Review,* "Playwriting and globalisation: Towards a site-unspecific theatre", 16:01, 97-113, 2006, DOI: 10.1080/10486800500451047

Regev, M. "Cultural Uniqueness and Aesthetic Cosmopolitanism", *European Journal of Social Theory,* Vol 10, No. 123, 2007.

Rice, E. *A Matter of Life and Death Programme,* National Theatre. 2007.

Rice, E. *Brief Encounter Programme,* Birmingham Repertory Theatre. September 2007.

Rice, E. *British Council Report on Kneehigh Theatre's Tour of China – The Red Shoes,* care of Falmouth University Kneehigh Archive, Falmouth University, 2001.

Rice, E. *Cymbeline Programme,* Lyric Hammersmith, 2006.

Rice, Emma. *Pre-show Talk for "Rebecca",* Birmingham Rep Theatre. 2nd May 2015.

Reilly, K. *Contemporary Approaches to Adaptation in Theatre,* Palgrave Macmillan, 2018.

Robins, D. "Flights of Fancy", *The Clifton Life,* 2010.

Ruhrmund, F. "Kneehigh's quickdraw 'pantomine' is full of laughs", *Western Morning News,* Published 24/12/02.

Ruhrmund, F. The Cornishman, "A very old man earns his wings" *Three Islands Project Hayle, Penwith, Cornwall,* "A Very Old Man with Enormous Wings – Evaluation Report", publishes 4th August 2005.

Ruhrmund, F. "Wild West comedy is a must see", *The West Briton Truro & Mid Cornwall Edition,* Published 09/01/03.

Saville, A. "The Tin Drum Review", *Timeout,* 11th December 2017, <https://www.timeout.com/london/theatre/the-tin-drum-review>, (accessed 22/02/2020).

Saunders, G. *British Theatre Companies 1980-1994,* Bloomsbury Methuen Drama, 2015.

Saunders, T.F. "Dead Dog in a Suitcase (and other love songs) review: Kneehigh turn The Beggar's Opera into an uproarious Punch and Judy show", *The Telegraph,* 24th May 2019, <https://www.telegraph.co.uk/theatre/what-to-see/dead-dog-suitcase-love-songs-review-kneehigh-turn-beggars-opera/>, (accessed 22/02/2020).

Schechner, Richard. *Between Theatre and Anthropology,* University of Pennsylvania Press, USA, 1985. 33-34.

Schulze, Daniel. *Authenticity in Contemporary Theatre,* Bloomsbury Publishing, 2016.

Shepherd, M. *The Kneehigh Creative Asylum,* Kneehigh Archive Falmouth University. 2012.

Shepherd, M. and Rice, E. *Kneehigh Theatre The Asylum Summer Season 2010,* Kneehigh Archive Falmouth University. 2010.

Shepherd, Mike, *Kneehigh Theatre Journal,* Kneehigh Archive, Falmouth University, 2013.

Shepherd, Mike. *Kneehigh Theatre – The Red Shoes – Report on British Council Tour to Syria and Lebanon,* Kneehigh Archive, Falmouth. 2002.

Shoaf, R.W. "Notes", *Second Series,* Vol. 56, No. 3, Mar 2000: 648-654.

Sierz, "Cymbeline", *The Telegraph,*2008.

Singh, A. "Emma Rice: it was a mistake for Shakespeare's Globe to hire me", *The Telegraph,* 18th December 2017, <https://www.telegraph.co.uk/news/2017/12/18/emma-rice-mistake-shakespeares-globe-hire/> (accessed 22/20/2020).

Skantze, P.A. *Itinerant Spectator,* Punctum Books, New York, 2013. 1-260.

Sklair, L. "Capitalist Globalisation: Fatal Flaws and Necessity for Alternatives", *Brown Journal of World Affairs,* Fall/Winter 2006, Vol XIII, Issue 1, 29-37.

Smelt, M. *Interview with Mike Shepherd and Maurice Smelt,* Kneehigh Archive, Recorded at Morrab Library, published 21st March 2000.

Smelt, M. *Interview with Sue Hill, Bill Mitchell and Maurice Smelt,* Recorded at 42 Weeth Lane, Camborne, 28th April 2000.

Smith, A. *National Identity,* University of Nevada Press USA.1991.

Snow, G. *The Stage,* "Brexit: what does it mean for the arts?", published 24.06.2016 <https://www.thestage.co.uk/news/2016/brexit-what-does-it-mean-for-the-arts/>.

Spencer, C. *The Telegraph,* "The Umbrellas of Cherbourg, Gielgud Theatre, review", published 23rd March 2011 < http://www.telegraph.co.uk/culture/theatre/theatre-reviews/8400463/The-Umbrellas-of-Cherbourg-Gielgud-theatre-review.html > accessed (11/04/2017).

Staniewski, W. with Hodge, A. *Hidden Territories – the theatre of Gardzienice,* Routledge, London. 2004.

Strachan, Alan. "Nick Darke - Playwright of maverick brio who found inspiration in his native Cornwall", *The Independent,* 14th June 2005.

Steger, M.B. *Globalisation - A Very Short Introduction,* Oxford University Press, Oxford. 2009.

Stoian, Linda. "Archive Review: Learning performance by archiving Performance." *Performance Research: On Archives and Archiving.* Ed. Gough, Richard. & Roms, Heike. *Vol 7. No.*4, Routledge, Dec 2002. 128-134.

Summer Schools in Cornwall 2001, Kneehigh Theatre, Kneehigh Archive Falmouth University.

Taylor, Diana. *The Archive and the Repertoire: Performing cultural memory in The Americas,* Duke University, 2003. 2-278.

The Asylum, Kneehigh Theatre, Kneehigh Archive Falmouth University, 2012.

The Asylum, Kneehigh Theatre, Truro: Cornwall, UK, 2010-2014.

The Ark, Carn Marth, 21st June 1999, Audience Survey Results 24/9/99, Kneehigh Theatre.

The Arts Council Consultation Paper 2011-12, Kneehigh Theatre.

The Cornishman. "Panto Sold Out", Published 19/12/2002.

The Dome Company, *Design Project,* 2005.

The Itch, Heligan & Trelissick Summer 1999, Audience Survey Results 4/11/99, Kneehigh Theatre.

The Kneehigh Plan 1997-2000, Kneehigh Theatre.

The Kneehigh Plan 1999-2001 Appendices, Kneehigh Theatre.

The Kneehigh Plan 1997-2000, Kneehigh Theatre.

The Lost Gardens of Heligan, <https://www.heligan.com>, (accessed 07/03/2020).

The Red Shoes Heligan Gardens 18-21 July 2000 Audience Survey Results 25/9/00, Kneehigh Theatre Company.

'The Red Shoes' Report on British Council tour to Syria and Lebanon October 2002, Kneehigh Theatre.

The Red Shoes Trevarno Estate Gardens 12-13 June 2000 Audience Survey Results 22/9/00, Kneehigh Theatre Company.

The West Briton Truro & Mid Cornwall Edition, "Kneehigh and Eden up for major award", published 24/10/02.

This is Cornwall, "Hayle Hosts Kneehigh", 4th August 2005 <www.thisiscornwall.co.uk>.

Three Islands Project "A Very Old Man with Enormous Wings" Report, 2003, Kneehigh Theatre & Wildworks.

Three Islands Project Hayle, Penwith, Cornwall, "A Very Old Man with Enormous Wings – Evaluation Report", 2005, Kneehigh Theatre.

Tregida & Milden. "Before My Time: Recreating Cornwall's Past through Ancestral Memory" Oral History, Vol. 36, No.1, Spring 2008, 23-32 Oral History Society

Thomas, J. *The Economic History Review* New Series, Vol. 20, No. 1, Apr 1967, 175-176 Blackwell Publishing on behalf of Economic History Review.

Tomlin, L. *British Theatre Companies 1995-2014,* Bloomsbury, 2015.

Tomlin, L. & Jackson, S. *Contemporary Theatre Review,* "Innocent tourists? Neo-colonialist narratives in contemporary performance", 16:01, 23-30, 2006, DOI: 10.1080/10486800500450940.

Trelissick Gardens 2-5 August 2000 Audience Survey, published 25/9/00, Kneehigh Theatre.

Trewhela, L. "Frock 'n' roll – yet another hit play", *The West Briton Helston & The Lizard Edition,* Published 18/03/2004.

Trewhela, L. "It's back to Cornish roots for masters of surprise", *The West Briton Redruth, Camborne & Hayle Edition,* Published 11th November 2007.

Trewhela, L. *Plymouth Live,* "Why no more Kneehigh Theatre is devasting for Cornwall", 1st April 2022.

Tripney, The Stage, "Wise Children" Review. 2018.

Trueman, M. "The church of the lost cause: inside Kneehigh's wild Cornish home", *The Guardian,* 18th September 2017, <https://www.theguardian.com/stage/2017/sep/18/kneehigh-the-tin-drum-cornish-home-mike-shepherd>.

Trust Limited Trustee's Report and Accounts for the year ended 31st March 2000, Kneehigh Theatre.

Trust Limited Trustee's Report and Accounts for the year ended 31st March 2002, Kneehigh Theatre.

Trust Limited Trustee's Report and Accounts for the year ended 31st March 2003, Kneehigh Theatre.

Tucker, Herbert F. "Spectacle." *A New Companion to Victorian Literature and Culture.* Oxford, UK: John Wiley & Sons, 2014. 299-311.

Vergnault, O. *In Your Area,* "Kneehigh Theatre to reinvent itself and thrive again thanks to Government recovery fund", 19th October 2020.

Watson, Ian. "The Bacchae", *What's on Stage Review,* 2004.

Walters, S. "Theatre Company Punchdrunk is back with the crash of the Elysium." *Manchester Evening News,* 2011 <http://menmedia.co.uk/manchestereveningnews/entertainment>.

Wang, G. and Yeh, E. "Globalization and Hybridization in Cultural Products: The cases of Mulan and Crouching Tiger, Hidden Dragon", *International Journal of Cultural Studies,* Vol 8, Issue 175, 2005.

Welton, M. *Emma Rice of Kneehigh Theatre in Conversation with Martin Welton 9th October 2012,* Queen Mary University of London.

Welton, M. "Chapter 15 – There are no Formulas: Emma Rice of Kneehigh in Conversation with Martin Welton", *Theatre and Adaptation: return, rewrite, repeat,* Laera, M (ed). Bloomsbury, 2014.

White, Rupert. "Jonathan Paul Cook on Footsbarn, communal living, and rural theatre", artscornwall.org, 17th May 2015, 1-11, <http://www.artcornwall.org/interviews/Jonathan_Paul_Cook.htm>.

Whitney, Hilary. "Why Kneehigh may roam far and wide, it will always return to its Cornish roots", *The Arts Desk,* 16 July 2011, <http://www.theartsdesk.com/print/4119>.

Whitney, Hilary. *theartsdesk.com,* "Q&A: Director Emma Rice", 16th July 2011, <   http://www.theartsdesk.com/theatre/theartsdesk-qa-director-emma-rice?page=0,1 > (accessed 11/04/2017).

Wiegand, C. "Shakespeare's Globe appoints Emma Rice of Kneehigh as new artistic director", *The Guardian,* 1st May 2015, (accessed 22/2/2020) < https://www.theguardian.com/stage/2015/may/01/shakespeares-globe-emma-rice-new-artistic-director>.

Williams, H. "Singing truth to power: How Kneehigh's new show uses mass karaoke to topple a dictator", *The Independent,* 7th August 2018, < https://www.independent.co.uk/arts-entertainment/theatre-dance/features/kneehigh-ubu-karaoke-alfred-jarry-asylum-cornwall-barns-mike-shepherd-a8479201.html>. (accessed 22/02/2020).

Wirtz et al. "Business Models: Origin, Development and Future Research Perspectives", *Long Range Planning,* Vol 49, 2016, 36-54. http://dx.doi.org/10.1016/j.lrp.2015.04.001 (accessed 24/07/2017)

Wood, A. "Did critics think Wise Children was a smart act?", *WhatsOnstage.com,* 19th October 2018, <https://www.whatsonstage.com/london-theatre/news/wise-children-review-roundup-old-vic_47848.html>.

Wozniak, L. "Review: Malory Towers at The Passenger Shed, Bristol", *Exeunt Magazine,* 19th July 2018, <http://exeuntmagazine.com/reviews/review-malory-towers-wise-children-theatre/ >. (Accessed 22/02/2020).

Wozniak, L. "Tin Drum Review", *Exeunt Magazine,* 2017.

Wright, S. *Performance,* "Cornish Past", Published 9th September 2005.

Wyver, K. "Kneehigh's Ubu! A Singalong Satire review – karaoke hell", *The Guardian,* 13th December 2019, <https://www.theguardian.com/stage/2019/dec/13/kneehighs-ubu-a-singalong-satire-review-shoreditch-town-hall-london> ,(accessed 22/02/2020).

Unesco, *Culture*, "Intangible Heritage", 2005
    <http://portal.unesco.org/culture/en/ev.php-URL_ID=2225&URL_DO=DO_>.
Young, I. "Shakespeare's Globe: The real-life drama that led Emma Rice to quit",
    BBC News, 19th April 2017, <https://www.bbc.co.uk/news/entertainment-arts-
    39645975 (Accessed 22/02/2020).

AUTHOR

Catherine Trenchfield is Team Leader/Higher Education Lead for the Creative Industries at Kingston College (University Centre South Thames College Group). In addition, she is the Course Leader for the BA (Hons) Acting for Stage and Media, validated by the University of West London, whilst being an Associate Lecturer with UWL. She formerly obtained her PhD at Royal Holloway University and MA at Rose Bruford College and has taught within further and higher education since 2002. She has maintained an international research profile, presenting her work on Kneehigh at conferences in Australia, Malta, Portugal, Ireland and the UK. Before becoming an educator, Catherine worked as an actor within theatre in education with Cragrats Theatre Company and West Midlands Children's Theatre.

INDEX